# Women, Faith, and Family

*Reclaiming Gender Justice through Religious Activism*

Samaneh Oladi

UNIVERSITY OF CALIFORNIA PRESS

University of California Press
Oakland, California

© 2024 by Samaneh Oladi

Library of Congress Cataloging-in-Publication Data

Names: Oladi, Samaneh author.
Title: Women, faith, and family : reclaiming gender
    justice through religious activism / Samaneh Oladi.
Description: [Oakland, California] : [University of
    California Press], [2024] | Includes bibliographical
    references and index.
Identifiers: LCCN 2023056333 | ISBN 9780520400443
    (hardback) | ISBN 9780520400450 (paperback)
Subjects: LCSH: Itilaf-i Islami-yi Zanan (Organization) |
    Shiite women—Iran—21st century. | Religion and
    politics—Iran—21st century. | Activism—Religious
    aspects.
Classification: LCC BP194.185.G43 2024 |
    DDC 297.6/50820955—dc23/eng/20240217
LC record available at https://lccn.loc.gov/2023056333

32  31  30  29  28  27  26  25  24
10  9   8   7   6   5   4   3   2   1

Women, Faith, and Family

*To Soudeh*

# Contents

# Acknowledgments

This book stands as a testament to the unwavering support and invaluable contributions of many individuals. During its formative stages at the University of California, Santa Barbara, I greatly benefited from the mentorship of Ahmad Ahmad, Kathleen Moore, Mark Juergensmeyer, and Mary Hancock. Their guidance was pivotal as I charted the early course of this work. As the project evolved, I was fortunate to engage in insightful discussions with esteemed colleagues. Cristina Stanciu, Christine Cynn, Melis Hafez, Antonio Espinoza Ruiz, Faedah Totah, and Rohan Kalyan deserve special thanks for their feedback, which was instrumental in refining several chapters.

The efforts of Eric Schmidt from the University of California Press in facilitating the book's publication are commendable. Likewise, Jyoti Arvey's contributions were crucial in guaranteeing a smooth publication journey. I'm also indebted to the anonymous reviewers whose insights greatly enriched the final manuscript. Furthermore, my gratitude extends to all the individuals who generously shared their insights through interviews. It's important to mention that the views and sentiments expressed during the conversations are those of the interviewees and may not align with my own views.

Funding and support from several institutions played a crucial role in this project's realization. I extend my thanks to the Jack Shand Research Grant, Society for the Scientific Study of Religion; the Center for Islam in the Contemporary World Research Grant; Virginia Commonwealth

University's Seed Award; the Joseph H. Fichter Research Grant, Association for the Sociology of Religion; the Virginia Commonwealth University's Humanities Research Center; and the Department of Religious Studies at the University of California Santa Barbara for their financial backing.

On a personal level, my friends, including Fariba Entehsari, Anita Daniel, Annam, Jeannette Love, Suzanne Dunn, Kathryn Murphy, and Jenny, and Maurice Bisheff, have been pillars of strength and encouragement.

I owe much to my family. I'm indebted to my father for instilling in me the value of education and for his endless love; to my mother, whose silent sacrifices speak volumes and from whom I learned the power of independence and perseverance; and to my siblings, for their continued support and love. The cherished memories of my grandparents, who left behind a legacy of love, continue to ground me. I am eternally grateful to Aba, who ignited my love for spirituality.

Last, my heartfelt thanks to my husband for his unwavering love and support throughout this journey, and to my beloved daughter, whose very presence has redefined and deepened my understanding of pure, unconditional love.

# A Note on Transliteration and Translation

In this book, I've employed the transliteration guidelines for Arabic and Persian from the *International Journal of Middle East Studies* with a few exceptions. Familiar terms such as *Qur'an*, *jihad*, and *hadith* are presented in their commonly recognized English forms without transliteration. For the English interpretations of Qur'anic excerpts, I've relied on Abdullah Yusuf Ali's translation with some adjustments. The translations of Persian interviews and supplementary content are entirely my own.

# Introduction

In July 2006, when I visited my childhood friend Leila in Iran, she expressed skepticism about my research, which looks at women's rights activism and the attempt to challenge hierarchal interpretations of Islamic scriptures. "Be careful not to be misled by the idea of liberating the Muslim woman," Leila warned me. "We don't need more Westerners telling us that we need to be saved from our culture and religion." Leila viewed my Western education and research topic as yet another instance of the West's cultural imperialism. She advised me to take a critical stance against Western hegemony over Muslim women's bodies and souls.

In 2008, when I visited Leila again, I found her in a state of despair. She had good reason for her distress: she had learned that her husband of fourteen years had entered into a polygynous marriage, and her whole world and faith had crumbled. Leila's husband justified his actions as an inalienable right sanctioned by Islamic law. Leila's reaction was not an uncommon one: "How can I maintain my faith when I see such injustice?" I was startled by her remarks and the shift in her attitude, especially considering her previous position where she had viewed criticism of women's status in Iran as an act of transgression against her Iranian culture and Islamic identity. "How could laws that are meant to uphold God's justice allow for such injustice?" she lamented. In a desperate attempt to hold on to her faith, Leila decided to join Itilaf-i Islami-yi Zanan (IIZ, Women's Islamic Coalition), an organization that used faith-based activism to advance women's rights within Shi'i Iran. Why, like the other women in the IIZ, did Leila believe that the most effective approach to advancing gender justice in Iran was to work within the framework of Shi'i Islam? What instigated the activism of such individuals, many of whom had not long ago fervently defended the gender policies of the Islamic Republic of Iran? For these activists, what are the possibilities and limits of achieving gender justice in the realm of family law within an Islamic framework? Is the conventional discourse of Islamic law susceptible to influence from the bottom up? This book unpacks these questions and takes an insider look into the practices adopted by IIZ and its critical engagement with faith-based activism to advance gender egalitarianism through engagement with women's jurisprudence.

By using IIZ's activism as a lens through which to view women's legal status, I tackle complex questions about the limits of women's agency within Islamic frameworks and argue that Muslim women's access to and use of religious resources have reinforced their position in gender negotiations. Female religious activists not only struggle against patriarchy and conventional frameworks but also cultivate a distinctive jurisprudence advanced by women that simultaneously challenges Western liberalism and religious orthodoxy. *Women, Faith, and Family* provides a nuanced portrait of Iranian women's faith-based activism and captures female activists' attempts at reforming women's legal status, while also challenging assumptions rooted in a secular-liberal feminism that has historically assumed an intrinsic discord between women's agency and religion.

The women's jurisprudence advanced by IIZ critically engages with sacred scripture with the intention of redefining itself. IIZ members utilize the term *women's jurisprudence* to describe the distinct method they apply when endeavoring to reinterpret Islamic jurisprudence. This critical form of women's jurisprudence is invigorated by the rhetoric and ideas given currency by reformist discourses. Women's jurisprudence advanced by IIZ is an evolving discourse on the interpretation of gender in Islam, grounded in independent intellectual investigation (*ijtihād*)[1] of the Islamic sacred scripture, which allows for women's experiences to be taken into account and incorporated into law. Through interviews, case studies, and textual analysis, I engage with debates about localized reformation within the Shi'i tradition and the nuances of female faith-based activism in contemporary Iran. Female activists' commitment to achieving gender justice exemplifies contemporary religious movements that are increasingly grounded in local tradition and that move away from both secularism and orthodoxy, toward religious egalitarianism. *Women, Faith, and Family* takes readers on a journey to reveal the social, legal, and political complexities faced by Iranian women as they challenge and engage with long-held cultural and religious beliefs.

## THEORETICALLY GROUNDING FAITH-BASED ACTIVISM

Since the turn of the twenty-first century, a coterie of Muslim writers and scholars have maintained an interest in and commitment to women's rights issues. The majority of their scholarship has focused on secular feminist movements, leaving the voices of faith-based activists systemically sidelined or marginalized. As we bear witness to a growing body of scholarship that looks at women's rights and religious activism in the Sunni tradition, the literature lacks a systematic treatment of women's legal status and religious activism in the Shi'i tradition.

Moreover the binary voices that claim to represent Muslim women emphasize how religion either has curtailed or violated women's rights or in contrast has afforded them the freedom to pursue rights they did not previously possess. The cacophony of voices that are competing to advocate for the Muslim woman have seldom focused on how women have influenced religious traditions and policy formation in Muslim-majority countries. To fill these voids, I examine Shi'i women's faith-based activism and how modern discourses on gender have shaped and been shaped by strategic negotiations between female activists and the state.

In analyzing women's faith-based activism in Shi'i Iran, I challenge two deeply embedded and opposing narratives about female religious activism in Muslim societies. The dominant narrative views female religious activists as victims and/or perpetuators of Islamic orthodoxy. The second, more peripheral narrative idealizes women's religious activism as part of a new feminist wave challenging the hierarchical Islamic legal system.[2] *Women, Faith, and Family* argues that such binary constructs that frame Muslim women as either perpetuators of or liberators from Islamic orthodoxy discount non-Western understanding of women's faith-based activism. The latter view, which positions secularism as a necessary precondition for achieving gender justice, can inadvertently marginalize the efforts of Muslim women's faith-based activism.

Given the diversity of religious movements and predicaments faced by contemporary Muslims, one can anticipate a perplexing array of labels ascribed to female religious activists. Women in Muslim-majority countries continue to face difficulty in representing their activism in any terms other than those of the dominant secular-liberal discourse. One of the more common descriptors attributed to Muslim women's religious movements is *Islamist*. The term *Islamist* is widely contested, as it is part of a Western terminology that falls short of capturing the complex social and political realities in Muslim-majority nations.[3] Furthermore, Muslim female activists do not share some of the fundamental considerations of Islamist movements that frame themselves as revivalist or militant, intent on liberating societies from corrupt practices out of a desire to return to an idealized form of Islam. The majority of Muslim female activists are neither attempting to revive an idealized form of Islam through excessive measures such as military action nor working to undermine Islamic law to make it accord with Western values.

In outlining the parameters of this study, framing the work of Muslim women activists as "feminist" is also problematized. This becomes particularly evident when considering contemporary women's rights activists; despite being beneficiaries of the previous generation of feminists, they are skeptical toward the very concept of feminism.[4] Women's rights activists have notably expanded on the rights discourse, a central component of secular feminism. Yet they strive to distance themselves from the label of feminism. This detachment is primarily due to feminism's association with secular Western values and the use of feminist rhetoric by colonizers and imperialists to justify conquest of Muslim-majority lands. Even though both religious and secular women are striving to achieve gender justice, mistrust toward Western secular values stems from a perceived hostility of secular-liberal feminism toward religion. This has resulted in the construction of an alternative movement among faith-based Muslim women activists that places religion at the center of their activism. By embracing an egalitarian interpretation of Islamic sacred scriptures, these Muslim women activists are advocating for a reformation of Islamic law.

The space afforded by liberal-secular feminism has historically excluded Muslim women's voices and experiences. In Iran, feminism has often been portrayed as the ultimate expression of *gharbzadigī* (Westoxification). The concept of *gharbzadigī* carries the negative connotation of a loss of Iranian cultural and historical identity through the adoption of Western ideas and values. This was exacerbated by the Pahlavi monarchy's (1925–79) imposition of top-down secularization and emancipation, which further alienated Iranian women, except for the elite population. The concept of *gharbzadigī*, which was popularized by the influential Iranian writer Jamal Al Ahmad in the 1960s, was predominantly linked to women's rights issues. The initial association of women's rights with Westoxification was made because women were deemed to be more susceptible to this particular phenomenon and its influence.[5] Furthermore, women's issues were strategically used by Western powers to undermine Muslims and exercise control over Muslim-majority lands.

Feminism has historically been perceived as a Western phenomenon with imperialist and elitist tendencies alien to the Iranian way of life. Thus feminist organizations have been viewed with suspicion. Although in contemporary Iran the concept of feminism has been evolving, traditionalists consider it to be a sign of *gharbzadigī* and to contradict an organic Iranian women's movement. The concept of *gharbzadigī* became central for the revolutionaries during the 1979 uprising that toppled the Pahlavi monarchy. The anti-imperialist position advanced by the revolutionaries emphasized independence from foreign influence in all aspects of life. Consequently, in contemporary Iran, the majority of women's rights organizations that are working within existing structures set by the state try to distance themselves from such loaded terms.

Some Muslim women activists also distance themselves from the concept of "Islamic feminism" because of the historical misappropriation of feminist rhetoric by Westerners to rationalize the assault on Islamic cultures and Muslim-majority lands.[6] The limitations of the secular liberal lens in analyzing Muslim women's activism have led to the emergence of a competing discourse that I refer to as *faith-based activism*. In an effort to move beyond the binary discourse of *feminism* and *Islamism*, I employ the term *faith-based activism* to signify religious activism that synthesizes Islamic values and social justice activism.

The term *faith-based activism* advances the notion that women possess agency and can transform their circumstances through empowering themselves. In this understanding of activism, empowerment is achieved through spiritual guidance and engagement with sacred scriptures. The term suggests cultivating and transforming one's religious conviction into social action by grounding women's rights in sacred scripture instead of secular values. More specifically, it is an approach that stands for justice and galvanizes a deeper connection between religion and social justice. Faith-based activism is thus a synthesis of the ideals of religious beliefs with the activists' zeal for justice, combined to create a strategic path to advance social, political, and legal reform. Considering the structure of the Islamic Republic, one of the effective means of advancing women's rights has been through localizing women's movements and formulating women's rights within an Islamic jurisprudential framework.

The reluctance of organizations such as IIZ to be associated with Islamic feminism is also rooted in the fact that they do not want to lose credibility among the 'ulama' (religious scholars) and traditionalist masses, whose approval is crucial for gaining legitimacy in their reinterpretation efforts to improve women's status within an Islamic context. Some female religious activists refrain from framing their activism as promoting absolute gender equality. Instead, they champion the idea of complementary roles for men and women, as endorsed by their faith. Therefore, instead of feminism, alternative terms such as *woman-centered*, *gender equity*, *egalitarian*, and *gender justice* have been used to advance causes related to gender justice within Islamic frameworks.[7] Furthermore, feminism is understood to be exclusively concerned with the welfare of women, without considering the needs of different members of the family and societal units. The association of feminism with secularism and by extension an exclusion of religion has further complicated any connection with this concept.

In their effort to dismantle gender hierarchies, IIZ adopts its own unique approach to addressing women's issues. In post-Revolution Iran, the two prominent approaches toward women's rights issues have been *sunnatī* (traditionalist) and *digar-andīshī* (reformist). In dealing with women's rights issues, the *sunnatī* approach adopts a cautious outlook toward both Islamic and secular feminism, while the *digar-andīshī* outlook is influenced by liberal ideals derived from Islamic feminism and the Universal Declaration of Human Rights. IIZ has constructed a third space in which elements of traditionalist and reformist thought come together. This hybrid approach revisits Islamic law and tradition by foregrounding female perspectives and experiences. Members of the IIZ employ the term *fiqh-i zanan* (women's jurisprudence) to characterize their unique approach to reinterpreting Islamic jurisprudence and to distinguish their activism. Women's jurisprudence utilizes a fluid and inclusive approach toward Islamic jurisprudence and builds upon a long reformist tradition in Iran. Through women's jurisprudence, these faith-based activists are promoting a method that amends legal rulings by problematizing and engaging with tradition without resorting to secularization.

Women's jurisprudence takes women's experiences into account when developing legal opinions in accordance with Islamic principles. It is holistic in its approach as it tries to make Islamic jurisprudence, which has been distorted by male bias, more inclusive. Considering that Islamic law is designed as prejudiced in favor of male values, IIZ believes that it is imperative to include women's perspectives and experiences. When interpreting legal rulings, members of IIZ rely on *ijtihād* while also using hermeneutic phenomenology, which incorporates women's perspectives. In doing so, they are shifting the legal paradigm, which has been traditionally male-centric, into a space where both male and female experiences and voices are accounted for and valued. What distinguishes Shi'i women's application of *ijtihād* from that of their Sunni counterparts[8] is that, in the Shi'i tradition, the door of *ijtihād* has always remained open, serving as the primary means for addressing legal matters. Thus Shi'i women employing *ijtihād* are operating within the orthodox framework of their own tradition.

Faith-based activists are simultaneously challenging and redefining the immutability of Islamic law as perpetuated by the state. As legal anthropologist Ziba Mir-Hosseini argues, it is important to recognize that such critical engagement with Islamic law does not mean that the sacredness of shari'a has diminished; rather, the modern nation-state's ideological utilization of shari'a and its infiltration into both the public and private lives of its citizens have created a pressing need for legal reform.[9] The interdependence of political and religious authorities in Iran requires any debate over women's rights to be within the confines of an Islamic framework.[10] The point of departure for a growing number of faith-based activists is the modern nation-state's authoritative role in enforcing traditionalist interpretations of law at the expense of more dynamic interpretations.

To bring about feasible change in women-related issues, political and religious authorities need to reevaluate Islamic jurisprudence in light of modern discourses on women's rights. The Islamic Republic of Iran finds itself in a precarious position where it has to deal with contradictory premises: on the one hand it must uphold the promise that Islam is compatible with women's rights, while on the other hand it endorses a hierarchical understanding of gender. Such contradictions have created an opening for women to develop counterdiscourses. These evolving counterdiscourses have contributed to changes in the gender policies of the Islamic Republic and have led to the reversal of some of the earlier policies adopted by the state.[11]

Iranian women's faith-based activism has been a contested ground for secularists and traditionalists. Secular feminists have embodied a

Western-inspired emancipation of women, particularly during the Pahlavi era. In this paradigm, women's liberation has been historically tied to modernizing their dress code, often challenging their traditional and cultural values. Contrary to secular feminists, traditionalists insist that "real liberation" for women, as understood in the Islamic tradition, lies in their modesty. For traditionalists, the focus on women's dress code is essential; they advocate for more modest attire as a means to shield women from the male gaze and exploitation, framing this as a path to women's freedom and safety.

Through an analysis of competing voices in the context of women's faith-based activism, I engage in a cross-fertilization of critical scholarship and move beyond the discourse on religious gendering to examine how women have influenced Islamic tradition and institutions. Most relevant to my research is the scholarship that theorizes how Muslim women are engaging in localized reformation through religious activism.[12] My scholarship draws on and contributes to the existing body of knowledge that highlights the ways Muslim women act as agents of change. Such change is sometimes in concert with and at other times independent of the state and tradition.

## RECLAIMING AGENCY IN IRANIAN WOMEN'S ACTIVISM

It is important to ground and analyze Iranian women's activism in the larger Shiʻi discourse on women's rights movements across the Middle East. In the context of Shiʻi women's activism in Lebanon, Lara Deeb's scholarship on women who are pious activists raises significant questions about publicly performed religiosity. To frame Shiʻi Muslim women's activism in Lebanon, Deeb uses the expression *public piety* and defines it as "understanding and practicing Islam correctly, sacrificing one's time, money, and life to help others; and supporting the resistance against Israeli occupation. Underlying all these values is a strong belief in the necessity of both spiritual and material progress."[13] Informed by Deeb's scholarship regarding the concept of piety, my study crafts an analysis of women's activism among faith-based activists in Iran who employ piety and political activism in order to bring about reformation and reinforce women's authority in both public and religious spheres. The emergence of new "Muslim publics" can be interpreted as an indication of growing pluralism, where conversations about the "authentic" interpretations of sacred scriptures are becoming increasingly inclusive.[14]

In Western discourse, the secular understanding of agency has become the dominant framework in constructing perceptions of women and feminism. Considering that feminism is central to secular discourse, the analysis of agency acquires a distinctive meaning in liberal feminism. In secular-liberal feminist discourse, *agency* acquires a distinctive meaning and is structured as the willingness to prioritize the interest of an individual over both society and religion, which are presumed to limit human liberty.[15] Anthropologist Lila Abu-Lughod asks: "In what way can scholars identify women's resistance without misattributing to them forms of consciousness or politics that are not part of their lived experience—something like a feminist consciousness or feminist politics?"[16]

Abu-Lughod's scholarship takes into account Muslim women's experiences and objectives when resisting dominant structures of power. While studies of unconventional types of resistance by women or minorities have provided us with alternative perspectives and expanded our understanding of how women navigate power structures, Abu-Lughod warns against a celebratory culture that idealizes such resistance.[17] To obtain a more comprehensive view of resistance, Abu-Lughod proposes that researchers examine different types of opposition to domination and their connection with structures of power. Such an outlook is imperative for my study as it locates the specific nexus and manner in which power is exercised. *Women, Faith, and Family* examines how Iranian female activists use a myriad of approaches to entice policymakers to reform family law. Specifically, women's involvement in the production of religious knowledge and their subsequent connection with influential political and religious authorities are brought to the fore. Through such complex and dynamic engagement, women's rights activists frame their call for gender justice as rooted in local values rather than influenced by Western ideals.

In thinking about women's activism, Saba Mahmood's work on female agency in Egypt also offers valuable insight. Mahmood examines the ways in which women's pious activities have political outcomes by disrupting power relations. In this context, women's religious and pious activities, which at times reinforce traditional gendered norms, can affect power relations in ways that allow for meaningful ruptures. As Mahmood argues, shifts in power relations do not have to take the form of resistance to domination. Her work explores the expression of religiosity within everyday acts of resistance that affect political decision-making, attitudes, and behaviors. In this vein, invoking religious scriptures and being involved in hermeneutic projects to advocate for women's rights are deemed as manifestations of agency with political outcomes.[18] This is a valuable approach for looking at how most female religious activists have asserted their agency within traditional and Islamic frameworks. These women have not fully taken on an overt or oppositional form of agency; rather, they partake in religious discourses, simultaneously perpetuating and resisting gendered norms. Through engaging in activities that are both political and sacred in nature, Iranian women activists play a critical role in advocating family law reform. By analyzing women's faith-based activism, my work looks at how power and authority interact and are negotiated as women strategically expose gender inequalities. This work challenges the assumption of many secular Western feminists that religion hinders, even undermines, women's agency.

The shadow of Western feminism over Muslim women's activism is reflected in the way Saba Mahmood problematizes some of the premises that support the postcolonial feminist portrayal of Muslim women. The secular assumptions underlying postcolonial feminist scholarship enforce a Western perspective on what is considered progressive versus regressive. Mahmood questions these secular-liberal biases and urges for a more inclusive model of agency.[19] An inclusive model of agency distances itself from rigid secular and liberal frameworks that perceive self-determination and absolute equality as central objectives in women's liberation projects.[20] It is important to use a broad definition of agency, one that is not confined to women's liberation from tradition and that includes a variety of endeavors women are engaged in, such as revolutionary movements, counterhegemony, and sociopolitical reform.[21]

Mahmood's unconventional notion of agency proposes that the embodiment of piety by women is a form of agency rooted in the practice of Islamic morality. While Mahmood's work is innovative and compelling, she generalizes women's religiosity when describing piety movements, offering limited detail on how power is distributed within different religious structures. Furthermore, there is little account of *how* and *why* such movements are becoming increasingly popular and the extent to which Muslim women activists both influence and are influenced by structures of power. In response to these queries, my work critically examines the activism of IIZ members in Iran, indicating a paradigm shift in power relations.

*Women, Faith, and Family* addresses some of the existing literature's reductive interpretations of feminist agency and justice, particularly in relation to Muslim women. If the feminist notion of justice and activism is based on a secular-liberal epistemology, it inadvertently reduces female activists into a limited perspective, suggesting that they can achieve true liberation only if they overtly contest structures of power. Such a liberal-secular model of agency does not account for the agency of Muslim women who are engaged in the production of religious knowledge in an attempt to reinterpret sacred scriptures. These women, while operating within the framework of their religious traditions—and thereby reinforcing its legitimacy—are covertly countering existing power structures by their strategic engagement with sacred texts. Therefore, if we are to truly grasp the nuanced agency of Muslim women activists, particularly in the context of Shi'i Iran, it becomes imperative to refine our conceptual framework of agency.

Within the secular feminist discourse, the advocacy of Muslim women for reform within a religious tradition that is frequently viewed as endorsing female subordination presents a conundrum. Nonetheless, the intermediary space that nurtures this form of activism transcends the conventional boundaries set by liberal and secular ideologies on gender parity.[22] Specifically, many female faith-based activists refuse to define their activism as resistance to gender inequality; instead they advocate for complementary roles for men and women as sanctioned by their religious tradition. Increasingly, we are witnessing women using religious language to advocate for their rights because of the affective and effective power and influence religious scholarship wields in traditional spaces. Female activists in Iran have come to recognize the powerful impact of religion in their quest to advance women's rights. Their familiarity with Islamic scripture works to their advantage and affords them the opportunity for increased political and public engagement. The outcome of such an approach is not an Islamic state but a localized civic society.

An examination of Iran's historical trajectory illustrates the disruption the 1979 Revolution posed to the prevailing modernization paradigms that had been influential since the 1950s.[23] The participation of Islamist women in the revolutionary movement problematized the binary construct of modernity versus tradition inherent in modernization theories.[24] A number of the women who actively participated in the Revolution, including Maryam Behroozi, Zahra Rahnavard, Monireh Gor, and A'zam Taleqani, later became affiliated with IIZ. The work of these individuals during and after the Iranian Revolution blurred the restrictive boundaries of the modern, the traditional, the progressive, and the regressive in relation to women's rights activism. Yet the scholarship on female religious activists in Iran is generally monolithic and cautiously gravitates toward early modernization theories when discussing religiosity and secularism.[25] As a result, Iranian women's faith-based activism is treated with suspicion and understood to be apologetic, while secular women's activism is presumed to be progressive and liberating for all women.

Drawing on anthropological research and case studies by prominent scholars such as Lila Abu-Lughod, Saba Mahmood, and Ziba Mir-Hosseini among others, this book offers a comprehensive exploration of Iranian women's faith-based activism by analyzing how these women reinterpret Islamic family law. By employing a concept of agency that expands beyond the model perpetuated by secular-liberal principles,[26] I look into how women are embodying faith-based activism to challenge hegemonic religious and traditional configurations in an effort to reform Islamic family law. Women's faith-based activism counters the reductive understanding of women's religious activism that has been perpetuated by radical Islamists, reinforced by Orientalists, and sustained by some feminists. *Women, Faith, and Family* challenges the secular-liberal feminist portrayal of Muslim women with limited agency while also contesting traditional feminist scholarship that exaggerates the opportunities afforded to Muslim women by measures that in effect restrict their courses of action.[27] In problematizing the binary of secular-liberal feminism and traditionalist religious activism, this book illustrates that such concepts are not mutually exclusive; rather, they intersect and inform one another.

It is important to point out that feminism and faith-based activism are not static categories; rather, they evolve in the process of their interactions. In her study of feminism in Islam, Zakia Salime describes this fluidity as the feminization of Islamist groups and the "Islamization" of feminist groups. The common threads in the theoretical dispositions of feminism and faith-based activism highlight the gaps in liberal-secular feminist theory, which depicts Muslim women as individuals in need of liberation as opposed to active agents of change with the power to transform state policies related to women's rights.[28] To move beyond the duality of Islamist and secular frameworks, it is essential for contemporary feminists to understand women's religious activism in terms of reformist and faith-based movements as opposed to regressive and reactionary ones. Striving to have their voices heard, these faith-based activists have brought women's rights issues to the forefront of the public consciousness.

Traditionally, women's activism in Iran has been associated with secular modernity as the path to women's empowerment. Although secularist discourses paved the way for women's entry into politics during the Pahlavi reign and primed Iranian women to participate in the 1979 Revolution, they have become less relevant to the current discourse on gender. In contemporary Iran, an effective means of advancing gender justice is through religious frameworks.[29] Female faith-based advocates such as those active in IIZ are restructuring the secular/religious dichotomy in women's activism. These women are disrupting the tradition of women's activism, which previously endorsed secular modernity as the only path to women's empowerment and liberation.

In religious activist circles, top-down political agendas that enforce universalist tenets such as equal rights for women have come under criticism. Secular feminists may inadvertently silence or erase the experiences of women from developing nations in their attempt to represent the experiences of women globally.[30] Anthropologist Arzoo Osanloo deconstructs and problematizes the ways in which employing the human rights discourse as a universal concept, at times puts it at odds with the local culture. Osanloo points out the importance of recognizing the historical circumstances in which the human rights discourse has been formed. According to Osanloo, "Rights, in general, and rights talk in particular, are cultural practices emerging from a European-American historical and political trajectory that includes colonialism and is shaped by global power relations."[31] Osanloo further argues that in order to fully comprehend the implications of human rights in societies like Iran, it is imperative to consider the various forms of representations of human rights in such societies.[32] Muslim women's rights groups avoid becoming entwined in the "human rights" discourse, which is primarily rooted in Western constructions. In alternative activism spaces, Muslim women's engagement in localized reformation through faith-based activism is gaining momentum. IIZ's decision to frame its activities as a quest for gender justice rather than to adopt the label of feminism reflects a commitment to their tradition while strategically avoiding state marginalization.

The study of Iranian women's faith-based activism is an attempt to understand how women's faith empowers them to seek gender justice in the Islamic Republic of Iran. It is important to note that the focus on faith-based activism does not mean Iran lacks aspiring secularist women's rights activists. Given that this book is looking at the Shi'i legal tradition's capacity to foster gender justice, I specifically focus on a coalition that works within the framework of the Islamic tradition and promotes women's rights through faith-based activism. Engagement from traditional elements in Iranian society in endorsing values consistent with gender justice could be viewed as an indication that women's struggle toward gender justice is becoming more prevalent and localized.

## METHODOLOGICAL APPROACH: NAVIGATING FAITH-BASED ACTIVISM

The scope of *Women, Faith, and Family* incorporates a blend of detailed case studies, ethnographic research methods, and textual analysis. To analyze Iranian women's faith-based activism, I examine the social, political, and faith-based activism of IIZ members through textual analysis, interviews, and participant observation. Through the use of interdisciplinary research methods, drawing on works in religious studies, women's studies, and anthropology, I approach women's faith-based activism textually and contextually, as well as in actual practice. I use a combination of anthropological, interpretive, jurisprudential, and theological methodologies in order to offer a nuanced look at women's faith-based activism that balances modernity and tradition. In conducting textual analysis to examine the works of Muslim female activists in Iran, I critically review primary sources such as organizational reports, selection of works written by female activists involved in IIZ, and other primary and secondary legal sources. By analyzing women's exegetical writings, this book examines the extent to which these women operate within an Islamic framework when negotiating their roles and rights with religious and political authorities. The book offers a critical understanding of the strategies Iranian women utilize to bridge the gap between Islamic jurisprudence and gender justice.

A detailed examination of the legal arguments presented by members of IIZ sets the stage in this book. After identifying and unpacking the key arguments, I turn to the sources informing these activists' arguments and the legal texts they draw upon in order to legitimize their cause. Specifically, I examine how these women draw on classical sources such as hadith commentaries and premodern jurisprudential texts in making the case for inclusive gender policies. This discussion offers insights into both premodern and contemporary juristic discourses on family law, addressing areas like polygyny and consent, temporary marriage and dowries, and evaluating the role of modern institutions on these subjects. The writings of influential premodern jurists such as al-Muhaqqiq al-Hilli (d. 1277), Shahid al-Awwal (d. 1385), and Shahid al-Thani (d.

1559), whose works are among the most extensively referenced in Shiʻi family law, are also critically examined. Additionally, the work of Ayatollah Ruhollah Khomeini (d. 1989) is considered in this study because of his authority and influence on modern Shiʻi legal rulings. By revisiting the traditional and modern legal arguments regarding family law, I explore the extent to which female activists' use of modern religious discourse draws from the Islamic tradition.

Drawing from textual analysis and anthropological methodologies such as participant observation and both structured and unstructured interviews, I delve deep into the activism of IIZ members. My interactions with these women provided insights into the nuances of their religiosity and agency. As I collected and examined my research findings from them, I engaged in a form of critical reflexivity that encouraged me to reflect on the intricacies of my identity as an Iranian Muslim woman, trained in Western academia. Although a few of the interviews were conducted in the United States, the majority of the interviews, which are in Farsi, were conducted in Iran. By adopting these methods, I familiarized myself with members of IIZ, attempting to learn the subtleties of their activism through questions as well as observation. In this way, the book seeks to examine religion and faith-based activism both textually and experientially.

In the quest to give an authentic account, prioritizing women's experiences offers a more accurate depiction of their lived reality. It thus becomes imperative for scholars to look beyond their own assumptions and engage with the experiences of the individual. In this regard, Dorothy Smith and Sandra Harding argue that feminist theorists need to incorporate the viewpoint of women by focusing on their lived experiences.[33] The tendency, particularly by poststructuralist scholars, to overly rely on religious text at the expense of women's experiences has resulted in a misrepresentation of their reality and a reductive understanding of resistance and how women embody their faith.

In an analysis of the relationship between Islamic law and women, it is important to holistically consider not only the law but also societal customs and practices. Investigating IIZ's faith-based activism requires situating these women's activism within the contexts of historical, religious, and sociopolitical movements. As historian Judith Tucker argues, it is not enough to examine only what the law states about women; it is equally important to consider how these laws have been interpreted and lived by Muslims.[34] By understanding how women decide to respond to or interpret their religious traditions, we can understand how religion is embodied in practice. The doctrines of a religious tradition are not necessarily reflective of the embodied concept of religiosity; religious living can best be discovered in the lived practices of the faithful.[35] Therefore, it becomes crucial to consider how Muslim women activists negotiate their rights within their respective environment and in so doing reestablish their authority in the religious discourse.

Studying the role of Iranian women in reforming family law through faith-based activism necessitates recognizing evolving power dynamics. Considering that Iran is among a handful of states upholding an Islamic court system, reformations in family law can significantly affect the country's Shi'i identity. Reformation of family law poses great possibilities for shifting gender paradigms and power dynamics. It is at times of reform that the shifting of power relations becomes evident, making the interaction among the state, women, and religious authorities particularly pronounced in these pivotal moments.[36] By framing this project in line with the way women, religious authorities, and the state negotiate and claim authority over family law, I highlight points of contrast and conformity among these three actors as well as the ensuing shifts in power relations.

One such shift took place in 2007, when the "Principlist"[37] government of Mahmoud Ahmadinejad proposed revisions to the Family Protection Bill. Some of the articles in the bill created unrest among women's rights activists in Iran, who labeled it the "Anti-Family Bill." The newly revised bill was controversial and was considered discriminatory toward women. The proposed reforms in the new bill particularly alarmed female activists and organizations that were ardent supporters of the Islamic Republic of Iran. One such organization, IIZ, had been actively engaged in faith-based activism to advance women's rights within Shi'i Iran.

## WOMEN, FAITH, AND FAMILY: AN INSIDE LOOK

The following chapters examine issues pertaining to women's faith-based activism and gender justice by taking a thematic approach to the study of Islamic family law. Framed within the context of IIZ, the book explores women's legal status and activism through various lenses such as marriage, divorce, custody, women's activism, and female religious authority. This study unfolds over the course of six in-depth chapters, each focusing on a different aspect of the interplay between faith-based activism and family law within the Islamic tradition in the context of Iran.

The first chapter, "Women's Activism: The Case of Itilaf-i Islami-yi Zanan (Women's Islamic Coalition)," explores women's faith-based activism, focusing on how activists have challenged restrictions on women's participation in the political and religious spheres. Through textual analysis, interviews, and participant observation, I examine the initiatives of IIZ to confront discriminatory policies within an Islamic framework. This examination highlights how IIZ's innovative adoption of women's jurisprudence strives for gender justice in the Shi'i tradition and deviates from conventional jurisprudential methods. Additionally, the analysis reveals the multifaceted nature of faith-based activism and the extent to which Muslim women's mastery and application of religious resources have empowered them. The chapter asserts that this empowered stance in gender negotiations has advanced significant transformation in the bedrock structures of Iran's legal institutions.

Building on these explorations, the second chapter, "The Intersection of Law, the State, and Women's Activism in Iran," contextualizes IIZ's activism by tracing Iranian women's activism since the twentieth century and the changes to women's legal status in the Iranian Constitution and Civil Code. This chapter explores the extent to which the legal standing of women in the realm of family law has been transformed since the Iranian Constitutional Revolution (1905–7). It further provides an overview of the process of codification of law in modern Iran and examines how the Islamic Republic of Iran instituted Islamic legal codes that were enforced by state officials in state courts. Subsequently, the chapter analyzes IIZ's efforts to reform the Constitution and support the Citizenship Rights Charter. The chapter argues that in their pursuit of gender justice, IIZ activists have reformed and renegotiated paradigms of gender and Islam, with their activism emerging as a potent force that has substantially redefined Iran's legal landscape.

The third chapter, "Itilaf-i Islami-yi Zanan and the Family Law Controversy," discusses IIZ's attempts to reform and challenge the 2007 Family Protection Bill. This section adopts a twofold approach: first, it demonstrates how the women active in IIZ tried to revive the egalitarian principle believed to be inherent in Islamic law through the cultivation of women's jurisprudence; and second, it shows how they challenged the Western framework of approaching gender justice through the prism of absolute equality. I argue that IIZ, by proposing an alternative family paradigm, is reforming Islamic family law while simultaneously arguing for its legitimacy. In this chapter, I examine the negotiations and discussions that took place between 2008 and 2014 involving IIZ, when the organization expressed public disapproval toward some of the discriminatory articles in the Family Protection Bill. IIZ has made substantial progress in contesting the Family Protection Bill, achieved through their active participation in the production of religious knowledge and their negotiations with religious and political authorities. This proactive engagement and faith-based activism in the sociopolitical and religious sphere has been instrumental in driving the reformation of Iran's legal paradigm.

The fourth chapter, "Islamic Family Law and Gender Politics: Legal Provisions of Family Formation," explores the foundations of the family unit and the different types of marriage recognized in Shi'i *fiqh* (jurisprudence) and the Civil Code, including temporary and permanent marriages. The chapter addresses the necessary preconditions that precede an Islamic marriage, including the proposal and engagement processes. Issues pertaining to the legal age of marriage and the role of legal guardians in legitimizing marriage for minors are also examined. This chapter provides further insight into the traditional Islamic marriage contract and dower and highlights the reforms suggested by members of IIZ. It also investigates modern state-sponsored reforms and depicts how women in Iran use dower as a bargaining tool to compensate for legal restrictions on women's rights. By examining the changes affecting the modern Muslim family, the chapter shows how IIZ members have reenvisioned and renegotiated fundamentals of the traditional family paradigm, thus emphasizing their significant role in shaping policy and influencing its implementation.

Transitioning from marriage to marital roles, the fifth chapter, "Navigating Islamic Family Law: Life after Marriage and Rights after Divorce," analyzes the raison d'être of the family unit, as well as a complex network of ideas and assumptions about the roles each member of the family plays in Shi'i jurisprudence and the Iranian Civil Code. This chapter demonstrates the interconnectedness of spousal maintenance and women's sexual availability, which constitute an integral part of classical Islamic marriage. Initially, a couple's duties, including the husband's *nafaqa* (obligation to financially provide for his wife) and the wife's *tamkīn* (obedience toward her husband), are discussed. Following this, the chapter delves into the legal ramifications of failure to uphold spousal duties. It then examines the three standard ways to dissolve an Islamic marriage in the Shi'i legal tradition—*ṭalāq* (divorce at the husband's behest), *khul'* (divorce at the wife's behest), and *tafrīq* (divorce by judicial order), as well as their ramifications. The chapter also offers innovative dimensions to the discussion on the breakdown of the family unit by examining the concept of *ṭalāq 'āṭifī* (emotional divorce) in the context of modern Iran. It further discusses how the traditional Islamic concepts of *ḥiḍāna* (custodianship) and *wilāya* (guardianship) have shaped family relations regarding custody and remarriage. The chapter then highlights modern reforms that have been suggested by IIZ to improve women's legal standing in matters pertaining to divorce and custodianship. This chapter concludes by arguing that IIZ members' commitment to faith-based activism, coupled with their participation in political discourse, has been integral in reshaping legal interpretations and institutional structures, particularly in the context of family law.

The final chapter, "Conclusion: Women's Involvement in Production of Religious Knowledge," chronicles the significant strides made by female faith-based activists in post-Revolution Iran. It sets the stage by examining the issue of female religious authority within the Shi'i tradition and analyzing the opportunities and challenges faced by women seeking to reclaim their position as religious authorities. This chapter makes a compelling case that female faith-based activists such as those active in IIZ have provided an alternative framework that recognizes Islamic principles of justice and utilizes them to call for comprehensive reform in women's legal status. These reforms are deemed as essential considering that the traditional construction of gender lends itself to injustice and inequality. By arguing that justice and equity are fundamental principles of Islam, IIZ activists have challenged patriarchal dominance and made progress toward achieving gender justice through political activism and epistemic authority. The concluding chapter suggests that women's faith-based activism and participation in the production of Islamic knowledge have transformed legal reasoning, legal institutions, and the nature of lawmaking in the Islamic Republic of Iran.

# CHAPTER I

# Women's Activism

*The Case of Itilaf-i Islami-yi Zanan
(Women's Islamic Coalition)*

In 2007, Mahmood Ahmadinejad's "Principlist" government proposed the Family Protection Bill. It met with broad disapproval from female activists, inciting a feeling of discontent. Across various sectors of society and organizations, faith-based activists ranging from *Islah-talab* (neoreformers) to *Usul-gara* (neotraditionalists) strategically united in opposition to the controversial bill, labeling it the "Anti-Family Bill." Each act of resistance emboldened them, amplifying their demands and bolstering their collective resolve. In 2008 this focus and determination led to the establishment of the IIZ Coalition. Positioning themselves as sociopolitical actors, the women active in IIZ did not cease their efforts to reform discriminatory laws, even when they met with resistance by the government.

The diversity of political and ideological convictions among IIZ's members was not only integral to the identity of the group but also key to its effectiveness. Some of these women endorsed traditionalist views on gender roles, while others advocated for a more open polity in which women would have access to equal opportunities and rights in public and private spheres. But it had become evident to all of them that reformist, traditionalist, and liberal activists should form a united front in their struggle toward gender justice. Combining their efforts to advance women's rights and improve the sociopolitical status of Iranian women, they partially succeeded in forcing the state to reform the Family Protection Law.

The majority of female activists involved in IIZ came from either middle-class or urban backgrounds. The Revolution had a relatively empowering effect on their public lives, encouraging new forms of social and political activism for women. As a result, a growing number of women from religious families, primarily those who supported the establishment of an Islamic Republic in Iran, gained prominence in public and political spheres. These women not only encouraged but insisted on reform to women's legal status. Their sociopolitical affiliations made the arguments they put forward difficult for the state to refute. This was partly because some IIZ members had training in Islamic sciences or connections to prominent religious and political authorities. This unique access to centers of power allowed them to strategically pressure influential authorities, enhancing the legitimacy of their gender justice demands in the eyes of the government, especially compared to their secular counterparts, who had historically framed their demands in secular terms.[1] Armed with the belief that gender equity was their Islamic right, IIZ activists were unified in demanding gender justice by engaging in religious reasoning.

Intrigued by these dynamics and the experiences of the activists, I embarked on an immersive research journey in the summer of 2008. I conducted semistructured, in-depth interviews over a span of five months in Iran with female activists from the IIZ Coalition. Continuing this exploration, I also conducted follow-up interviews in 2012 and 2014, as well as two sets of online interviews, one in 2019 and one in 2021. The interviews were conducted in Farsi, transcribed, and later translated into English. Throughout the analysis, a recurrent theme that emerged from the interviews was that the framing of the questions provoked emotional responses from the interviewees, particularly when the terms *feminism* or *Islamist* were used. At times when I used these terms, the interviewees expressed doubt about my intentions as a researcher and voiced concern about whether I was accurately conveying the complexity of their ideas and experiences. These encounters spurred me to reevaluate my positionality and the complexity of my own "shifting identifications"[2] in relation to the participants in the study.

Some of the prominent figures I interviewed included the founder of IIZ, the founder of the Zaynab Society,[3] and the former vice president for women and family affairs in President Hassan Rouhani's cabinet. In addition to these conversations, I closely examined the Coalition's website to access content produced by IIZ members and to gather insights into the organization's activities throughout the country. Since 2015,

IIZ has moved its platform fully online to adapt to the changing technological and political landscape in Iran. Recent years have seen a noticeable increase in the online presence of female activists, which has turned cyberspace into a public forum. In Iran, online platforms encourage lively debates and exchange of ideas and allow women and activists to tackle subjects that are deemed to be controversial. To avoid being accused of going against the interests and principles of the state, writers at times use pseudonyms to explore controversial issues that challenge the status quo.[4] Although most content on IIZ's websites is published under real names, there are instances when members of the Coalition use pseudonyms to discuss politicized issues depending on the political climate, and at times some material is even removed to evade unnecessary scrutiny from the authorities.

One criterion for selecting IIZ for my research was that it is one of the few Iranian coalitions in which neotraditionalist and neoreformist women from different ideological and political backgrounds have united in their efforts and strategies to advance women's causes within an Islamic framework. After experiencing the co-opting of women's movements by the state, the 'ulama', or secularist currents throughout the last century, faith-based Iranian activists have come to realize that one of the most effective ways to advance their rights is through localized women's activism and popular support. They have also recognized that in order to effectively promote women's rights in a theocratic state, it is important to engage with religious discourses that appeal to both traditionalist masses and the state. In a direct reflection of these realizations, the interviews and information gathered made it all the more apparent that a counterdiscourse had developed in Iran with the aim of disputing the gendered practices of the state through religious activism. In light of Iran's state of flux, both socially and politically, the transformation of Iranian society and the Iranian polity has compelled many IIZ activists to reassess and modify their views regarding women's rights. In light of IIZ members' pragmatic approach, it is not unexpected that the reforms they demand are at times influenced by situational imperatives.

The IIZ Coalition's founder, arguably the most vocal member of the organization, had formerly been the secretary of Jami'a-yi Zaynab (Zaynab Society). Being politically active during the Iranian Revolution emboldened these activists to criticize unjust laws toward women. Like many other members of IIZ, the Coalition's founder had lived under both secular and religious legal systems. During the Pahlavi era, reforms related to women were strictly enforced by secular elites and did not adequately represent the lived realities of the majority of Iranian women, which were frequently dictated by traditional and cultural norms that differed significantly from the ideals promoted by the elite. Then, following the Revolution, a number of rulings instated throughout the Pahlavi reign were retracted and replaced with new laws based on religious readings of women's rights. What may have been unprecedented is that after the Revolution, newly empowered religious women who had been marginalized under Pahlavi rule began to express their objections toward some of the discriminatory policies of the Islamic state that were enacted in the name of religion.[5]

After 2008, IIZ, which had initially engaged with the urban and educated women of Tehran, expanded its reach into several other cities and rural areas across Iran through both in-person and online platforms. The Coalition's emphasis on gender justice and human dignity aligns with its mission of challenging patriarchal views toward women. Some of the central objectives of this organization include advocating women's jurisprudence, empowering women, eradicating discrimination, promoting Islamic ethics, and strengthening the family unit. IIZ also focuses on improving women's status as individuals and as part of both the family unit and society. Embracing an Islamic outlook toward women to advance their independence and dignity is another priority for this organization. The Coalition advocates change and reform in the legal, cultural, and educational domains in an effort to assert egalitarian principles in relation to women's rights.

Members of this civil society network come from various organizations, including Jamiyyat-i Zanan-i Jumhuri-i Islami (Women's Society of Islamic Republic), Anjuman-i Zanan-i Musalman-i Pazhuhishgar (Muslim Women Scholars Association), and Jami'a-yi Zaynab (Zaynab Society). Most women active in the Coalition are prominent social, religious, or political figures who have in the past supported and contributed to the ideals of the Islamic Republic of Iran. These women predominantly reference Ayatollah Khomeini's support of women's involvement in political affairs. In the initial phase of the Iranian Revolution, Ayatollah Khomeini publicly legitimized women's involvement in social and political spheres and encouraged women to take part in the election process, not so much to exercise their right to vote as to fulfill their religious obligation. Women who in the past had found their voices to be silenced or drowned out now had a vested interest in ensuring the maintenance of the new revolutionary state. While these women appreciated the sociopolitical mobility they had gained in post-

Revolution Iran, secular activists felt that their demands and historic role in advancing women's rights were being systematically sidelined and began resisting the newly established Islamic Republic.[6]

Several prominent figures have a special status or hold a central position in IIZ. These include the late Maryam Behroozi (d. 2011), chairwoman of the Jami'a-yi Zaynab and the first female member of the post-Revolution parliament; Soheila Jelodarzadeh, a reformist, three-term parliamentarian, and active member of the Hizb-i Islami-yi Kar (Islamic Labor Party); Masoumeh Ebtekar, first female vice president of Iran, former head of Sazman-i Hifazat-i Muhit-i Zist (Department of Environment), and cofounder of the Institute for Women's Studies and Research; Shahindokht Molaverdi, former vice president for Women and Family Affairs; and Zahra Shojaei, reformist politician and advocate of women's rights. A number of IIZ members wield greater religious or political legitimacy due to their close ties to influential political or religious families. These include the late A'zam Taleqani (d. 2019), daughter of the prominent Ayatollah Mahmoud Taleqani; and Faezeh Hashemi, whose father, Akbar Hashemi Rafsanjani, was Iran's president for two consecutive terms. Both are women who have gained political influence and, in Taleqani's case, a certain degree of religious authority, partly attributable to their connections to religious or political figures.

Several high-profile members of the IIZ Coalition are religious women who were marginalized or imprisoned during Pahlavi rule. Religiously educated women like Maryam Behroozi, whose work centered on teaching Qur'anic studies to other women, were initially not viewed as threats to the monarchy. However, when Islam became a rallying point for resisting the Shah's rule, they were banned from the religious education of women and Behroozi herself was detained.[7] The Iranian Revolution, which led to the formation of a theocratic state, brought the custodian of shari'a to power. These women initially threw their full support behind the Islamic Republic and sought to elevate women's legal status through involvement in political discourse. However, after the Iran-Iraq War (1980–88), a growing number of female activists became increasingly dissatisfied with the gender policies of the state. Instead of turning their back on the system, most of them chose to work within the narrow spaces available in the political architecture to demand improvement in women's legal status. A critical approach adopted by these activists has been to challenge hierarchal interpretations by reinterpreting religious scripture through a more egalitarian lens. IIZ members recognize the challenges posed by the entrenchment of patriarchal paradigms in Iran's legal and political systems. In their view, these paradigms, and the gender stereotypes they promote, undermine the cause of advancing justice and equality. Consequently, they argue that legal rulings that pertain to women's rights must be issued in consultation with women.

A closer look at Jamiʻa-yi Zaynab, a leading organization within the IIZ Coalition that advocates women's involvement in political domains, offers important insights. Jamiʻa-yi Zaynab, the *Jumhuri Khah* (Republican) branch of the women's party, was established under the orders of former chief justice Ayatollah Mohammad Beheshti[8] and enjoyed the support of Ayatollah Khomeini. Acknowledging the positive impact of women's political activism, Khomeini advocated for their direct involvement in the political process. He also played a constructive role in bolstering the activities of the Zaynab Society by supporting partial funding for the organization. To assert the legitimacy of their activism, Jamiʻa-yi Zaynab and IIZ reference Ayatollah Khomeini's endorsement of women's engagement in the political domain. The late founder of the Jamiʻa-yi Zaynab, Maryam Behroozi, stated, "It is an honor for us to be the only association that Imam [Khomeini] allowed to use the Imam's share.[9] The Imam's outlook was actually very positive toward women and their political activities."[10] Throughout the sixteen years of Behroozi's presence in Parliament, and despite her traditionalist outlook and affinity with the *Usul-gara* (neotraditionalists) faction, she succeeded in changing some of the discriminatory laws affecting women, including ones related to divorce and retirement.[11]

The name Jamiʻa-yi Zaynab (Zaynab Society) was strategically selected. Zaynab, the granddaughter of Prophet Muhammad, is known for her leadership and courage in standing up against unjust authorities. In a speech given on the anniversary of the birth of Zaynab, Behroozi declared Zaynab to be a role model for herself and other Muslim women. Behroozi asserted that despite historical attempts to suppress women's activism and participation in the political sphere, since the early days of Islam women like Zaynab have been persistent in their mission to speak up against injustice. Islam, Behroozi argues, encourages women to engage in social and political activism.[12] Thus the discrepancy between men's and women's rights can be attributed to the lack of women's participation in religious and political domains. Behroozi has invited women and officials from various political parties, ministries, and city councils to join the common cause of advancing women's participation in politics. Faith-based activists like Behroozi further emphasize the benefits of the Revolution for women, including the provision of safe spaces for women to advance in society. The women involved in this organization assert that because of the Islamic nature of the Iranian Revolution, eradicating all forms of discrimination, particularly those targeting women, should be at the heart of all policy.

According to IIZ members, one of the central objectives of the Revolution was to entrust Iranians with political and legal autonomy and put an end to foreign influence. Carrying out Islamic justice thus became a prominent goal and the national slogan of the new political structure in post-Revolution Iran. For IIZ activists, Islam's conceptualization of women as liberated, independent, and powerful individuals motivated them to join the struggle against the Pahlavi monarchy. IIZ defends Islamic principles pertaining to gender justice because these very principles empower women to resist discrimination and propel them to oppose policies leading to the oppression of women in the name of Islam.

In the years following the Revolution, women who were not represented in the Pahlavi monarchy demonstrated their capabilities in various sociopolitical realms. But despite their contributions, women's share in positions of power has consistently remained minimal. This is a far cry from the Islamic justice that was promised during the early days of the 1979 Revolution. In their strategic effort to stay loyal to the ideals of the Revolution, IIZ has called for a reevaluation of women's status within the current structure and has demanded greater inclusion of women in politics, decision-making bodies, and the power structure. IIZ argues that when a society claims to be Islamic, its social and political constructs should promote justice and be inclusive. These female activists maintain that all the manifestations of oppression and discrimination against women need to be abolished for justice to prevail in a meaningful way. As asserted by IIZ, Islamic tradition upholds the belief that men and women originate from one essence and have equal ethical and social value. However, religious activists criticize the state for failing to create spaces where the full dignity of women can be honored.

For IIZ, honoring women's dignity means going beyond performative measures and allowing women from all walks of life to enter the public sphere in pursuit of justice and equality. In evaluating different governments' performance over the course of four decades since the Iranian Revolution, IIZ contends that although women have advanced on the educational and economic fronts, they remain underrepresented in decision-making positions; men continue to monopolize institutional positions of power and marginalize women. Despite women's active engagement in the

Revolution, the metaphorical glass ceiling has prevented them from reaching positions of power. IIZ reiterates that "throughout Islamic history, many women have stood at the vanguard of leadership. However, state-imposed policies and laws have stunted women's contribution to leadership at the local and national level. State policies that marginalize women have only intensified discriminatory practices in recent years, compelling women into roles confined to domestic responsibilities and significantly undermining their empowerment and leadership potential."[13] The limited number of women who have been offered leadership roles often find themselves conforming to the agendas and expectations of their male colleagues out of concern for maintaining their positions. Some of them have adopted a more conservative approach in order to navigate such environments and institutions.[14]

During President Rouhani's administration, in 2013, IIZ succeeded in nominating one of their members, Shahindokht Molaverdi, to become the vice president for Women and Family Affairs. Molaverdi is a women's rights advocate and firm believer in equal opportunity for men and women. But there is still a need for greater systemic change to empower women and provide them with equal social and political opportunities. IIZ activists say it is imperative for women to have a voice and an active presence on the Expediency Council and in the Assembly of Experts— influential bodies that hold responsibilities such as electing and removing the Supreme Leader as well as revising the Constitution.

In 2014, in a letter to President Rouhani, IIZ specified its expectations from the government. The letter charged that although over the years women had proven their political and individual capabilities, their involvement in policymaking and their presence in positions of power remained minimal. Members of IIZ demanded that the president uphold revolutionary principles and urged the government to take necessary measures to include women in the decision-making process. The activists offered various strategies to challenge prejudicial policies that posed a threat to women's autonomy and the family structure. They demanded "an Islamic Republic where all citizens, regardless of their gender, have equal opportunities and rights," and asserted that "based on the teachings of Islam, women are equal to men in terms of their human dignity. If women's dignity is not preserved, families will experience growing tensions and face the possibility of dissolution."[15] Similar letters have been communicated to President Ebrahim Raisi, who came to power in 2021. They are only the most recent of IIZ's many appeals to the government to stop the violation of women's rights.

IIZ members point out that although in the past men monopolized positions of power in political, legal, and religious institutions and women were confined to the private sphere, the 1979 Revolution promised to change that paradigm. These faith-based activists contend that women and men have equal civil rights and should be provided with equal opportunity to be active in social and political domains. Addressing the gendered nature of Islamic family law, which has limited women's participation in public life, they seek to resolve the tension between traditional conceptions of womanhood and women's public activities by adopting an approach that balances women's family commitments with their career requirements. Additionally, they urge public and private institutions, along with the state, to collaborate constructively to maximize women's involvement in the power structure. Specifically, they call upon the state and public institutions to offer women incentives to enter the workforce by providing childcare services and maternal paid leave.

The IIZ Coalition has made strides by focusing on issues affecting women and by engaging in various forms of activism, including petitioning the government, engaging in discussions with prominent religious and political authorities, and holding press conferences in an effort to problematize the infallibility of religious-based laws that are discriminatory toward women.[16] These faith-based activists are employing religious discourses to infiltrate male-dominated domains that have previously been closed off to the public, particularly women. In retrospect, the existence of a "religious public sphere" has created a space that allows these women's rights activists to thrive.[17]

## IIZ'S PERSPECTIVE ON GENDER EGALITARIANISM

IIZ's activism is grounded in both pragmatic and neoreformist approaches. The Coalition engages with a broad range of ethical and legal issues in order to advance gender justice. Formulating their distinct strategy and activism within a Shi'i legal framework has allowed these women to exceed the achievements of secular activists in post-Revolution Iran. IIZ's unique approach toward women's rights has fostered a space where the movement for gender justice is viewed as organic and localized, as opposed to a mere imitation of Western paradigms of gender equality. These women's rights activists are adamant about not abandoning their cultural and religious traditions in order to undermine androcentrism. Instead, they are working within current cultural, traditional, and religious norms as they advocate for women's rights by adopting religious language to convey their demands.

Despite their demands for gender justice reform, female activists from the IIZ Coalition are careful to avoid identification as feminists or secularists. When asked whether IIZ considered itself as an integral part of the feminist movement, Zahra Shojaei, a former politician and an IIZ member, replied:

> The feminist movement must be defined first. The term has many interpretations and definitions in our country. Feminism itself is an ideological movement that underwent changes throughout history. The first, second, and third waves of the movement do not have the same goals and employ different strategies to achieving their stated aims. Therefore, we cannot know with certainty whether the current movement in our country is influenced by feminism. In fact, browsing through our historical struggles toward justice and freedom only reaffirms this point that the women's social movement in Iran is national and organic, rooted in our own local values. Our own school of thought [Shi'i Islam] provides a far more efficient framework for achieving justice for women than anything Western feminism has to offer.[18]

Some members of IIZ criticize secular Western feminists for functioning as an extension of neoimperialist policies and consider Western feminist ideals to be detrimental to the progress of women in the Global South.[19] These faith-based activists also take issue with Western representations of Muslim women and are wary of the cultural hegemony that has been a signifier of Western feminism. Members of IIZ are well aware of the stigma attached to such concepts in Iran's political landscape, and they acknowledge the existence of a complex history and political culture that problematizes these terms. It is imperative for faith-based activists not to be labeled as feminists or advocates of human rights law if they are to escape the backlash and controversy associated with the terms *human rights* and *feminism*.[20] Consequently IIZ has chosen a pragmatic approach by disassociating itself from such concepts in order to avoid drawing unwanted attention from authorities.

These terms may no longer carry the same degree of negative connotation among the younger generation of Iranian activists, mostly because of different lived experiences. Newer generations of Iranian women face unique challenges, different from the ones experienced by traditionalist women such as IIZ members who lived under the Pahlavi monarchy. For most members of IIZ who experienced life prior to the Revolution, it has become increasingly clear that they need to take into account the experiences and socioeconomic circumstances of a younger generation of Iranian women in order to become more influential and address their demands.[21]

IIZ has also made a conscious decision to frame its activism as a quest for gender justice as opposed to gender equality. Though in the postmodern era the idea of justice without equality is often deemed futile and subversive, scholars such as Kecia Ali argue that activists and reformists "must take care not to be blinded by the commitment to equality, and the presumption that equality is necessary for justice, as classical exegetes were by their assumptions about the naturalness of male superiority and dominance in family and society."[22] IIZ members acknowledge that society's understanding of gender justice and rights has transformed over the years. Thus they propose a unique interpretation of gender equality and justice that resonates with the lived experiences of the majority of Iranian women and varies from what they perceive to be the feminist ideals of absolute equality. These religious activists believe that although justice is a basis of gender equality, absolute equality is not a requirement for gender justice.[23] IIZ cautions against fixating on declarations such as "Women are identical in all manners to men," because they consider such statements to be generally politically motivated.

The fact that IIZ is advocating gender justice as opposed to gender equality does not essentially mean that they are promoting unequal treatment of men and women. The Coalition recognizes that the biological differences between men and women can create circumstances where justice may require different treatment under the law. IIZ also holds male jurists partially accountable for unjust rulings because their androcentric views foster a culture where inequality and injustice are disguised as gender differences. Members of IIZ believe that while certain verses in the Qur'an do assign specific roles to genders based on biological differences, the intention is to foster harmony rather than to perpetuate patriarchy.[24]

The activists involved in IIZ consider both legal and ethical reform as means to achieve gender justice in the public and private spheres. These women, with their attachments to both sociopolitical and religious activism, have become a powerful force for change in gender relations despite facing internal and external resistance. During the initial research phase, I found that the IIZ Coalition had been targeted for criticism by both conservative religious authorities and secular feminists. The conservative religious authorities cast doubt on IIZ's interpretation of the role of women in Islam by expressing reservations about whether members of the IIZ Coalition had the appropriate training to be producers of Islamic knowledge. The secular feminists viewed women's involvement in religious discourse and faith-based activism as antithetical to women's rights. Given IIZ's willingness to work within the framework offered by the Islamic Republic and to negotiate with the state, they perceived it to be guilty by association. Despite these criticisms, IIZ activists continue to regard Islamic tradition as a means and necessity for realizing gender justice in the context of Iran.

Members of IIZ are not only activists but pragmatic experts who effectively collaborate with one another to avoid exploitation of women's causes by politicians. In an interview, the founder of IIZ stated, "Based on decades of experience, one of the issues that continues to harm women's affairs is the politicization of their movement, which usually lends itself to political exploitation. When politicized, the resources used to solve women's problems become a breeding ground for political parties to gain more power and influence."[25] Consequently, this organization is careful to ensure that women's issues are not sidelined and manipulated by politicians and political agendas.

## WOMEN'S JURISPRUDENCE: TOWARD AN EGALITARIAN EXEGESIS

The active engagement of women's rights activists in reinterpreting sacred texts and employing religious language is crucial to establishing their legitimacy in the public and political spheres. IIZ members' knowledge of legal tradition and their willingness to engage with 'ulama' and at times with the state have created a space where activists challenge policies that encourage polygyny, men's unilateral right to divorce, and temporary marriage, among other legal measures deemed to be discriminatory toward women. These women's religious knowledge has aided them in their attempt to reinterpret Qur'anic verses that lend themselves to gender hierarchy. Faith-based activists are engaged in an egalitarian rereading of religious texts in their pursuit of family law reform. These women are eager to point out how men's "misguided" interpretations of Islamic texts have harmed women's prospects for gender justice. In response to a long history of injustice, IIZ suggests a reinterpretation of Islamic texts from an inclusive perspective that takes into account women's lived experiences. Such reinterpretation can be achieved through women's jurisprudence that includes female perspectives in the processes of interpretation and legal decision-making.

Navigating this landscape where religious texts and gender justice intersect, IIZ argues that existing gender injustices, hierarchies, and stereotyping are primarily rooted, not in sacred scripture, but in misinterpretations or patriarchal readings of it. IIZ's conception of women takes root in Qur'anic verses emphasizing that man and woman are created from a single soul (*nafs*). Further, IIZ points out that according to the Qur'an (4:1), God does not differentiate between men and women with regard to their value. The Qur'an states, "The dearest of you to God is the most virtuous" (49:13). According to IIZ, this verse means that the elevated status of humans is based on their faith (*īmān*) and their adherence to the ethical principles of Islam, not their gender. Building upon this understanding, IIZ observes that in the Qur'an women are treated as equal to men in moral stature, notwithstanding their biological differences. For IIZ members, the Qur'an's story of Adam and Eve exemplifies Islam's stance on the equal worth of men and women, without assigning an authoritative or subordinate position to either.[26] IIZ is of the belief that this foundational view should govern all the cultural, social, economic, legal, and political dimensions of an Islamic society. Members argue, however, that the Islamic Republic of Iran has failed to base its principles on this central Islamic premise. Various leaders have used national and international podiums to claim that the Islamic Republic elevates the status of women, and the official stance of the Islamic Republic is that there is no difference between men and women in terms of human rights and responsibilities. But the state does not enact laws and regulations that substantiate such claims. The founder of IIZ asks, "If such proclamations are true, why is the state reluctant to implement regulations that are in conformity with Islamic teachings? Is it not true that Islam is about justice and against discrimination?"[27]

IIZ recognizes that within the Islamic tradition, God has created men and women with different potentialities and capabilities, an aspect they perceive as an expression of divine wisdom. These varied capabilities should stimulate human curiosity and learning, not serve as grounds for exploitation. IIZ reasons that gender differences are not a license for domination, as God will hold those who transgress the rights of others accountable to their actions. The Coalition asserts that the hierarchal notion that men are superior to women is erroneous, as it contradicts God's commands in the Qur'an. Members of IIZ argue that the problem women face is not inequality but rather domination. Accordingly, one of the effective means of disrupting domination and transgression is highlighting the multivalent interpretations of the Islamic tradition.

IIZ argues that the Qur'an offers a discursive and multidimensional framework on gender relations. This model does not strictly adhere to either egalitarianism or hierarchy, with some Qur'anic verses underscoring gender equality and others assigning distinct roles to each gender.[28] IIZ's approach to the issue of gender is unique in that it is based on religious and cultural moral paradigms. These faith-based activists rely on egalitarianism as a fundamental principle, while simultaneously acknowledging the biological differences between men and women as specified in sacred texts. IIZ's distinct stance on equality and justice speaks to the realities women face on the ground. This stance is starkly different from the feminist ideals of absolute equality. The Coalition asserts that although justice is a cornerstone of gender equality, absolute equality is not a necessary marker of justice. Through an emphasis on justice and equity instead of absolute equality, IIZ engages in discourses that reconfigure the meaning of justice and equality and acknowledges their variations in different societal and cultural contexts. Thus it resists a reductive reading of complex issues, particularly with regard to women and men's rights and duties. By acknowledging the categorical differences that exist between men and women, the Coalition offers an alternative model that reflects the history, needs, and experiences of Iranian women.

IIZ members draw on Islamic tradition to argue for women's greater social and political involvement. For example, the Qur'an states that faithful men and women are one another's "guardians" (9:71). This reference is considered a reminder to believers to refrain from inflicting harm on one another and instead to perform good deeds (3:110). Members of the IIZ Coalition understand these Qur'anic verses to mean that religious and political authorities are in constant need of supervision and guidance. Therefore, it is the religious obligation of all Muslims, including women, to monitor the actions of authorities so as to prevent them from making unfair and unjust decisions.

Further, these activists believe that by actively participating in the sociopolitical domain, women can progress toward the ideal of a Muslim woman, fulfilling their religious duties as *khalīfa* (God's representatives on earth). They draw attention to Qur'anic verses that emphasize human beings' responsibility as *khalīfa* (2:30), and through an egalitarian reading of the notion of *khalīfa* they argue that women and men are equally responsible in upholding their *khalīfa* duties. The systemic discrimination that women face indirectly violates women's agency and by extension undermines the Qur'anic principle that considers men and women to be God's representatives on earth. Thus the Islamic concept of *khalifa* affords these faith-based activists a space to demand greater involvement for women in social and political realms as a moral and spiritual responsibility. These activists do not view a woman's engagement in society as a violation of her responsibilities as a mother and wife.

In advancing their model of the ideal Muslim woman, IIZ looks to the Qur'an and Shi'i history for role models. Prophet Mohammad's daughter Fatima and his granddaughter Zaynab serve as models of women who defied the restrictive social conventions of their time and fought for social and political justice. Fatima is one of the exceptionally strong and brave women in Islamic history. On many occasions, she was left to singlehandedly defend Prophet Muhammad and never failed to stand up for justice. She stood her ground and refused to back down from her claim to legitimately inherit Fadak.[29] In one of the interviews, an IIZ member states, "Our role model is Fatima bint Muhammad. There are a lot of significant points in her life that modern-day women can use as a guide. Her relationship with her husband, children, society, and even government is very meaningful. She was a vocal critic of the authority of her time. Given that our goal is to serve people in an Islamic society, we should also voice our concern over injustices perpetrated in the name of Islam."[30] IIZ also highlights the role of female leaders throughout Islamic history, citing instances such as the influential socioeconomic status and leadership role held by Muhammad's wife, Khadija, during times of resistance, as well as the role of Fatima al-Ma'suma, the sister of the eighth Shi'i imam, revered for her political acumen and her significant role as a religious leader.[31]

Another renowned advocate of social justice in Shi'i history is Zaynab bint Ali, the daughter of Fatima and sister of Husayn ibn Abi Talib, the third Shi'i imam. Following the infamous battle of Karbala and after witnessing most of her family members massacred, including her brother Husayn, Zaynab confronted and spoke out in fiery public orations against Umayyad authorities who had rallied a strong army. In the epic story of Zaynab in the context of Karbala, she became the heroine of a tragic day in Shi'i history by delivering powerful speeches and speaking truth to power.[32] Zaynab is also believed to have played a vital role in protecting the life of the fourth Shi'i imam, Zayn al-Abidin, during and after the battle of Karbala. Modern Shi'i intellectuals have drawn attention to the symbolic significance of the courage and honor of women like Zaynab, whose empowered lives continue to inspire and motivate Shi'i women through the ages.[33] Narratives of strong women like Zaynab create an aura of legitimacy and authority similar to those of the infallible Shi'i imams.[34] IIZ capitalizes on this discourse and elevates Zaynab as the pinnacle of piety and activism and as a model for Muslim women. Members of IIZ, like Maryam Behroozi, celebrate Zaynab's prowess as a social justice activist but also honor Zaynab's commitment to her family as a wife, mother, and sister. For individuals like Behroozi, Zaynab is a reminder of how public and private commitments can coexist in a society.

The Qur'an itself contains verses about formidable women like Asiya, the wife of a pharaoh who lived centuries before the emergence of Islam. Asiya is portrayed as someone whose way of life should be admired and emulated by all true believers (66:11). She epitomizes the ideals of virtue and strength and is considered to be one of the most exceptional women throughout history. Her superior character and unadulterated faith have turned her into a role model for all Muslims, men and women. The Qur'an also depicts another influential woman, the Queen of Sheba, a sovereign ruler adept in political negotiations. Her story (27:29) underlines women's intellectual competence and their ability to be in positions of authority and leadership. For IIZ, the Qur'an's representation of the Queen of Sheba is a clear indication that Islam does not prevent women from taking on leadership and political roles. By praising the Queen of Sheba's wisdom and negotiation skills, the Qur'an discredits the discriminatory hadiths and biased views perpetuated by conservative male jurists.

In post-Revolution Iran, the state made use of strong Shi'i female figures to exalt women's status. As a result, the traditionalist ruling elite in Iranian society increasingly acknowledged women's broader intellectual and political potentials. The decision to commemorate the birthday of Fatima, the daughter of Prophet Muhammad, as Woman and Mother's Day is a gesture seen by many as an acknowledgment of women's high status in Islam. These decisions align with Ayatollah Khomeini's stance regarding the importance of women's political and leadership roles in the social and political spheres. But although many political and religious leaders emphasize that women's position in society must improve, in reality women's calls for change have gone unheeded and their progress has been resisted at every turn. In spite of all that women have achieved before and after the Revolution, they are still facing numerous obstacles in their efforts to attain gender justice.

In light of these challenges, IIZ emphasizes the importance of enhancing female representation at decision-making tables. Societal problems are not exclusive to men, so women should have more prominent participation in policy-making institutions. The Coalition believes that traditional gendered norms have historically affected how policy is formulated and enacted. Women's absence from decision-making and the omission of their voices have meant that legal rulings and policies that directly influence women's lives are biased and ineffective. Because men do not experience the lived reality of women, women's issues are relegated to the periphery and deprioritized. Consequently, IIZ claims that policies that neglect to incorporate women's perspectives are inadequate and invalid.

Early on in its activist practice, IIZ identified two main causes behind hierarchal and discriminatory rulings pertaining to women. The first cause is a reliance on the male perspective as the standard for decision-making. It is important to recognize that hierarchal rulings do not only result from a desire to maintain male norms but are also influenced by methods of interpretation. The second cause of legal discrimination is the limitations of traditional Islamic jurisprudential methods. To encourage a paradigm shift in the direction of gender egalitarianism, faith-based activists resort to three principles in their practice of women's jurisprudence. The first principle, *ijtihād*, entails diligent effort to interpret Islamic teachings and derive legal judgments through critical analysis of religious texts. The second principle is that *fiqh* rulings should be in line with the Islamic values of justice (*'adl*). The third principle emphasizes that women's perspectives need to be included in jurisprudence and the hermeneutical process of interpreting religious scripture.

IIZ's involvement in women's jurisprudence, grounded in *ijtihād*, aims to rupture the discursive boundaries of patriarchal rulings. IIZ argues that *ijtihād* can be used to reshape current policies related to women so that they better reflect the state of knowledge today. Considering that the door of *ijtihād* never closed in Shi'i legal thought, Shi'i women do not face the same limitations as their Sunni counterparts in this regard. The centrality of *ijtihād* in women's jurisprudence, and its ability to adapt to contemporary reality, create a space in which women can advocate for gender egalitarianism within a Shi'i framework. Along with a justice-oriented approach and the incorporation of women's perspectives and experiences, this strategy forms a bridge between contemporary realities and past traditions, while concurrently adjusting Islamic law to cater to the needs of Muslim societies.

As the debate between the state, the 'ulama', and women continues to ebb and flow, women's jurisprudence has proven to be an effective approach to promoting egalitarian principles in a manner that aligns with the demands of all three actors. Proponents of women's jurisprudence question the practicality of traditional jurisprudential methods without rejecting them altogether. These faith-based activists are interested in offering an alternative method within the broader tradition of Islamic knowledge. Members of IIZ believe that male Islamic scholars have overlooked women's experiences when interpreting and extracting laws from sacred scriptures. To meet the needs of women in the post-traditionalist era, these faith-based activists are utilizing women's jurisprudence in their attempt to redefine tradition in the age of modernity. Such an approach enables IIZ members to adhere to the principles of their faith while also restoring the long-neglected ideals of plurality and inclusiveness as the fundamental tenets of juristic discourse.

By utilizing women's jurisprudence, faith-based activists employ an interpretive methodology that embraces the holistic spirit of the law. Through highlighting the fallibility of human effort to capture divine intent, these activists call for the reassessment and reformation of discriminatory aspects of Islamic laws pertaining to women. Arguing against a formal and literal interpretation of Islamic law, they speak out against scriptural literalism. They warn that an excessive emphasis on law shifts attention away from the values and principles that constitute the essence of Islam, particularly its emphasis on justice. Women's jurisprudence does not lose sight of the underlying purpose of the law and advances an interpretative method that considers both the letter of the law and its spirit.

The existing laws in Iran predominantly reflect some of the most traditionalist views and interpretations of Islamic scriptures, overshadowing the diversity of interpretations among various jurists. This monolithic approach, largely employed by traditional male scholars, not only disregards the dynamism and diversity of Qur'anic interpretations but also indirectly claims an absolute understanding of God's truth, which can be deemed as *shirk* (cardinal sin) in and of itself.[35] Contrarily, women's jurisprudence, utilized by IIZ, strategically uses dynamic and diverse interpretations espoused by both male and female scholars. In this vein, the IIZ Coalition has developed a robust legal apparatus capable of addressing women's issues in contemporary times. By challenging traditional gender frameworks through women's jurisprudential reasoning, IIZ seeks to advance gender justice within an Islamic framework.

IIZ also recognizes that current discriminatory policies toward women are not solely rooted in traditional jurisprudential methods. A vast majority of these discriminatory policies are shaped by the normalization of male experience. In their efforts to reconstitute gender egalitarianism, IIZ is in effect undoing patriarchal interpretations of the Qur'an by invoking women's voices and experiences in the hermeneutic process. Interpreting Islamic sources through a lens that incorporates the experiences of men and women is seen by IIZ as a strategy to simultaneously afford women leverage and empower them. By focusing on women's jurisprudence, these women attempt to circumvent the seemingly inflexible laws related to women.

While criticizing some jurists' hierarchal interpretation of religious texts, IIZ advocates for a more nuanced interpretation of the Qur'an and hadith.[36] This approach seeks to situate Islamic teachings within specific times and places, differentiating between context-bound directives and the eternal ethical principles of the Qur'an. The exegesis conducted by IIZ members focuses on contested verses that lend themselves to gender hierarchy through male-biased interpretations. One of the prime examples relates to verse 4:34, which is considered to be the foundation of gender relations in Islam. This Qur'anic verse from which the concept of *qiwāma* (protection) is derived reads: "Men are the *qawwāmūn* (protectors and maintainers) of women, because Allah has given the one more [strength] than the other, and because they support them from their means. Therefore the righteous women are *qānitāt* (devoutly obedient), and guard in (the husband's) absence what Allah would have them guard. As to those women on whose part ye fear *nushūzan* (disloyalty and ill-conduct), admonish them (first), (Next), refuse to share their beds, (And last) *ḍribūhunna* [beat them (lightly)]; but if they return to obedience, seek not against them Means (of annoyance): For Allah is Most High, great (above you all)."[37]

To challenge the traditionalist reading and translation of the above verse, IIZ has attempted to deconstruct the term *nushūz* (disobedience). Although *nushūz* can be applied to behavior on the part of either spouse, most jurists use it exclusively in relation to the wife's responsibilities, or lack thereof, toward her husband. But IIZ argues that when the Qur'an refers to an obedient woman, there is no indication that the obedience is in relation to her husband. Rather, obedience should be understood in terms of obedience toward God. In the context of marital relations, obedience is required only in matters that do not contradict Islamic teachings. IIZ concludes that as far as the interpretations of Qur'anic teachings are concerned, obedience should be toward the Creator and not God's creations. According to IIZ, jurists who interpret this verse to imply the domination of men over women are going against the Islamic principle of justice. The Qur'an explicitly addresses both men and women without discrimination and urges them equally to uphold Islamic standards (33:35).

The female activists of IIZ do not limit themselves to reinterpreting the Qur'an, as they also question the prominence of hadith literature. IIZ recognizes that jurists' understanding of the Qur'an is negotiated through other sources of knowledge such as hadiths. Many of the biased understandings of the Qur'an arise when hadiths are given greater prominence than the underlying message of the Qur'an.[38] For instance, the Qur'anic position that men and women originate from a single soul (7:189) contradicts hadiths that attribute different characteristics to men and women. Interpreting Qur'anic principles by embracing patriarchal hadiths undermines the Qur'an's message of justice.[39] IIZ argues that even authentic hadiths must be disregarded when a ruling is not in harmony with the core values expressed in the Qur'an, reached through human reason, and consistent with women's dignity. These faith-based activists argue that hadiths that emphatically foster discrimination should be disregarded because their content contradicts the Qur'anic vision that grants spiritual and socioeconomic equality to women.[40]

The Coalition differentiates between the Qur'anic representation of women and the depictions found in certain controversial hadith narrations. While the Qur'an depicts women as empowered and strong in their faith, many hadith narrations reinforce biased stereotypes that portray women as flawed in their faith. IIZ maintains that some hadiths categorically contradict the Qur'an, and others go against Qur'anic ethics and human logic. One oft-cited hadith that is considered demeaning toward women is attributed to 'Ali ibn Abi Talib. the first Shi'i imam, cited in *Nahj al-Balagha*: "Women are imperfect in faith, deficient in shares of inheritance, and deficient in intelligence."[41] The explanation provided by reformist jurists for such disparaging expressions toward women is that 'Ali made these statements in the Battle of the Camel (656 CE), initiated by Prophet Muhammad's wife 'A'isha, which broke unity among Muslims and led to the death of many devoted followers of the Prophet.[42] In line with their reformist stance, IIZ argues that these statements are unfounded, as they contradict the Qur'anic ethos of justice and dignity.

Empowered by the inclusive spirit of the Qur'anic representation of women, IIZ faith-based activists have been vocal in their critique of patriarchal interpretation of sacred scriptures that adversely affect women. They argue that the traditional approach to jurisprudence has thus far failed to generate lasting reforms or to effectively address the concerns of Muslim women today. IIZ has presented women's jurisprudence as an alternative to the male-dominated interpretation of Islamic texts and as a means of making Islamic law compatible to the needs of society. Members describe legal rulings that foster discrimination in any realm as the result of male-centric views of the world and the use of traditional jurisprudential methods. Women's jurisprudence has afforded IIZ the opportunity to challenge such laws.

The activism embodied by IIZ is not an isolated, spontaneous phenomenon but rather an ongoing effort, part of a historical process that has been shaped by preceding generations of women who championed their rights and laid the groundwork for contemporary activism. The ensuing chapter will delve further into this interconnectedness by examining the broader trajectory of Iranian women's movements, beginning with the instrumental Constitutional Revolution of 1905, an event that ignited women's political consciousness and laid the foundation for subsequent advancements in women's rights. By situating the activism of IIZ women within this broader historical framework, the next chapter aims to link their struggles with those of their predecessors.

# CHAPTER 2

# The Intersection of Law, the State, and Women's Activism in Iran

The status of Muslim women and their public and private roles is a complex and contentious topic that has involved the state, women, and 'ulama' in dynamic debates. In the pursuit of gender justice and societal transformation, Iranian women have been advocating for policy reform through sociopolitical and religious activism dating back to the early 1900s. To adequately contextualize the activism of IIZ within this broader sociohistorical continuum of Iranian women's activism, it is imperative to trace the origins and evolution of women's rights movements in Iran. IIZ's activism is a continuation of the women's rights movement, which took root during the Constitutional Revolution (1905–11). This chapter offers a comprehensive sociohistorical overview of this context, situating women's faith-based activism in contemporary Iran within the broader frame of their drive for gender justice within the country's legal and political structures. Highlighting the trajectory of Iranian women's activism, this chapter analyzes their strategic maneuvers that have simultaneously challenged and circumvented the political and legal contours of Iran since the twentieth century. Additionally, it examines the role that women and 'ulama' have played in the fluctuating status of women's legal rights within the Iranian Constitution and the Civil Code, from the Constitutional Revolution to the present day. This inquiry underscores the intricate interplay between gender, religion, and law, offering valuable insights into the challenges and triumphs in the struggle for women's rights in Iran.

The establishment of the constitutional monarchy at the dawn of the twentieth century in Iran marked the initial emergence of the complex interplay between traditionalism and modernism, a dynamic that has remained central to the discourse surrounding women's rights in the country. The current chapter will further explore this ongoing struggle, integral to understanding the sociopolitical milieu of Iran and the position of women within it, by examining key elements of the Constitution and the Civil Code during their inception, as well as the significant changes that they underwent throughout the Pahlavi monarchy and following the establishment of the Islamic Republic. It is imperative to underscore the cascading impact of different codifications initiated throughout various periods. Each legislative change or reform has invariably sent ripples through the societal fabric, affecting women's rights and their societal roles. Consequently, a thorough exploration of these codifications reveals how female activists have navigated this complex interplay of tradition and modernity. This chapter sheds light on the dynamism and flexibility of these activists, their strategic negotiations, and their pursuit of gender justice within the framework of Iran's sociocultural and legal landscape.

## MODERNITY, RELIGION, AND WOMEN

Historically, Islamic law has provided Muslims with a comprehensive and practical guide on how to govern their societies and families. As one scholar of Islam, John Esposito, observes, "Islamic law has remained central to Muslim identity, for it constitutes the ideal social blueprint for the good society,"[1] and family law is at its heart and soul. Traditional Muslim family law provided a comprehensive approach to major aspects of family life, marriage, divorce, and custody that was compatible with premodern Muslim society. So long as the constitution of Muslim society remained the same, family law was relevant and attuned to the needs of its times. Thus the classical view of family law remained effective until contemporary times.[2]

Despite its historical efficacy, Islamic law's transition into the modern world, particularly in relation to women's rights, has been fraught with challenges. The creation of the modern nation-state and the codification of laws have not necessarily advanced Muslim women's legal standing. A key turning point was the enactment of the 1917 Ottoman Law of Family Rights, which set the stage for the gradual codification of Islamic family law in the Middle East. Prior to this juncture, Islamic family law was subject to the interpretations of presiding judges and influenced by the specific jurisprudential school they followed, thus allowing for a level of uncodified jurisprudence.[3] As historian Judith Tucker notes, Islamic courts displayed elements of both flexibility and diversity as they took into account the individual's needs and social realities. However, this trend did not last as modernity encroached in the nineteenth century and Western progress eclipsed traditional structures in Muslim communities. The emergence of modernity was followed by a period where the state ultimately utilized modern mechanisms to exert greater control over the courts through the codification of Islamic law.[4]

The journey from the premodern era, governed by traditional religious and legal systems, to the nation-state, characterized by rationalized bureaucracies and technocratic rule, led to profound sociopolitical and legal paradigm shifts.[5] The transition resulted in a complex situation—across social, legal, and political realms—that women's organizations like IIZ continue to wrestle with. In the past, the law was the purview of the 'ulama', to whom ruling elites were accountable.[6] But the advent of modernity and the establishment of new governments saw the state become the primary regulator of the law. In Iran after the 1979 Revolution, jurists assumed the roles of both creators and enforcers of divine law. This novel development introduced further complications as the emerging state had to negotiate the fine line between tradition and modernity.

Modernity's aim was to advance the quality of human life through progress, justice, and rights. The secular modernity introduced in nineteenth-century Iran was manifested through the Constitutional Revolution, and the 1907 constitutional amendments were likewise inspired by secular ideals and Western models of progress and nation-state building. However, modernity more broadly was introduced through cultural imperialism and economic colonization.[7] The state's top-down imposition of modernity was met with revolutionary resistance by the masses, who viewed it as a Western imposition and a mechanism to exploit resources. One can position women's rights organizations, including IIZ, as emerging alongside and as continuing these revolutionary movements.

The type of modernity that emerged in Iran after the nineteenth century gave rise to nationalist and Islamist discourses. The nationalist discourse imitated the European model of progress and merged it with the assertion of a pre-Islamic identity. According to historian Afsaneh Najmabadi, the type of Iranian nationalism that existed in the early 1900s was not so much antiforeign or anti-West as it was against religion and despotism. The Islamist discourse, on the other hand, attempted to modernize Islam by combining Iranian values with those of Twelver Shi'ism.[8] Throughout the twentieth century and as a result of the direct interference of foreign powers in Iran, there was a shift in the Iranian sociopolitical landscape, including a rise in antiforeign sentiments. These sentiments peaked during the 1940s, when the British controlled much of Iran's oil revenue, and later transitioned to anti-American sentiments when the United States dominated the economic and political sphere and supported the Pahlavis' repressive policies. They unfolded concurrently with other changes, mainly the rift between the government and civil society.[9]

The evolution of the Islamic perspective was marked by a secondary trend, which revolved around the dissociation of Islam from the modernist faction, largely due to the intensified association of the Pahlavi monarchy with modernists. Before long, Islam was branded as traditional and regressive, the antithesis to modernity. Islamist trends, characterized by anti-Pahlavi and antiforeign sentiments, began to emerge by the 1950s. This societal shift culminated in the 1979 Revolution, when an anti-imperialist, antinationalist, antisecular Islam emerged. In the decades that have passed since the Islamic Revolution, an understanding of Islam has arisen that is both oppositional and conforming to state policies. This nuanced understanding is evident in faith-based organizations such as IIZ. This form of Islam represents a continuation of the antistatism that led to the 1979 Revolution.[10] As a result of the dynamic interplay and friction between the state, opposition forces, and civil society actors, a distinct Islamic movement has emerged within the sociopolitical landscape of Iran.

## IRAN'S POLITICAL SYSTEM DURING THE CONSTITUTIONAL REVOLUTION

Striking the right balance between modernity and tradition is an ongoing struggle facing most Muslim nations, and this is certainly an issue for Iran. In fact, much of Iran's struggle in the past one hundred years, including the Constitutional Revolution and the 1979 Revolution, has revolved around the tensions between modernity and tradition. These revolutions remain key milestones in the country's modern history and have left a lasting mark on Iran's political, social, legal, and cultural domains.[11]

The Iranian political system preceding the 1905 Constitutional Revolution was the embodiment of a lineal and dictatorial monarchy where kings unilaterally ruled over all aspects of society. Iranian citizens did not influence their country's domestic or international policies. The judiciary system consisted of religious courts that drew on Ja'fari jurisprudence from the Shi'i sect of Islam. The religious judges presided over cases and issued rulings consistent with their own personal knowledge and interpretation of religious law.[12] Hence, it was not uncommon for different jurists to have different rulings on the same issue. The diversity of opinion among judges was accepted as a fact of life, considering that historically the work of traditional Islamic interpretation had been both flexible and adaptable to changing conditions.[13] Religious judges of the time would remain the highest legal authority in their jurisdiction so long as they accepted the sovereignty of the king over the nation.

However, a notable shift began in the early nineteenth century as the call for 'adālat (justice) echoed powerfully among intellectuals and the masses. Social and political actors who pursued an ideal society were motivated not only by the revolutions in Turkey and France but also by Islamic principles, as evidenced by their association of 'adālat with social justice and citizenship rights.[14] In the context of Persian-Islamic governance, the appeal to "justice" provided a foundation that lent legitimacy and urgency to the diverse demands of various sectors ranging from 'ulama', to merchants (bāzārīs) seeking political and economic justice, to women's rights groups calling for gender justice in the public and private realms.[15] This demand for justice continues to be expressed by religious activists such as IIZ because of its centrality to both the Shi'i tradition and Iranian tradition.

The quest for an ideal society led the reformists of nineteenth-century Iran to acknowledge the importance of the written code of law. One of the most prominent ideas of that era was that establishing constitutional order could advance social justice as well as the develop and preserve Iran's independence in the face of foreign domination. The reformists argued that adoption of a constitutional order could curtail the influence of the monarch and lead to the dispersion of power.[16] However, reformers were not able to advance a systematic and efficient model of governance because of their overreliance on Western political thought and institutions. This stalled the advancement of an intellectual tradition that could have acted as a mediating force between the state and the increasingly influential 'ulama'.[17]

The religious, political, and socioeconomic realities at the turn of the twentieth century caused a rift between advocates and opponents of the constitutional government. A number of activists and preachers recognized the importance of securing the backing of prominent 'ulama' to endorse constitutional reform. By aligning themselves with these religious figures, the constitutionalists avoided being labeled as "Westernized."[18] In a strategic move to advance justice and strengthen their position in society, a number of proconstitutionalist 'ulama' decided to join the cause of the reformists in their effort to advance constitutionalism.

Three distinct groups emerged as key players in what came to be known as the Constitutional Revolution. The first was constituted by the 'ulama', including individuals such as Sayyid Mohammad Husayn Tabataba'i and Sayyid 'Abd-Allah Behbahani. In the early stages of the Constitutional Revolution, these 'ulama' considered the "rule of law" to be synonymous with the implementation of shari'a.[19] The second group consisted of the *bāzārī* merchants, whose perspectives on constitutionalism were influenced by populist preachers in favor of the Revolution. These merchants shared not only discontent with the ruling establishment but also a collective aspiration to improve their own economic and political status. The third group consisted of Western-educated intellectuals, including the offspring of high-profile officials.[20] Several notable personalities within this circle had affiliations to the Qajar dynasty (1789–1925). Their ability to mediate between the state and the constitutionalists made this group an asset to the constitutional movement.[21] The constitutionalists' efforts to establish a modern system of governance in part depended on greater participation and support by women in the public sphere. In turn, the participation of women in the Constitutional Revolution gave them experience in organizing themselves to demand gender justice.[22] A number of historians believe that the early twentieth-century Constitutional Revolution in Iran was the breeding ground for the Iranian women's rights movement.[23] The activism of organizations such as IIZ can be understood as a continuation of women's rights movements that proliferated following the Constitutional Revolution.

Moving into the immediate aftermath of the Constitutional Revolution, increased pressure from constitutionalists forced the Qajar monarch, Muzaffarud-Din Shah, who came to power in June 1896, to issue a declaration in favor of the Constitution. In 1906 he finally accepted the creation of an elected parliament, which regulated the king's power. Despite the secular inclination of some constitutionalists, the traditionalist outlook remained the dominant discourse for many members of the newly founded parliament. As a result, Parliament passed laws that denied women the right to participate in parliamentary elections. For instance, Article 10 of the electoral law prohibited women from voting, while Article 13 denied them the right to run for parliamentary seats.[24] But although the traditional mindset toward women persisted, the Constitutional Revolution acknowledged the importance of people's involvement in shaping their destinies and succeeded in introducing people to new ideas such as the interaction between civil society and the state.[25]

## WOMEN'S ACTIVISM DURING THE CONSTITUTIONAL REVOLUTION

Women's rights activists in Iran have been promoting gender justice and legal reform since the Constitutional Revolution. They have taken advantage of any opportunity, no matter how small, to express their grievances and demands. The individuals who led various women's rights movements during the 1900s, most of whom came from upper-class circles and intellectual families, also had an active presence in both constitutionalist and nationalist movements.[26] According to Hamideh Sedghi, women's participation in the constitutional movement was reminiscent of the Tobacco Protests of the early 1890s.[27] Like their predecessors, these women expressed strong nationalistic and anticolonial sentiments and aspired to an independent Iran that would no longer fall victim to foreign hegemony. They demonstrated their commitment to the constitutionalist and nationalist cause by going to extraordinary lengths, including disguising themselves as men and participating in battles in northwestern Iran. It was in this region that the renowned national commander Sattar Khan spearheaded a rebellion against both the Qajar dynasty's oppressive rule and Britain's escalating influence over Iran's internal affairs.[28] Beyond these visible and dramatic demonstrations of their commitment, women also strategically formed clandestine organizations and courageously took part in street protests, riots, boycotts, and armed clashes.[29]

In 1906 female activists held an assembly where they advocated for schools to be set up for girls. In the same year, women's rights organizations held meetings to openly deliberate on the political and social realities of Iran.[30] And over a span of four years starting in 1907, women became increasingly active as they established a number of organizations, including the Revolutionary Women's Forum and the Women's Freedom Forum, that not only sought the expansion of educational opportunities for women but urged that women be allowed to vote and become members of Parliament.[31] But their calls for gender justice and equality were sidelined by nationalistic demands, and they met with backlash from the conservative members of society, who saw their movement as backed by foreign powers and condemned their values as antithetical to the cultural norms in Iran. Consequently, the authorities shut down these organizations along with several schools affiliated with them, even though the founders of most of the girls' schools were Muslim women connected to renowned religious elites. These women had strategically incorporated religious education into the schools' curricula in hopes that critics of girls' education could not reject it as un-Islamic.[32]

Partly because of the pressure applied by these organizations, less than a decade later Iranian society witnessed an increased number of educational institutions for girls, and formal education came to be viewed as essential for women. In spite of these advances, the opportunities provided by Iran's educational system mostly benefited affluent and urban citizens.[33]

The aftermath of the Constitutional Revolution provided women with the opportunity to express their views on various issues in constitutional newspapers. For nearly two decades after 1908, several women's newspapers and magazines were published.[34] Further, the political movement led by upper-middle-class women in the early twentieth century succeeded in setting up health clinics, schools, and assemblies that addressed women's concerns. Yet these advances, along with women's active involvement in the Constitutional Revolution, did not translate into the realization of basic rights such as voting for women.[35] To protest these shortcomings, a number of prominent women wrote to the Parliament demanding greater involvement in Iran's political and civic processes.

The women's rights movement in Iran has been fraught with challenges since the early 1900s. Throughout the Constitutional Revolution, women struggled to become subjects, not just objects of debate about their own rights. Women's engagement in the Constitutional Revolution emboldened them to demand greater justice, notably advocating for restrictions on polygyny and men's exclusive right to divorce. While the legal rationales for suppressing women's rights were based on interpretations of scripture, most activists calling for greater rights for women were hesitant to critique religious texts themselves. Instead, they directed their criticism toward men and conservative clerics, highlighting the discrepancies between scripture and their assertions. In a parallel manner, contemporary women's rights organizations, such as IIZ, criticize literal interpretation of sacred sources by traditionalist 'ulama' and practice women's jurisprudence in their pursuit of gender justice.

## POLITICAL AND LEGAL STRUCTURE
## IN THE PAHLAVI MONARCHY

When Muzaffarud-Din Shah signed the Constitution of Iran in 1906 in one of the last acts of his rule, the path of progress took a new direction. The weakening Qajar rule gave way to the Pahlavi monarchy in 1921, a change brought about by a successful military coup. With Reza Shah at the helm as the first Pahlavi king, a political cabinet was swiftly put together, intended to facilitate his grand plans of modernizing and reforming Iran. Central to this modernization project were women's issues, marking a new phase in the ongoing quest for gender justice in the country.

Reza Shah embarked on his sixteen-year reign with a focus on fortifying the military and broadening the reach of state bureaucracy. The newly crowned king transferred the responsibility of educational institutions and the judicial system to the state. Historically, these institutions had been under the jurisdiction of 'ulama'. This move toward secularization by the Pahlavi monarch led to growing dissatisfaction among the 'ulama', local tribes, and the new intelligentsia. As these radical changes continued, the once-celebrated Constitution was gradually emptied of its significance, turning into a hollowed-out symbol of its former self.

Despite mounting resentment and resistance, Reza Shah remained unyielding in his strategy of top-down secularization and modernization.[36] But the tides of power were soon to shift dramatically. In 1941, Reza Shah was forced to abdicate by the Allies in the aftermath of the Anglo-Soviet invasion, and his son, Mohammad Reza, ascended to the throne. Throughout the reign of the new king, significant modifications in the government's policy took place as the system of constitutional monarchy was once again revitalized. Mohammad Reza Shah pledged his allegiance to the parliamentary government, even as a constitutional monarch. In this era, the authority of the prime minister and Parliament was partially restored. This trend continued until the new king was on the brink of being overthrown and replaced by then prime minister Mohammed Mossadegh. The democratically elected prime minister helped nationalize Iran's oil industry, which was seen as a threat by both internal and external powers. However, the period of parliamentary governance came to an abrupt end in 1953 when a US-backed coup d'état ousted Mosaddegh.

To strengthen his position following the coup, Mohammad Reza Shah called for reforms that collectively came to be known as the White Revolution. The recommended policies included land reform and the eradication of illiteracy, which benefited women. The White Revolution also introduced significant changes for women, allowing them to vote, run for elected office, and serve as judges.[37] While the White Revolution was promoted as a progressive leap toward modernization, the Shah's political intentions to legitimize the Pahlavi dynasty were clear. His calculated move did not proceed as anticipated and faced opposition from both secularists and the 'ulama'. The secularists opposed the Shah's abuse of the Constitution and his decision to dissolve the Parliament. The 'ulama', on the other hand, opposed the White Revolution reforms, particularly land reform and women's suffrage.[38]

The Pahlavis based much of their policymaking on a constitution that had sought to include both the tenets of Western liberal democracy and Islamic law.[39] But Mohammad Reza Shah did not tolerate political opposition and persecuted many of his outspoken opponents. His secularization of social and political institutions contradicted the traditional ruling system in Iran. He also kept traditional Islamic institutions from accessing their financial assets. And the Shah further overlooked his constitutional obligation to form a committee of Islamic legal scholars to ensure that parliamentary rules and procedures would not contradict Islamic law.[40]

A number of Mohammad Reza Shah's decisions, such as taking the title of "King of Kings" in 1976 and altering the Islamic calendar to an imperial one, ignited widespread disapproval among various social actors. In response to escalating criticism, the Shah defended his actions and plans by professing allegiance to the Iranian heritage while underscoring the importance of Western acculturation. Such actions were perceived as the severing of Iran's connection to its Islamic roots. The Shah's Westernization and secularization policies with regard to women were criticized for their purported role in compromising the status of women as guardians of Islamic traditions.[41] Before long, the 'ulama' and university students, including women and intellectuals, who sought major reform and disapproved of the Shah's growing dependence on Western powers formed an opposition alliance in their quest for social and economic justice. The top-down modernization and legal reforms of the Pahlavi era propelled the country toward modernity. However, the autocratic tendencies of the regime prevented it from securing the support of the masses. The strong show of force displayed by women, including religious and Marxist activists, in opposition to the Shah's reforms reflects the complexities of Iran's sociopolitical landscape. It was within such complex spaces that some of the prominent members of IIZ, including A'zam Taleqani and Maryam Behroozi, began their activism.

## CIVIL CODE AND FAMILY LAW IN THE PAHLAVI ERA

The rise of the Pahlavi dynasty in 1925 marks the initiation of the modern Iranian legal system, which affected women's status and legal standing. One of the important initiatives undertaken during the Pahlavi reign was the codification of family law. This process began in 1928 with the formulation of the Iranian Civil Code (*qānūn-i madanī*). Subsequent codification of Islamic family law was enacted in 1967, under the Pahlavi monarchy, and later following the 1979 Iranian Revolution. The Iranian Civil Code consisted of regulations that directly and indirectly affected every social and civic aspect of an individual's life. Written at the turn of the twentieth century, it comprised three parts: property law, law of evidence, and laws of personal status.

The process of creating the articles of the Civil Code was spearheaded by a delegation composed of the Council of 'Ulama' and lawyers proficient in Western legal systems. While the Pahlavi monarchy assured the 'ulama' that the Civil Code would align with Islamic principles, in reality most Islamic concepts were not implemented and European codes were endorsed instead. The law of evidence seems primarily derived from the civil codes of European nations such as France, Belgium, and Switzerland, and laws regarding contemporary issues not directly addressed in Islamic law, such as nationality and legal residency, were adapted from international private law.[42] The shift, however, did not entirely disregard Islamic law. Particularly laws regarding property and personal status largely conformed to it. In these areas, many articles reflect a codification of majority opinions within the Shi'i *fiqh*. More than eight hundred provisions of the first volume of the Civil Code, on property law, are derived from Shi'i legal texts.[43] Similarly, despite the diminishing role of the 'ulama' in defining and administering the law, the commission entrusted with drafting the 1928 Civil Code relied heavily on Shi'i legal texts[44] as sources informing the personal status law. This reliance carried substantial implications, directly affecting women's legal rights and their status within the family unit.[45]

In this complex interweaving of Islamic and Western legal systems, another important initiative was the establishment of the special courts to arbitrate over matters related to family law. Though these courts were perceived as a progressive step toward modernizing the country's judicial system, they were not necessarily to the advantage of women, who had limited access to them and who were more likely, in matters of marital discord, to find recourse in consulting with local religious figures. As the new institutional arrangements considerably curtailed the 'ulama''s power, many of the abuses women endured went unnoticed and unrecorded.

By the 1930s, Shi'i laws on marriage, divorce, and custody were included in the Civil Code.[46] The legal codification of the Iranian Civil Code represented the first designated family law codification. The subsequent codification of Islamic family law manifested in the enactment of the Family Protection Law (FPL) in 1967. The law was more favorable toward women in matters of divorce, marriage—including age of marriage—custody, legal guardianship, and travel. It also granted women the right to become judges and lawyers.[47] This was followed by additional reforms in 1975, when the FPL included amendments that awarded equal access to custody for both men and women. Another sign of reform during the Pahlavi era came about when family protection courts were set up to deal with marital disputes among other issues. Furthermore, the FPL incorporated rules for the registration of divorce and marriage.[48]

As the newly enacted FPL broadened circumstances under which women could secure a divorce, it signified a positive change in the marital rights of women. Such conditions included the husband's imprisonment for five years or more, his entry into a polygamous relationship without the first wife's approval, and his contraction of a disease harmful to family members. Since women's equal opportunity for divorce was in conflict with Islamic legal norms, the FPL required individuals to stipulate the right to divorce in the marriage contract.[49] Islamic law acknowledged the validity of these terms, but the state's enforcement of such private agreements and contracts was unclear. Prior to the 1967 FPL, it was the responsibility of the wife and her family to negotiate the woman's rights to divorce, which were rarely granted given the traditional social structure of the time.[50]

The Pahlavi monarchy was given credit for the progressive FPL and presented it as an important achievement in women's rights and an essential step toward modernization. By the time the FPL was implemented, it came under the direction of the Women's Organization of Iran, sponsored by Ashraf Pahlavi, the sister of the Shah.[51] Yet despite the touted benefits, the close ties between Ashraf Pahlavi and the Shah raised doubts about the legitimacy of the reforms. Notably, many secularists opposed such reforms, associating the FPL with Mohammad Reza Shah's reign, a period characterized by co-optation of women's rights organizations in Iran.[52] Resistance came not only from secularists but also from 'ulama', who collectively condemned the reforms.

As the Pahlavi monarchy faced crises of legitimacy, so too did its modernization and Westernization initiatives. Successive waves of opposition ultimately led to the overthrow of the Pahlavi monarchy and the triumph of the Iranian Revolution. By the time of the 1979 Revolution, there was a resounding demand from both the masses and the elite to discard Western models in favor of Islamic ones.

## WOMEN'S ACTIVISM DURING PAHLAVI RULE

With the end of the Qajar dynasty and the beginning of the Pahlavi monarchy, the first phase of the women's movement came to an end. What had begun as an organic movement inspired by grassroots sociopolitical change during the Constitutional Revolution gradually came under the sway of the top-down secularization and modernization project of the new state.[53]

Throughout the Pahlavi monarchy, women's legal status underwent significant transformation. To curb the influence of Islamic institutions within society, policies adopted by Mohammad Reza Shah altered the status of women in both social and political realms.[54] The amendments to Articles 10 and 13 of the previous electoral law in 1964 were among the most notable changes. The revised law ultimately granted women the right to vote and run for parliamentary positions.[55] Further reflecting the top-down approach to women's liberation, the Women's Organization of Iran was founded in 1966, directly sponsored and managed by the government. Even though such actions were well received by some of the elite, they faced resistance from many others within the general public. A majority of women viewed these reforms as a misguided attempt to impose Westernization and undermine their culture.

While the Pahlavi monarchy initiated a transformative era for women's legal status, it was also marked by a surge in women's organizations. However, the state maintained a firm grip on these organizations by bringing them together under the auspices of the High Council of Women's Organizations. This maneuver significantly curtailed the autonomy of women's organizations in Iran.[56] The council, established by the Pahlavi family and backed by the state, managed to consolidate control over independent groups over several years. As a result, any group that declined to join this overarching organization risked being disbanded.[57]

Although the top-down Westernization of Iranian society did not challenge patriarchy, it effectively modernized and secularized it.[58] The modernization project of Mohammad Reza Pahlavi advanced women's status through the FPL, but in reality the majority of Iranian women did not reap the benefits of these reforms. In this context, the state's patriarchal nationalism and Western-style feminism molded an agenda to monopolize the Iranian women's movement and identity.[59] As a result, the Pahlavi monarchy and feminist organizations were linked with Westernization, an association that persists even today.

Throughout the twentieth century, women active in state-sponsored feminist organizations supported the monarchy's White Revolution, launched in the 1960s. The land distribution component of these policies enriched a new group of commercial farmers but harmed the lower strata of the rural population. Consequently, during that era, feminism became associated with an elite class that was unaware of the needs of women from the lower classes.

The White Revolution further intensified these divisions by exerting pressure on women to remove their headscarves and *chador*s (a large cloth that covers the body, leaving the hands and face exposed). In this respect it continued, though with less violent enforcement, the "unveiling" initiative made compulsory by law in 1936 by Mohammad Reza Shah's father.[60] Under both of their reigns, the monarchy portrayed its secularization and Westernization efforts as means to liberate women from obsolete cultural and religious practices, positioning them as the only ways that modernization could be achieved. But as Zohreh Sullivan notes, "The liberation of women, though not necessary to the larger agendas of modernity, becomes a troubled sign of its possibilities, limits, blind spots, and discontents."[61] Considering that many women preferred to stay in domestic spaces rather than appear uncovered in public areas, the participation of numerous middle- and lower-class women in public spaces for work and education was curtailed. This led to increased isolation and a heightened dependency on men.[62] The opponents of such modernization policies viewed them not only as a violation of their Islamic identity but also as cultural imperialism: an imposition of Western ideals of women and a forced separation from their own cultural heritage. While some who supported Reza Shah's unveiling project viewed it as an inevitable step toward modernization, others critiqued the brutal ways these policies were enforced. The repressive measures taken by the Shah would instigate Islamist reactionary movements that ultimately led to the 1979 Iranian Revolution.[63]

During the Pahlavi monarchy, substantial reforms were implemented in the educational sphere, most notably allowing women to enroll in Tehran University for the first time in 1935. Despite this advancement, the conditions for young girls at the university were far from ideal. Many Iranian families who were against Reza Shah's unveiling policies and opposed mixed schools refused to allow their daughters to pursue their education in these institutions. Nevertheless, the presence of privileged women at this prestigious school was noteworthy.[64] Through the top-down enforcement of modernization, women's status began to change, albeit for a small sector of society. During Reza Shah's rule, there was little political or social reform or enfranchisement for women.[65] In addition to not granting women suffrage, Reza Shah's legal reforms did not address family law issues such as polygyny, divorce, and inheritance, and patriarchal structures continued to be reinforced in both public and private spheres.[66]

When Mohammad Reza Pahlavi initially came to power in 1941, women's issues were not a priority for the ruling establishment. However, 1963 proved to be a year of transformation and liberation for women as they obtained the right to vote and run for Parliament, and their voices began to be heard in social and political spaces.[67] Women started working in civil services and governmental agencies, and increasingly they enrolled in higher education institutions. As a consequence of urbanization and the dream of a better life, many families migrated from small rural towns to cities.[68] These migrations gradually led to women's increasing contribution to the workforce and engagement in the public sphere. The enactment of the FPL in 1967 was also a milestone for women's rights.

But although the reforms of the Pahlavi era had the stated objective of modernizing Iran, their hasty implementation led to greater social segregation for many women.[69] Despite their intent to modernize Iran, these reforms predominantly benefited a select group of women from the upper-middle social class, enabling them to advance in social and political circles. However, they fell short of fostering extensive engagement of women in leadership positions that could effect policy reform.

Throughout this period, women's political activities were neither organic nor independent but rather unstable, underdeveloped, and dependent on the ruling establishment.[70] Gender disparities grew as women faced the costs of social, occupational, and income inequalities.

These disparities, along with the sponsorship of state feminism, slowed the support for and progression of the women's movement.[71] As Louise Halper argues, despite Pahlavi's attention to women's issues, women's rights causes were deeply influenced by the Left's opposition to the ruling system. The political participation of mainstream Iranian women did not materialize in any meaningful way during the Pahlavi monarchy. On the contrary, women were visibly present in the 1979 Iranian Revolution as part of the resistance that opposed Pahlavi rule.[72]

Against the backdrop of these dynamics and the ensuing 1979 Revolution, the landscape of women's rights movements ushered in a transformative period with the promise of authentic freedom, justice, and dignity for women. Several high-ranking members of IIZ were particularly active during this pivotal time, simultaneously leading and participating in various women's organizations. These women pressured the male religious revolutionaries to address women's issues.[73] The leader of the Revolution, Ayatollah Khomeini, emphasized Islam's interest in social justice and criticized the monarchy's degradation of women despite its ostensible commitment to feminism. Khomeini's stance, among others, led to the widely held belief that advancing women's rights was a priority for the revolutionaries.[74]

## POLITICAL AND LEGAL STRUCTURE OF THE ISLAMIC REPUBLIC OF IRAN

More than seventy years after the Constitutional Revolution, the 1979 Revolution changed the course of history in Iran. Prior to the 1979 Revolution, a number of laws with secular undertones were implemented in the country that improved women's legal standing. At the time these laws were enacted, they faced opposition from the 'ulama' and the traditionalist masses. Lacking religious patronage, they failed to obtain the support of a considerable segment of the population. The fatwas issued by 'ulamas' like Ayatollah Khomeini also undermined the legitimacy of these laws. The Pahlavi monarchy eventually succumbed to widespread public resistance, and the popular uprising in 1979 brought the Islamic Republic to power.

The establishment of the new state was founded on a range of diverse and at times contradictory premises. Merging religious and political leadership, the Islamic Republic of Iran created a complex dynamic between religious authorities and the masses. As a pivotal premise of its ideological ethos, the government vowed to center Islamic justice, aiming to restore the justice exemplified by the first Shiʿi imam, ʿAli ibn Abi Talib.[75] The unique aspect of this newly formed state, compared to other Muslim nations, is the prerequisite for the leader to be a high-ranking Shiʿite religious authority, aligning with the concept of *vilāyat-i faqīh,* which translates to "the comprehensive authority of the jurist." Initially, the religious nature of the state made it difficult for female activists to challenge some of the discriminatory laws implemented by the new state leadership. In the early years of the Revolution, the ʿulamaʾ wielded both social capital and political influence, enabling them to enhance, impede, or overturn any articles in the Constitution or the Civil Code. Organizations like IIZ often found themselves aligning with the ruling elite despite changes in some of the laws that were detrimental to women.

This complex dynamic was further solidified by the overwhelming influence of Ayatollah Khomeini. Such was his authority that challenging the head of state seemed almost inconceivable. Furthermore, it was Ayatollah Khomeini who had originally advanced the theory of *vilāyat-i faqīh,* which granted absolute power to the Supreme Leader. During the 1920s, Khomeini, who would lead Iran's revolution half a century later, was deeply inspired by the Platonic vision of the philosopher-king. Elements of the Islamic Republic were eventually shaped by Ayatollah Khomeini's interest in Islamic mysticism and his study of Plato's *Republic,* as he used principles derived from these philosophies to inform the structure of the state.[76] Khomeini had come to believe that for a political system to engender virtuous citizens, it had to be governed by an enlightened minority. His political treatises on the ideal Islamic state emphasized the fusion of religion and the state within an Islamic framework.[77] Khomeini believed that the ʿulamaʾ were the rightful guardians of the republic and inherited the responsibilities of guidance and leadership passed down from Prophet Mohammed and the imams.[78] His vision forever changed the relationship between the state, ʿulamaʾ, and women.

One of the first issues that was subject to a referendum after 1979 was the Iranian Constitution, which greatly affected women. The Council of the Islamic Revolution (Shura-yi Inqilab-i Islami), established on the basis of the orders of Ayatollah Khomeini, had been made responsible for drawing up a draft constitution with the interim government and approving the final form that would be presented for voter ratification.[79] The postrevolutionary constitution, which drew on the 1958 Constitution of the French Republic as well as the 1907 Constitution of Iran, can be described as a fusion of theocratic and democratic principles.[80] Articles 1 and 2 of the Constitution bestow sovereignty in God, while Article 6 requires elections for both the presidency and the Majlis (Parliament). Nevertheless, all of these measures are contingent on the authorization of the Supreme Leader (*vilāyat-i faqīh*) and the Guardian Council (Shura-yi Nigahban). The Guardian Council, succeeding the committee of five *mujtahid*s from the 1907 Constitution, wields broader authority. Composed of twelve jurists, this council splits evenly between clergy with expertise in Islamic law, appointed by the Supreme Leader, and civil jurists nominated by Parliament.[81] One of its major duties is to review all laws passed by Parliament to ensure that they align with the Constitution and Islamic law. The modified constitution was no longer a mere republican constitution that was made compatible with Shi'i Islam. Instead, it became primarily shaped by Shi'i tenets of leadership and governance.[82]

With the rise of anti-Western rhetoric in the postrevolutionary space, crucial amendments to the Constitution were more readily accepted. This shift provided much-needed leeway for conservatives to undermine Western-style reforms, including those pertaining to women's rights. Despite this, the new constitution initially acknowledged women's issues. For instance, Article 20 affirmed the equality of men and women before the law, while Article 21 focused specifically on women's rights issues within the framework of motherhood and family.[83] However, the amendments to the Constitution ratified by the state in 1989 did not bring about substantial improvements in laws pertaining to women's rights. Instead, the focus shifted to facilitating greater political and socioeconomic participation for both men and women, as outlined in Article 3 of the Constitution. In the span of several years, all secular legislation was gradually removed and replaced with Islamic legal principles. Inspired by continued revolutionary zeal, which was partly fueled by the ongoing Iran-Iraq War, organizations like IIZ continued to work within the structures offered by the government. During such turmoil, these organizations did not exert substantial pressure on the state or the 'ulama' to advocate for women's rights.

Political scientists have been deeply intrigued by the resurgence of the Islamic legal framework following years of secular legislation. One of the compelling arguments is that in contrast to many Western nations, Iran did not experience the Industrial Revolution. The Western ideals of Enlightenment were introduced to the Iranian public, but the society lacked the robust economic, industrial, and political mechanisms to critically analyze these new concepts. In essence, the Pahlavis' "modernization" initiatives were a superficial outcome of modernity that was exported from the West to Iran.[84] The reemergence of the Islamic legal structure after years of secular laws has also been attributed to Iran's traditional society, where religious values historically played an influential role in people's lives. Secular changes in the 1907 Iranian Constitution backfired because of the refusal to acknowledge and reflect strongly held beliefs and social norms in the legal system.

In the postrevolutionary era, the political and religious elite attempted to merge aspects of religious law with those of a more secular nature. A prime example of this can be seen in the presidency of Mohammad Khatami (1997–2005), during which a shift back to foundational principles rooted in the country's constitution was adopted as a strategic political trend. Khatami promised to make Iran an Islamic democracy, governed by the rule of law, and he notably established the Supervisory Committee for the Constitution to protect constitutional principles. Consequently, throughout his presidency civil society experienced a much-needed revival, supported by Iranian youth and women's rights activists.

Khatami's reformist initiatives empowered nongovernmental organizations that focused on women's issues. By the end of the reformist era, more than 450 NGOs that worked to improve the status of women had come into being. The diversity of these organizations reflected the pluralistic nature of Iranian society. They adopted differing strategies and ideologies in their efforts to center women's concerns and improve their social and political standing in society. While some of them embraced a secular outlook in addressing women's rights causes, many chose to work within the established religious framework in the Islamic Republic of Iran.

The shift in the civil society landscape of Iran presented women with a unique opportunity to once again play a significant role in the civil society discourse.[85] Though Khatami's administration did not establish protective measures to prevent subsequent administrations from disbanding women's organizations, the political discourse that emerged during this period came to have a lasting impact on the women's rights movement.

The political tide in Iran shifted significantly when Mahmoud Ahmadinejad assumed the presidency in 2005. Soon after Ahmadinejad came to office, conservative forces dominated all branches of government. As a result of this swift political change, civil society institutions were suppressed, impeding the activities of a growing number of grassroots movements actively seeking policy reform. In an unexpected reversal, Ahmadinejad reestablished the Supervisory Committee for the Constitution. The Committee, which was originally established during Khatami's presidency, was responsible for reporting violations of constitutional principles and recommending modifications to laws and regulations to better align with the Constitution's objectives. The Guardian Council, which considered itself the sole supervisory organization in the Islamic Republic of Iran, had always resisted the formation of such a body.

The political forces supporting Ahmadinejad's newly established government closed down numerous civil society organizations and stifled the media. Nevertheless, discussions over the rule of law and constitutional rights continued to intensify. In such a politically charged climate, many women, 'ulama', and reformist intellectuals began to express their views on the compatibility of Islam, human rights, and dignity. Grand Ayatollah Husayn 'Ali Montazeri, who passed away in 2009, forcefully argued that shari'a and human rights law can coexist harmoniously. He reasoned that dignity is the prerogative of every individual and that the Islamic state must therefore honor and protect human rights and dignity.[86]

In June 2009, Iran's tenth presidential election made history once again. Although Ahmadinejad was declared victorious with approximately 63 percent of the votes, the opposition candidates contested the outcome, and their millions of supporters took to the streets to protest what they believed to be election fraud. Their movement, which came to be known as the Green Movement, sparked the largest protests since the 1979 Revolution. Although it was suppressed, its significance in Iran's modern political narrative has been acknowledged. During this time, the quest for equality and social justice among Iranian women gained momentum, with many protests spearheaded by women.

Navigating the political landscape during Ahmadinejad's tenure proved increasingly challenging for social and political activists, particularly those advocating for women's rights. Undeterred by these obstacles, women's rights organizations like IIZ innovatively collaborated to demand gender justice, specifically concerning amendments to the Family Protection Bill. The intensity of their activism led to modifications of several discriminatory provisions within the bill. In 2013, Iranian politics grabbed headlines again when moderate candidate Hassan Rouhani went on to become the president with the support of the reformists. Rouhani's campaign pledge to create a Citizenship Rights Charter generated excitement among civil society actors. The Charter, developed by two hundred prominent lawmakers and academics across different fields, articulates citizens' rights and empowers individuals to become familiar with their political, legal, economic, cultural, and social rights.

The Citizenship Rights Charter proposed by Rouhani's government is in line with former president Mohammad Khatami's "Plan to Respect Legitimate Freedoms and Protect Citizenship Rights," which was approved by the Guardian Council though never enforced.[87] Rouhani's proposed charter draws on its predecessor and a number of international human rights treaties and was written in accordance with the Iranian Constitution and Iranian customs and traditions. Nevertheless, getting it adopted is a monumental task, given that it must simultaneously satisfy the 'ulama', international human rights organizations, and conservatives and reformists in Iranian society.

Although some of the Charter's articles are ambiguous, it represents a stride toward safeguarding citizens' rights and fostering civil society growth. In terms of women's rights, the Charter assures women of equal opportunities for social and political engagement. Women are afforded the opportunity to play an active role in policymaking, legislation, and management positions.[88] The Charter stipulates that all citizens, especially women and children, must be protected from violence, including verbal and physical abuse within public and private realms.[89] Furthermore, women have the right to appropriate job opportunities and are entitled to receive pay equal to men's.[90] Women also have the right to access and form their own social, cultural, and artistic groups and organizations.[91]

When Rouhani proposed the Charter, some of the more conservative members in his government argued that many of its articles did not align with Islamic values. On the other end of the spectrum are civil rights activists who have maintained that the Charter does not go far enough to uphold the rights of women and minorities. Such debates over citizenship rights and constitutionalism has been described as a sign of "gradual replacement of Islamic legalism with a political practice based on the interests of the state."[92] But although the moderate success of republicanism as manifested in Rouhani's election provided a platform to advocate for a revision of the Constitution in hopes of restoring certain democratic rights, the Charter, which is draft legislation, has no enforcement guarantee. Iran's new conservative president, Ebrahim Raisi, who assumed office in August 2021, has not addressed the Citizenship Rights Charter, implying a lack of intention to implement it.

## CIVIL CODE AND FAMILY LAW IN THE ISLAMIC
## REPUBLIC OF IRAN

In the wake of the numerous debates and changes surrounding the Citizenship Rights Charter, another critical area of transformation deeply affecting women's legal status was the overhauling of Iran's Civil Code and Family Law in post-Revolution Iran. After the Revolution, traditionalist perspectives held sway in most state-controlled areas, resulting in the reinstatement of Islamic law. Consequently, numerous secular laws were either revoked or revised.[93] Among the most critical legislation that was overturned was the Civil Code, which was replaced with an Islamic Civil Code. Significant revisions were also made to the Family Protection Law of 1967. The revision of the Civil Code and family law after the Revolution had a significant impact on women's legal status. In attempting to navigate the complexities of Islamic law, particularly issues not previously addressed, the 1967 FPL was used as an interim guide until new legislation could be enacted. Over time, the revisions to family law in the Civil Code that were introduced in the Islamic Republic have increasingly echoed the 1967 Family Protection Law, indicating an ongoing change in the approach to women's rights and legal standing in Iran, which has become less traditionalist.[94]

The special civil courts for family law that had been established during the Pahlavi era were closed down after the Revolution, and family-related issues were integrated with other civil affairs in general courts.[95] But the general courts proved incapable of resolving family matters, so the government was forced to once again establish separate family courts.[96] The purview of these recently formed family courts encompassed matters such as marriage, divorce, dowry, compensation for domestic work, child custody and visitation, issues of insubordination, guardianship, remarriage, and terms stipulated in the marriage contract. In addition to these changes, the Expediency Council ruled that female advisory judges could be appointed to collaborate with the highest judge, since women had been banned from being appointed as judges after the Revolution.[97]

Since the Islamic Revolution, the Civil Code has seen significant changes, with dozens of articles systematically removed, modified, or substituted, leading to mixed outcomes. Female parliamentarians and women's rights groups like IIZ have mounted resistance against some of the more stringent laws with adverse effects on women, advocating for legislative amendments and striving for legal equity in a complex sociopolitical landscape. Despite their efforts, the results have been varied, reflecting the ongoing tension between women's activism and conservative legal frameworks.

The replacement of the Iranian Civil Code with the Islamic Civil Code is one of the enduring contested issues influencing gender equality discourse in Iran. Considering the Civil Code's expansive reach into both public and private aspects of an individual's life, jurists and women's rights groups scrutinize recommended revisions meticulously. While it might initially seem that efforts to secularize legislative and judicial institutions reverted to conventional understandings of Islamic law after the Revolution, in reality the state had to accommodate various viewpoints before modifying the Civil Code.[98] For instance, the traditionalist stance on *mahr* (dower)[99] did not initially support the adjustment of *mahr* to consider the rate of inflation. However, under pressure by female parliamentarians like Soheila Jelodarzadeh, who was also a member of IIZ, Parliament amended Article 1082 of the Civil Code to accommodate their demands.[100] Such adaptations epitomize the complex dynamics at play between groups advocating a firm return to shari'a and those championing a more reformist approach.[101]

In alignment with the evolving dynamics that led to modifications in the Civil Code, a significant political shift occurred as the twenty-first century dawned. Iranians reelected reformist president Mohammad Khatami (1997–2005) and voted for parliamentarians who campaigned on platforms promoting women's rights and reforming family law. To implement their electoral pledges, reformist MPs presented numerous bills with the intention of ending some of the legal discrimination faced by women in Iran. However, the Guardian Council rejected most of these bills, including a proposal to join the international Convention for the Elimination of Discrimination Against Women (CEDAW).[102] Contrary to previous instances, the Guardian Council did not have the last word, and an impasse ensued. To end the gridlock between the Guardian Council and Parliament, the Expediency Council intervened, and more than half of the suggested bills were ratified. These bills included stipulations to revise the earlier Civil Code, increase the age of marriage, and change divorce and custody laws in favor of women.[103] A number of prominent women's rights activists—who later became members of IIZ—brought public awareness to the Guardian Council's problematic role and succeeded in gathering considerable support from a diverse array of women's rights activists, both secular and religious.

Nevertheless, the momentum of this change proved to be short-lived. In 2004, as conservatives regained majority control in Parliament, the progression of reforms came to an abrupt standstill, in stark contrast to the strides made by women's rights activists in the previous years. The conservative parliament's resistance to reform only made women's rights activists more determined in their drive for gender justice. One of the initiatives undertaken by female activists was a campaign aimed at changing gender inequality laws in Iran. Launched in 2006, it was referred to as the "One Million Signatures" campaign, modeled after Moroccan women's activism in the 1990s.[104] With regard to family law, the campaign sought to secure equal rights in marriage and inheritance and put an end to polygyny.

Throughout the presidency of Mahmoud Ahmadinejad (2005–13), numerous attempts were made to end reforms to family laws, which had gained momentum during Khatami's presidency. In 2007, Ahmadinejad's government presented a controversial bill to Parliament entitled the Family Protection Bill. This new bill sought to reverse the postrevolutionary amendments and to hinder the progress made in family law during Khatami's presidency. Some of the most contentious provisions of the proposed bill included Article 22, which removed the necessity to register *mut'a* (temporary marriages), and Article 23, which made polygyny easier for men by permitting polygamous marriages depending on the man's financial capabilities. Another controversial component of the bill was Article 25, which levied taxes on women's *mahr* if it surpassed a specified amount. These contentious articles raised concern among women's rights activists, including members of IIZ, who joined forces to challenge them. Despite some controversial articles undergoing changes during Rouhani's presidency, the rights and legal status of women have remained areas of conflict between women and the state during Ebrahim Raisi's presidency.

## WOMEN'S ACTIVISM DURING THE ISLAMIC REPUBLIC OF IRAN

The significant political engagement of women in the years leading up to the 1979 Revolution profoundly influenced Ayatollah Khomeini during his years in exile. As Azadeh Kian points out, the leader of the Revolution advanced an interpretation of Islam that assured women's political and social rights.[105] Khomeini also commended women for their active role in the Revolution, declaring, "You are the leaders of the movement. You have shown the path and we have followed you. I recognize this and I am your servant."[106] By affirming women's political and social rights in the Islamic tradition, Khomeini highlighted women's duty to become politically active.[107] IIZ members have often gained legitimacy for their activism by referencing Ayatollah Khomeini's documented statements about the importance of women's involvement in politics and social arenas.

While supporting the rights of women to be politically active during the Revolution, Ayatollah Khomeini adopted concepts such as self-determination and democratic government to address women's issues. For Khomeini, "Democracy is incorporated in the Qur'an, and people are free to express their opinions and to conduct their acts. Under the Islamic government, which is a democratic government, freedom of expression, opinion, and pen will be guaranteed for everyone."[108] Such inclusive statements appealed to both secular women, whose activism had been undermined or systemically curtailed during the Pahlavi monarchy, and traditional women, who were systematically excluded from Pahlavi's modernization project.[109]

The 1979 Revolution awakened a sense of agency among a growing number of middle-class and traditional women who had previously remained distant from the sociopolitical sphere during the Pahlavi reign. It created an environment conducive to the participation of Iranian women in the sociopolitical arena in the name of "oppositional Islamic femininity," effectively challenging and altering traditional notions that had prevented women from engaging in public life.[110] Khomeini's endorsement of women's political and social involvement played a significant role in this shift. Women's newfound empowerment prompted them to enter the public domain at an unprecedented pace. What had once been a movement limited to the elite now became a national outcry for justice and equality.

The traditionalist 'ulama' were intent on guiding women back to what they perceived to be their primary roles as mothers and spouses. Traditional jurisprudence, advocated by these 'ulama', stated that men and women are different in their essence and should complement one another in their duties. Hence, the notion of gender equality was rejected and gender complementarity became central.[111] But Ayatollah Khomeini, in contrast to traditionalist 'ulama', encouraged women's presence and activism in the public sphere. He strongly contended that "women's role in society is more important than men's. Women are active in all aspects, but they also raise children who will become active."[112] He also maintained that "God is satisfied with women's great service. It is a sin to sabotage this [women's activity in the public sphere]."[113] The explicit endorsement from Ayatollah Khomeini for women's political involvement served as a crucial stepping-stone, facilitating women's path to positions as MPs during the first three parliamentary sessions held between 1980 and 1988.[114]

Through the endorsement of women's political involvement, a reciprocal relationship was formed, with women in return expressing their support for the newly established government. This relationship was particularly evident in the initial year after the Revolution, when a constitutional referendum in the Islamic Republic was held, obtaining overwhelming public approval, with over 99 percent of the vote. Leading up to the referendum, Ayatollah Khomeini stated that "all of you [women] should vote. Vote for the Islamic Republic. Not a word less, not a word more. . . . You have priority over men."[115] In a public show of support for women's political involvement, Khomeini stressed that "women have done more for the movement than men, for their participation doubles the power of men. Men can't remain indifferent when women take part in the movement."[116] Khomeini's stance on women's sociopolitical rights underwent a gradual but at times significant shift after the Revolution. Though when he came to power he suspended the Family Protection Law implemented during the Pahlavi era, during the Iran-Iraq War Khomeini expressed more support for the demands of women who had supported the Revolution and now sought more representation and rights. The growing calls from women involved in Iran's social and political arenas, including notable members of IIZ, led Khomeini to make a number of pragmatic decisions that opened the way for greater participation of women and activists who had pledged their allegiance to the Islamic Republic. Historically, women's causes had been used instrumentally to rally support for various political agendas. Recognizing this challenge, women's rights activists started to explore new avenues to voice their concerns, refusing to be marginalized by a system that was not primarily concerned with women's rights issues.

The turn of events following the 1979 Revolution led to renewed calls for the establishment of women's organizations. Khomeini supported women's groups that aligned with the Revolution's ideals and could potentially offset the sway of secular and Western feminist currents. The Jam'ah-i Zanan-i Inqilab-i Islami (Women's Society of the Islamic Revolution) came to the fore as the leading organization that brought together women's rights advocates with this specific objective. This organization was created to raise women's awareness concerning the identity of "authentic Iranian Muslim women."[117] The majority of its members were educated and came from the middle and upper classes. A number of these women were also affiliated with IIZ and elite religious and political families. This prominent participation of women during the Revolution, in conjunction with their high-profile connections, served to underscore the potential and capacity of women as active participants in the sociopolitical landscape, thus cultivating a fresh understanding and appreciation of women's roles in these areas.[118]

While progress seemed destined for previously marginalized traditional and religious women, elite secular women, known for their activism in women's rights, experienced setbacks on various fronts, including their access to public life. This added another layer of complexity to the evolving sociopolitical dynamics stemming from the Revolution. For instance, requiring the hijab became a way of excluding secular female activists, who opposed it, from the few positions of power that were available to women. In a show of force, women came to the streets just months after the Revolution to oppose mandatory hijab, which they considered a dangerous precedent. The diverse groups that took part in the protests included the Women's Society of the Islamic Revolution and communist groups like the Revolutionary Union of Militant Women.[119] But despite these women's strong objection, the masses remained silent, which was interpreted as tacit acceptance of the state's policies.

The justification for hijab came mostly in the larger context of the Islamic notions of modesty and equity in relation to women. In one instance, Ayatollah Khomeini stated that "in the Islamic system, women do have the same rights as men. They have the right to study, work, own property, they have the right to vote and to be elected. The only differences between men and women are natural and biological ones. According to Islam, women should wear the veil, but chador is not necessary."[120] Despite such proclamations, the *chador* became almost mandatory for women who had a vested interest in entering the political arena or pursuing careers in the public sector. The same hijab that had prevented previously marginalized women from accessing public spaces was now being used as an instrument of oppression toward women who had had more privilege and access to the public space in the Pahlavi monarchy.[121]

Women's roles and activism shifted yet again during the 1980s. When Iraq attacked Iran in 1980 with the promise of reaching the capital Tehran in a matter of days, the country immediately went into survival mode and mobilized all resources to resist the invasion. While in the immediate aftermath of the Revolution women had expressed a variety of demands in relation to their rights, throughout the eight-year war that ended in 1988, few if any instances of overt expressions of women's rights activism were witnessed. One way women did become hypervisible throughout the war was when they received military training and were allowed to join the army and support Iranian military forces behind the front lines.[122] In support of women's demand to join the military forces in defending their country, Ayatollah Khomeini referenced women in early Islamic history who had taken part in war and helped families of martyrs. The heroic acts of several women during the eight-year war continue to be retold by the state through interviews, documentaries, and publications.

The presence of women in historically male-dominated spaces also paved the way for the appointment of women to new political and military positions. A prominent example is Marziyeh Dabbagh Hadidchi, who was appointed as a military commander in the western province of Hamedan during the war years. Hadidchi also became renowned for her role as Ayatollah Khomeini's bodyguard when he was exiled in Paris. She became a trusted ally and a permanent member of Ayatollah Khomeini's inner circle until his death. She led a delegation to the former Soviet Union and personally gave a handwritten letter from Khomeini to the former president of the Soviet Union, Mikhail Gorbachev, in 1989. Hadidchi was also active in women's rights causes and chaired the Association of the Women of the Islamic Republic for a quarter of a century starting in 1987. After the war, the state would establish the Office of Women's Affairs. The primary objective of this organization, which maintained a direct connection to the president's office, revolved around enhancing the economic, social, cultural, and political status of women.[123]

Since the Revolution, over 30 percent of the female population in Iran have been able to access the workforce and become income earners. Women's more visible and increased presence in public and educational spaces has helped in their struggle for equality and justice.[124] Essentially, it was women's active participation in social and political life following the Revolution that led to their increased demands for gender justice. By the late 1980s, traditional and religious women who were emboldened by the Revolution were becoming disillusioned by limited improvements in the gender policies of the state. Instead of resigning themselves to this situation, they began to propose policies and initiatives with the intention of reforming the system they had categorically supported in the past.[125] What ensued was the mobilization of female activists who used their knowledge of religion to raise awareness on women's issues.[126] Such faith-based activism continues to be employed by contemporary women's rights organizations such as IIZ.

Women's rights organizations have come a long way over the past one hundred years to be able to unite in meaningful ways despite fundamental differences. The prerevolutionary period saw an increased presence of middle-class women in organizations that advocated women's rights. Women's organizations underwent another important transformation during the reformist era in the Khatami presidency (1997–2005). The reformist era saw the development of a collaborative dialogue within women's organizations. This created an avenue for in-depth debates about women's rights, which posed challenges to the conventional norms of the prevailing system.[127] The scholarly dialogue cultivated during this time greatly influenced the advocacy efforts of women's rights coalitions such as IIZ.

Politicians, particularly the reformists, often highlighted women's issues during election campaigns but once in positions of power would take minimal action to reform discriminatory policies. These politicians frequently capitalized on their concerns to make electoral gains but failed to fulfill their promises. Reformists in positions of power were more concerned with advocating for democracy and considered the problem of gender inequality to be peripheral. The female MPs in power between 2000 and 2004 in the reformist government of Khatami formed a women's coalition that made explicit efforts to push a women's rights agenda. They sought to ratify the UN Convention on the Elimination of Discrimination Against Women (CEDAW) and proposed bills that would amend the Civil Code with regard to such issues as age of marriage, access to divorce, and inheritance. But the Civil Code has proved rather inflexible and difficult to reform. The reformers lobbied government officials and influential 'ulama' in support of their cause and succeeded in getting important measures passed in Parliament. But the Guardian Council rejected the majority of these measures.[128]

In the postreformist era, women's rights groups attracted individuals across a wide political and ideological spectrum, including traditionalists, reformists, and secularists who sought to advance gender justice through policy reform. In so doing, they became part of the growing cluster of activists disenchanted by the divide between the ideals of the secular state and the realities of the Islamic one.[129] In this context, women's rights activists informed by different aims and aspirations decided to join forces in an effort to advance women's causes. The initial disagreements among diverse women's groups did not deter them from collaborating with each other. These activists sought alternative ways to circumvent the barriers they faced by finding shared ground and undertaking a number of initiatives to improve women's status. This newfound sense of unity, although liberating and unique, has not resolved all their differences. For instance, secular feminists oppose shari'a-based family and criminal codes, while religious activists seek to reform religious-based laws by problematizing patriarchal readings of sacred scripture. Despite these differences, women's rights activists, including members of IIZ, have managed to find enough common ground to form a united front when addressing gender-related issues in Iran.

One subject of contention that has not escaped women's critical gaze in post-Revolution Iran is the Constitution. Shahindokht Molaverdi, the former legal analyst of IIZ and vice president for women and family affairs, has highlighted some of the legal deficiencies of the Constitution that affect women's rights. In an interview she stated, "The Constitution, as the chief guarantor of people's individual and social rights, plays a significant role in providing a model for other laws in the country. Therefore, as an important frame of reference, the Constitution should not contain any expression that undermines women's independence. The language adopted by the Constitution must be in a manner that circumvents the use of any expression or term that implies the superiority of one gender over the other."[130]

Women's rights activists from a variety of ideological and political camps have offered a gender-based critique of the Constitution. In 2005, Iranian women from a wide range of sociopolitical backgrounds gathered to voice their concerns about the limited rights granted to women in the Constitution. Following this protest nearly one hundred women's organizations signed a declaration and formed the largest independent women's mobilization since the fall of the Pahlavi monarchy.[131]

Women's rights activists, particularly members of IIZ, have emphasized that the Constitution highlights women's role in public and private spheres and that its introductory section explicitly endorses women's human rights. But they argue that its perception of women continues to be grounded in a traditional gender role framework. Such conventional conceptualization confines women's function to their role in the family unit. It also perceives women as dependents, primarily tasked with fulfilling their responsibilities as wives and mothers. The role of women outside these realms is not recognized or defined. For instance, Article 19 of the Constitution considers Iranian citizens to have equal rights regardless of their race, language, and tribal affiliation but remains silent on whether gender can be a source of discrimination.

Women's organizations such as IIZ argue that the Constitution's legal ambiguities and promotion of vague concepts can result in varied interpretations and inconsistent decisions. They urge lawmakers to revise laws and regulations that are at odds with the principles, goals, and values of the Constitution. For example, according to Article 987 of the Civil Code and Article 41 of the Constitution, "Citizenship of Iran is the unquestioned right of all Iranians. The government may not deprive any Iranian of his/her citizenship, except at their own request, or if they take up citizenship of another country."[132] However, in reality Iranian women lose their citizenship if they marry a foreigner. There is also dissonance between Article 28 of the Constitution, which refers to people's freedom in choosing jobs, and Article 1117 of the Civil Code, which gives the husband unilateral rights to prohibit his wife from working in a job that he does not deem to be in the interest of the family. Another discrepancy relates to the guardianship of children. According to Article 21 of the Constitution, the criteria for guardianship are based on the mother's capability and merits, but Articles 1252 and 1251 of the Civil Code strip the mother of guardianship if she chooses to remarry. IIZ argues that in order to reconcile conflicting and discriminatory regulations against women, both patriarchal laws and problematic cultural traditions must change. They also recognize that although legal equality is necessary, it is not sufficient. Legislators should acknowledge the equality of men and women without disregarding their natural differences, so that men and women's distinctive natures are not used as grounds for discrimination.[133]

Articles 20 and 21 are among the few articles in the Constitution that explicitly address women. According to Article 20, "All citizens of the country, both men and women, equally enjoy the protection of the law and enjoy all human, political, economic, social, and cultural rights, in conformity with Islamic criteria." Similarly, Article 21 states that the government should ensure women's rights in all domains. This article aims to foster a favorable environment for the restoration of women's rights, both materially and intellectually. It further promises the protection of mothers, particularly during pregnancy. Indeed, the Constitution states that one of its primary objectives is to revive the revered role and duties of motherhood. However, IIZ members have pointed out that one of the contentious issues for women is balancing their motherhood duties with their citizenship responsibilities. Specifically, Article

43 of the Constitution declares that "the plan for the national economy must be structured in such a manner that the form, content, and hours of work gives individuals sufficient time to engage in intellectual, political, and social activities." In practice, though, government measures have led to extended maternity leaves, the closure of state-operated kindergartens, and a progressive reduction in working hours for women. According to members of IIZ, these policies are aimed at forcing women back into the private sphere instead of facilitating the conditions for their contribution to the economy and society. For IIZ, a key approach to boost women's participation in both public and private sectors is for the government to alleviate the challenges working women face by offering measures and structural support, bridging the divide between household duties and societal roles.

The task of amending the Constitution, however, is complicated by women's lack of representation on the bodies that make such changes possible. Considering that amendments to the Constitution are largely controlled by the Guardian Council, women from across conservative and reformist camps argue that the Constitution hinders its own intent by blocking women's strides toward better societal status.

In response to significant advocacy from civil rights activists and women's organizations like IIZ, Rouhani's government eventually implemented the Citizenship Rights Charter in 2016. The Charter strives to eliminate violations of citizens' rights but falls short of challenging men's monopoly over the Constitution. Elaheh Koolaee, a former MP and a member of IIZ, argues that some of its positive aspects include the "direct reference to women's rights to education without gender discrimination. This article is in contrast to some of the discriminatory policies in recent years that targeted women and excluded them from majoring in a range of fields of study that were deemed to be more appropriate for men." While acknowledging the efforts made by legislators of the Charter, Koolaee recommends that the Charter address the patriarchal structures and traditions in society that constrain women's independence. IIZ also asserts that the government should eliminate the social, political, and legal barriers to women's active citizenship and should ensure that women are provided equal opportunities across diverse sectors, including political roles.[134]

According to Koolaee, the Charter overlooks the growing presence of women in the public sphere, particularly in economic and political life. The former reformist MP states, "This Charter primarily addresses women's rights in the family unit and dismisses their role as independent individuals. There is little attention paid to the extensive presence of women in the public sphere, particularly in economic and political realms. Women's right to run for president and their presence in various religious and political councils are pressing concerns that were not addressed in the Charter. Although Rouhani's presidential slogan was based on equal opportunities for women, there has not been sufficient attention paid to these issues."[135]

Ashraf Boroujerdi, a member of the Socio-Cultural Council for Women and Family Affairs during Rouhani's presidency and a prominent figure in IIZ, similarly argues that a significant limitation of the Charter is its focus on women's rights solely within the family context, neglecting to recognize women as independent entities. Women have been placed in the same category as children and the elderly, while men's citizenship rights are addressed in a separate category. IIZ contends that categorizing women with minors and the elderly reveals how lawmakers view women. This perspective reinforces the notion that women, like children and the elderly, require guardianship and are therefore unable to make decisions independently. It inevitably discriminates against women and places them in an inferior status compared to men. Another controversial aspect of the Charter centers on women's social and political rights to equal opportunities. The Citizenship Rights Charter neglects to address women's representation in decision-making bodies as well as their status in educational, scientific, and technological fields. Yet despite its limitations and absence of legal enforceability, the Citizenship Rights Charter is viewed by numerous activists as playing a role in advancing civil society and raising citizen consciousness in Iran.

IIZ points out that while ideally there should be no distinction between the citizenship rights of men and women, addressing these issues separately by employing equity-driven affirmative action could be a way to rectify the long-standing neglect of women's rights. Acknowledging both the disparities between men and women and the vital necessity of safeguarding women's rights could serve as a provisional solution to the systemic biases women encounter within the legal and judicial systems. However, substantial and lasting reform requires broad-based, concerted efforts that are simultaneously social, political, and legal.

Though women's rights activists have pushed for reform of the Iranian Constitution and the Civil Code, they also draw on and at times tactically appropriate some of the government's own definitions of rights and responsibilities toward citizens as laid out in these documents. Using Article 20 of the Constitution as a reference—which guarantees that all citizens are protected by the law and are entitled to human, political, economic, social, and cultural rights—activists advocate for the recognition and empowerment of women's agency. Faith-based activists achieve their goals by strategically navigating local customs ( '*urf*), reinterpreting civil law, and drawing upon their understanding of sacred scriptures. Their effectiveness also relies on maintaining a constructive dialogue with the religious scholars and authorities in Islam. In practicing their faith-based activism, IIZ members display refashioned selves, drawing on both cultural and religious values, to redefine notions of rights and responsibilities within the Islamic legal code.

As women's struggles for justice persist, post-Revolution Iran has witnessed an emerging women's rights movement determined to challenge and change entrenched power structures. The reformist years in Iran created a space for female activists to establish advocacy groups independent of government-run organizations. Despite the challenges posed by powerful conservative forces, women's rights organizations have shown remarkable resilience. Their determination and resilience have allowed them to continue advocating for change and pushing for advancements in women's rights in the face of significant obstacles. Even in the current restrictive economic and social setting, women continue to announce their demands. A notable testament to this defiance emerged in 2022. In urban regions across Iran, women began to overtly resist the state-imposed hijab. These acts of resistance were not isolated but echoed by different faith-based women's organizations and activists, who openly supported women's right to choose their attire. On Iranian social platforms, religious women showing support for those not adhering to the state-mandated Islamic dress code have faced intense opposition from conservatives. These women's resistance underscores a significant trend in contemporary Iranian society and marks a crucial step toward personal freedom and self-expression.

Women's ongoing activism has also translated into the government being forced to compromise on its gender policies. Women from religious and secular backgrounds have temporarily bridged their ideological differences, uniting in their efforts to eradicate gender-based inequalities. In this collaborative environment, they have jointly tackled various gender-related issues such as the modernization of family law, the necessity for women's greater political involvement, and the need to make women's concerns political and social priorities.[136]

The century-long struggle of Iranian women for gender justice that began to take shape following the Constitutional Revolution has gone through various changes in recent decades, even though Iran continues to be primarily a traditional nation. The Constitutional Revolution promoted women's involvement in social and political life and paved the way for women's participation during the Pahlavi monarchy.[137] For a long period, educated women with secular backgrounds were at the forefront of the struggle for women's rights, particularly throughout the Pahlavi monarchy. However, it was not until faith-based activists joined the struggle that women's rights issues became household conversations. In the path toward gender justice, women's rights activists such as those from IIZ have armed themselves with in-depth religious knowledge, challenging discriminatory policies enacted under the guise of religion and culture.

Moving forward, the next chapter will explore the distinct approach of faith-based activism that IIZ employed to counteract the discriminatory Family Protection Law proposed by Mahmoud Ahmadinejad's government. It will discuss the alternative vision for family law outlined by members of IIZ and will scrutinize the arguments they formulated against biased stipulations within the suggested bill. This examination will offer a more comprehensive understanding of these women's activism and the extent to which their faith-based advocacy was instrumental in challenging the controversial aspects of the Family Protection Bill, ultimately shedding light on the profound impacts of their activism.

# CHAPTER 3

# Itilaf-i Islami-yi Zanan and the Family Law Controversy

The contention over Islamic family law transcends the issues of women's rights within the family unit and the role and reach of Islamic law in society. It exposes the power relations that exist between the state and female activists. While the Islamic Republic of Iran as a sovereign entity has had a hegemonic hold on regulating and implementing family law, female activists contest the state's power by attributing authority to other sources, including the Shi'i tradition, *'urf* (custom), and the Constitution.[1] By tracing the challenges and possibilities that emerged from contesting the state's hegemony over modifying family law, this chapter examines the complex ways in which the Iranian state compels female activists to seek innovative approaches to structure their interpretation of gender justice in the proposed Family Protection Bill.

Islamic family law has been at the center of an ongoing debate in Iran since the early 1900s. The Iranian Civil Code of 1928 is considered the first official attempt to codify family law. The second major change in relation to family law can be traced back to 1967, when the Family Protection Law was formally introduced during the reign of Muhammad Reza Pahlavi. After the fall of the Pahlavi monarchy, the Islamic government rejected aspects of the Family Protection Law and introduced some amendments to it. The amended Family Protection Law and the 1928 Civil Code dictated Iran's family law until 2007, when a new Family Protection Bill emerged, filling a legal gap that had existed since 1979. This shift marked a departure from established legal traditions.[2] The

Principlist government of Mahmoud Ahmadinejad proposed several major changes to the bill that affected the Family Protection Law of 1967 and the progressive amendments made during the tenure of reformist president Mohammad Khatami.

In the subsequent exploration of this newly proposed family law, the focus will be on the activism of Itilaf-i Islami-yi Zanan (IIZ). Their interpretations of the legislation and their proposed alternative "family paradigm model" will be highlighted. This chapter specifically examines the arguments and rationales that emerged between 2008 and 2014, involving members of the IIZ Coalition who challenged some of the proposed amendments to the Family Protection Bill introduced by Ahmadinejad's government. A number of controversial bills were introduced that engaged the attention of female activists. While I cannot hope to cover all the responses issued by IIZ, this chapter will specifically focus on their campaigns against polygyny. IIZ's strategic reinterpretation of Islamic family law is anchored in their family paradigm model. Skillfully leveraging this model, IIZ has crafted a potent counternarrative to the state's stance, leading to meaningful legal transformations.

## THE FAMILY PARADIGM MODEL

To fully comprehend the family paradigm model proposed by IIZ, it is imperative to locate the roots of the laws practiced by Muslims. Contemporary legal norms in Muslim societies, particularly as they pertain to gender relations, are an amalgamation of Islamic jurisprudence, *urf,* and nineteenth-century conceptualizations of gender.[3] Modernization brought about the codification of laws and forced Muslim societies to adhere to personal status laws that were not necessarily based on Islamic legal principles. These personal status laws were gendered, with the man perceived to be the head of the household. Consequently, male authority was perpetuated and protected by the modern nation-state. The modern state's attempt to codify family law created a space where the notion of the nuclear family became central to the family system. Informed by such discourse, a man's role came to be defined as the head of the household, while the woman's role remained confined to that of mother and housewife.[4]

Social realities have prompted lawmakers and social justice activists to deliberate on alternative solutions that better reflect the normative realities of the twenty-first century. As indicated, one of the fundamental components of Islamic family law is the concept of justice, which is central to the Shiʻi tradition. However, our understanding and interpretation of that concept have been subject to historical evolution. Given that changing social realities have led to the modification of legal solutions, it is inevitable that the notion of justice, as applicable to premodern social contexts, can no longer meet the needs of citizens living in the modern nation-state. It is in this context that IIZ questions whether some of the premises on which Muslim family laws are based have any significant bearing on today's realities.[5]

Over the past four decades following the Revolution in Iran, people's views regarding women's role in society have greatly changed. Men no longer object to women's participation in the public sphere, and women are increasingly aware of their rights. The majority of young Iranian women are interested in balancing their family life with a career. This signals a shift from the traditional family structure, where men were considered as the sole economic providers and women were expected to be content with their roles as housewives and mothers. Members of IIZ contend that in contemporary Iran most women believe that couples should share economic and household responsibilities, including raising the children.[6] However, the majority of male Muslim jurists continue to reinforce the premodern idea that men have authority over their family because of their role as economic providers. By these jurists' interpretations, a man's financial responsibility toward his family translates into authority over them. In reality, as Judith Tucker argues, the construction of gendered roles and the perception of men as the head of the family unit have influenced the public sphere and limited women's authority in the public realm.[7]

Shahla Aʻzazi, a sociologist and an active member of IIZ, points to another aspect of the changing nature of the family structure in Iran: "When we examine the process of change, we realize that the Iranian family has undergone significant transformation throughout the past two decades. In modern societies, in both the East and the West, people's understanding of the concept of family is rapidly changing. In Iran, this change is visible with the increase in the number of marriages that are based on companionship and love. Women are no longer content with only having their financial needs met. Couples believe a loving home, partnership, and emotional support are what makes for a stable and nurturing relationship and leads to marital bliss."[8] Further, according to Aʻzazi, "The time when extended families used to live together is long gone. The changes in society, particularly in the realm of employment, have led to the development of a new kind of nuclear family that consists of the father, mother, and children."[9] High divorce rates in Iran have also given rise to the emergence of single-parent households.

According to IIZ, jurists and politicians have ignored these profound transformations. Their attempt to reimpose traditional family values has consequently been ineffective by a wide margin. A'zazi maintains, "Many politicians try to restore the traditional model of family in place of the new family structure. These efforts do not appear to be succeeding, particularly in terms of long-term impact. The future of Iranian families, which is currently undergoing transition, is difficult to predict. But the current situation is indicative of extensive changes to the family structure. These changes are visible in the choice of a spouse, the formation of families, the birth of children, and the increase in the rate of divorce."[10]

Government statistics over the past two decades show a steep decline in the marriage rate, an increase in the rate of divorce, and a noticeable increase in the age of marriage.[11] But the ruling system has not caught up with the realities of Iranian society. Although there have been several attempts to reform Islamic family law, the solutions offered have been insufficient and inconsistent. Members of IIZ are advocating for a comprehensive and inclusive Islamic family law informed by women's jurisprudence. Such an approach is based on the Qur'anic principles of justice and compassion, which are central to the family paradigm.

IIZ believes that the problems plaguing the current family law system stem from two contentious paradigms: the individualistic paradigm and the equality paradigm. The individualistic paradigm places either men or women at the center of the decision-making process. When men are placed at the center and their opinions are directly reflected in the laws and rules governing the family unit, the outcome is a patriarchal society. Patriarchal interpretations of religion through history have clearly had harmful effects. Meanwhile, a secular feminist approach can also lend itself to problematic binaries by disregarding men's views. Members of IIZ maintain that similar to a patriarchal reading of the law, a feminist approach can undermine the legitimacy of the legal system. Embracing a feminist philosophical disposition, IIZ members argue, can be perceived as pleading on behalf of a particular population while ignoring the rights of another group. The employment of paradigms where one form of dominance is replaced with another has been criticized for being reductionist and reactionary. In such paradigms, women's experiences are depicted as similar across different religions, traditions, social classes, and races. Such an outlook lends itself to the essentialist view, suggesting that women possess innate attributes that solidify their understanding of femininity.[12] Rejecting both these approaches, IIZ advocates for a model that looks at family law holistically and includes the experiences of women and children, which have been historically marginalized.

The equality paradigm, according to IIZ, also suffers from limitations. The language of gender equality is grounded in Western traditions, so it is not necessarily the prevailing language used to address gender regulation in developing nations. IIZ argues that the equality paradigm has found its way into international laws such as the Convention on the Elimination of All Forms of Discrimination Against Women (CEDAW). As Rema Hammami notes, such international institutions have been influential in disseminating the concept of gender equality by utilizing it in their gender policies.[13] IIZ's problem with the Western perception of gender equality stems from the belief that the Western model overlooks differences between men and women. For IIZ, equality does not imply that men and women's differences, particularly in terms of their biological and reproductive abilities, should be overlooked. Instead, they believe the law should take women's experiences into consideration, particularly ones related to pregnancy, childbirth, and nursing, instead of complying with male norms. What IIZ appreciates about the Islamic model of family law, regardless of its deficiencies, is that it acknowledges women's ability to bear children. In doing so, it mandates men to financially support their wives, recognizing their contribution to domestic life and family roles. This support can manifest through *nafaqa* (maintenance) and compensation for breastfeeding.

The rhetoric of gender equality becomes even more complicated with women's entry into the workforce and public life. Despite a more prominent presence in the workforce, the burden of caregiving as well as domestic responsibilities continues to fall on the shoulders of women. IIZ perceives the predominant Western discourse on gender equality as exerting a conceptual oppression on women. In the framework of gender equality, women are either overwhelmed mothers and wives or self-interested individuals who forsake family responsibilities to focus on their careers.[14] In many Western countries, inclusive governmental policies and support have decreased potential disparities. However, middle-class women across the Middle East grapple with reconciling the notions of being exemplary wives and mothers, yet also professionals.

While equality is viewed as crucial to justice, the Western equality paradigm, as understood by IIZ, does not adequately recognize the differences between men and women. IIZ believes that true gender equality goes beyond simply treating both genders identically. Their concern is that the Western equality paradigm tends to generalize, failing to consider individual needs, capabilities, and constraints. The Coalition is of the belief that the Western equality paradigm has a penchant to neglect the rights and needs of children as well. This phenomenon, described by Anver Emon as "the paradox of equality," invites an idiosyncratic understanding of justice, where treating diverse groups of people differently takes precedence over the adoption of a single homogenous model for the treatment of everyone.[15] A fundamental question raised by IIZ is whether different legal rulings for men and women always result in discrimination. These faith-based activists are advocating gender justice in the legal system that is informed by women's jurisprudence as a meaningful alternative.

IIZ recognizes that a legal judgment rooted in a specific historical setting may have different interpretations across diverse circumstances. Therefore, sheer legal equality might not effectively challenge the deeply rooted advantages of men and could potentially weaken women's bargaining power within the family framework. If absolute equality were strictly implemented in family law, women's entitlements such as *nafaqa* (financial maintenance by their husband), *mahr*, remuneration for childcare, and payment for domestic work would risk being eliminated.[16] Thus IIZ believes that not every difference should be categorized as discrimination. In this manner, the Coalition is taking into account the difficult social and economic situations Iranian women might face in the absence of such financial support.

In an effort to address the shortcomings of the equality paradigm, IIZ offers an alternative that they call the "family paradigm model." The family paradigm model embodies a holistic approach that emphasizes the purpose and intention of marriage and raising a family. According to this framework, family-related laws should prioritize the collective welfare of the family as a whole rather than the desires of its individual members. This model emphasizes placing the welfare of the family at the center of government policies. This is in conformity with Article 10 of the Constitution, which stresses that the family is the fundamental unit of society and that all rules and regulations should strengthen the family structure. IIZ envisions an Islamic family paradigm that is rooted in women's jurisprudence while also cultivating Islamic virtues. This organization maintains that an effective family paradigm model has to include and regulate the experiences of women and children in accordance with Qur'anic principles of justice and compassion.

The family paradigm model is an important step to merging the rights of the spouses, children, and close relatives until an equilibrium is reached. Within this model, the rights and duties of individuals in a family unit are interconnected and reciprocal. The central premise of this paradigm is to steer away from individualism and be part of an organized family system that perpetuates a culture of compassion, generosity, and justice. IIZ contends that in such families a sense of peace and security flourishes and there is a strong focus on the spiritual development of every family member. In this spiritual journey, both men and women are responsible for cultivating an environment that nurtures a sense of well-being as they support one another. Among the parents' responsibilities in the family paradigm model is the necessity to foster an atmosphere where the children become acquainted with their Islamic rights and duties.

For IIZ, the family paradigm model is informed by the Qur'an's comprehensive understanding of family. In the first verse of the chapter on women, the Qur'an[17] advises human beings to worship God and be virtuous in order to be shielded from wrongdoing. The verse encourages individuals to uphold their responsibilities toward their family and kin, and cautions against adopting overly individualistic or patriarchal attitudes. The Qur'an (4:21) emphasizes the importance of honoring *mithaq ghaliz* (marriage covenants) and views the family as the bedrock of righteousness. IIZ contends that the Qur'an sets forth guidelines that aim to preserve the sanctity of the family structure.

Drawing from women's jurisprudence, IIZ classifies the Qur'anic principles related to family duties into six distinct parts. The first principle underlined by IIZ is about dignity and respect. This point is reinforced in a Qur'anic verse (4:21) that asks, "And how could you take it [anything you have given a first wife] after you have been intimate with each other, and they have taken from you a solemn covenant?" This verse emphasizes the responsibility of men toward their spouses and reminds believers that marriage is a divine covenant and agreement, which is different in nature from worldly contracts. It distinguishes marriage contracts from business contracts by highlighting the sacred nature of marriage vows. IIZ stresses that by neglecting marital obligations, believers are undermining their sacred vows not only toward their spouse but also in relation to God.

The Qur'an's emphasis on the principle of dignity is also evident in the context of separation and divorce. The Qur'an (2:237) stresses that a couple should respect one another's rights and behave righteously toward

each other at all times: "If you divorce your wives before the consummation of the marriage and the amount of dowry has been fixed, pay your
wives half of the amount of their dowry unless she forgoes the demand
for payment. To forgo such a demand is closer to piety. Be generous to
each other. God is well aware of what you do." In accordance with
Qur'anic principles, dignity and fairness are central to all human relations, particularly with respect to the family, and men and women should
continue to respect one another even after the dissolution of marriage.

The second Qur'anic principle cited by IIZ is the principle of *mawadda
wa raḥma* (love and compassion). The Qur'an (30:21) states, "And of
His signs is that He created for you from yourselves mates that you may
find tranquility in them; and He placed between you affection and mercy.
Indeed in that are signs for people who reflect." IIZ interprets this verse
to mean that a marital union should be based on love and mercy and the
coming together of two individual bodies and souls. Being married, IIZ
contends, should not be restricted to meeting your sexual needs. As such,
individuals are encouraged to create a peaceful and compassionate
environment where they can realize their full potential. Although these
faith-based activists acknowledge the importance of sexual relations and
procreation in marriage, they also emphasize that a marital union should
be centered on mutual respect, love, and a sense of security.

The third Qur'anic tenet regarding family relations is the principle of
*ḥusn* (goodness). Repeatedly discussed in the Qur'an, the concept of
*ḥusn* offers a template for couples and provides them with guidelines on
how they should treat one another. The Qur'anic emphasis on this principle is quite explicit in that in the last section of the chapter "Al-Baqarah," *ḥusn* is mentioned on ten different occasions. IIZ references this
chapter in the Qur'an (2:228) in its effort to highlight the scope of rights
and responsibilities assigned to couples. IIZ has readily embraced the
concept of *ḥusn* and has argued in favor of incorporating this ethical
principle in various dimensions of family law.

From an Islamic perspective, after a marriage contract is signed, rights
and responsibilities are assigned to the couple. The couple's rights are
divided into the two categories of financial and nonfinancial. With regard
to financial rights, the Qur'an states (2:233), "Upon the father is the
mothers' provision and their clothing according to what is acceptable."
The nonfinancial right is that couples treat each other well, adhering to
*al-maʿrūf* (good behavior). The Qur'anic recommendation to treat
women well is explicitly stated in the following verse (4:19): "O you who
believe! Ye are forbidden to inherit women against their will. Nor should

you treat them with harshness, that you may take away part of the *mahr* you have given them, except where they have been guilty of open lewdness; on the contrary live with them on the basis of kindness and equity. If you take a dislike to them it may be that you dislike a thing, and Allah brings about through it a great deal of good." For IIZ, maintaining a strong family bond is dependent on the respectable and peaceful demeanor of the couple toward one another. IIZ's understanding of the Qur'anic principle of *al-ma'rūf* is reflected in its emphasis on good behavior toward the spouse as an indicator of the depth of one's faith. To support its stance, IIZ also references Article 1103 of the civil law, which stresses the importance of the constructive behavior of couples toward one another.

The fourth Qur'anic principle pertaining to family relations is the principle of peace and reconciliation. The Qur'an states (4:128), "If a wife fears cruelty or desertion on her husband's part, there is no blame on them if they arrange an amicable settlement between themselves; and such settlement is best; even though men's souls are swayed by greed. But if you do good and practice self-restraint, Allah is well aware of all that you do." This verse refers to circumstances under which the relationship between a husband and wife becomes strained. If the tension prevails, it can lead to irreconcilable differences. In such situations, the Qur'an advises couples to either reconcile or part ways amicably. In essence, couples are invited to practice self-restraint and forgo their individualistic desires, which can have a detrimental impact on the family. The possibility of reconciliation is further emphasized in the Qur'an (4:19), where couples are encouraged to resolve their differences and refrain from disagreements for the sake of the family. According to IIZ, such verses demonstrate that men are more likely to abuse their authority and power, which is why the Qur'an warns them against such behavior. Essentially, the principle of *al-ma'rūf* underlines peaceful reconciliation and the precedence of the family's interests over that of the individual.[18]

For IIZ, the fifth principle highlighted in the Qur'an with regard to family relations is related to the avoidance of harmful behavior (*la ḍarar*). The Qur'an highlights (2:231), "And so, when you divorce women and they reach the end of their '*idda* (waiting term), then either take them back in a fair manner or let them go in a fair manner. And do not take them back to hurt them or by way of transgression; whosoever will do that, will indeed wrong himself." This verse advises men to act justly and in good faith toward their spouses in cases of separation. On the basis of this verse, men are warned against forbidding their wives from divorce by being verbally abusive toward them or using force or exerting undue pressure. In a similar vein, the Qur'an (65:6) states, "Lodge them [in a section] of where you dwell out of your means and do not harm them in order to oppress them. And if they should be pregnant, then spend on them until they give birth. And if they are nursing, then give them their payment and confer among yourselves in the acceptable way." Referencing this verse, IIZ highlights the importance of laws that prevent men from restricting their spouses or abusing them. Furthermore, IIZ cites other Qur'anic verses (58:2) to assert that any abusive or dishonorable behavior (*ghayr ma'rūf*) should be punishable by law. The family structure prescribed by the Qur'an supports the wife's independent financial rights and stresses the importance of engendering a space where women's spiritual, social, and sexual rights are acknowledged and honored. Such a holistic view of family illustrates the nuances of rights and duties within the family unit.

The final principle, which is central to women's jurisprudence and informs all the other principles, is justice. IIZ reasons that justice forbids believers to restrict the rights and sovereignties of others. The Qur'anic principle of justice condemns any discrimination against women through various forms of domination and gender hierarchies. IIZ references different verses in the Qur'an[19] to illustrate that God does not oppress or burden His creations. The oppression faced by women is the consequence of discrimination and male supremacy, which is rooted in the misinterpretation of sacred scripture.[20] Advocating for women's rights in many Islamic communities has not meant pursuing equality as such but rather pushing back against domination. These faith-based activists argue that an effective strategy to prevent domination is to emphasize the Qur'anic notion of *ḥudūd Allah* (God's boundaries). This concept is referenced at least six times in the chapter al-Baqarah (2:229 and 2:230), cautioning against crossing God's accepted limits.[21] Members of IIZ view these verses as indicative of the importance of acting in a just manner toward one another.

IIZ asserts that Qur'anic teachings affirm gender justice, and the Qur'anic creation story (49:13) sets the ground for this: "Oh humankind. We have created you from a single pair of a male and a female and made you into tribes and nations that you may know each other. The most honored of you in the view of God is the most righteous of you." In light of the fact that men and women originate from a "single soul," they should enjoy equal authority to exercise their agency. The aforementioned verse contains no suggestion of a hierarchy between men and women; what differentiates human beings is their piety and virtue, not their biology.[22]

IIZ also relies on the Qur'anic paradigm of morality, which holds men and women to the same standards and urges them to be simultaneously morally responsible and spiritually aware. This paradigm is highlighted in chapter 33, verse 35 of the Qur'an, which states, "Muslim men and women, believing men and women, devout men and women, true men and women, men and women who are patient and consistent, men and women who humble themselves, men and women who give to charity, men and women who fast, men and women who guard their chastity, and men and women who engage much in God's praise; for them God has prepared forgiveness and great reward." This Qur'anic ethos advances substantive equality between men and women, recognizing their unique capabilities and promoting jurisprudential rulings that protect the rights of both men and women.

In addressing the contested issue of women's rights in Islam, members of IIZ argue that the principles of humanity and justice must be given prominence in Islamic rulings over specific provisions found in Islamic law. IIZ reasons that the rulings of previous male jurists have been influenced by particular historical contexts. Therefore, *fiqh* rulings that appear to advance inequality between men and women are viewed as being either male-centric or appropriate for a particular sociohistorical context. Hence, it is mandatory to reinterpret principles of *fiqh* in new social contexts where modern realities and women's experiences are considered. Informed by this understanding, IIZ advocates for a more inclusive and holistic family paradigm by relying on women's jurisprudence. IIZ's family paradigm model presents a model of gender relation that transcends the equality paradigm and includes Islamic ethics in relation to marital issues and gender justice. Within it, the family unit is given priority over the individual, and the rights and duties of the husband, wife, and children are interconnected and reciprocal.

By incorporating these Qur'anic principles into the family paradigm model, IIZ offers an alternative framework that recognizes the Islamic principles leading to justice and utilizes them to call for a comprehensive reform of family law. Such reform is deemed essential, as the current state of family law continues to adversely affect women's lives. For these faith-based activists, envisioning reformed laws that reflect central Islamic principles such as justice is not difficult considering that reform has been an integral part of the Muslim legal and ethical tradition. Given that justice is a fundamental principle of Shi'i tradition, it should also regulate the rights of husbands and wives within a family unit.

## IIZ AND THE DYNAMICS OF THE FAMILY
## PROTECTION BILL

The journey of family law in Iran spans many periods of resistance from women's rights activists. This resistance reflects the continual struggle for gender justice and the decisive role female activists have assumed in driving transformation within the realm of family law. The Family Protection Law of 1967, later modified in 1975, marked a critical milestone in the modernization of legal provisions concerning women. Yet influential religious leaders such as Ayatollah Khomeini criticized it for shifting matters of personal status, such as marriage and divorce, from the realm of Islamic legal authority to the civil legal system. Ayatollah Khomeini, denounced the FPL as contradictory to shariʿa and Muslim family customs.[23] After the 1979 Revolution, when Khomeini returned from exile, he put the FPL on hold and replaced its family courts with new special civil courts to ensure that legal rulings pertaining to family would be compatible with Islamic law. The move was perceived as a direct attempt to retract the advancements achieved in family law throughout Pahlavi rule. This trend of replacing family courts continued intermittently until 1994, when the Law of Formation of General Courts was implemented in a critical step toward restructuring the courts in Iran.[24] The enactment of this law led to the dissolution of special civil courts, and general courts became the new legal bodies that oversaw family disputes alongside other legal matters. The subsequent judicialization of family law after the Revolution signified a gradual Islamization of the legal system.

As legal anthropologist Arzoo Osanloo points out, despite the initial dissolution of the legislative body, Civil Code, and courts following the Revolution, the Islamic Republic reinstated them following Khomeini's criticism and subsequent suspension of the Family Protection Law. This led to the resurgence of a legal system that prioritized individual rights. This dual legal framework enforced the shariʿa through codification, unsettling the prior equilibrium between shariʿa and state law. The fusion of these legal systems emerged as a compromise among diverse groups, leading to a unique postrevolutionary state structure.[25] This structure was neither purely a realization of Khomeini's vision of an Islamic government nor a replica of the European republican model but rather a unique blend. As the Islamic principles adapted to the republican state format, they revitalized liberal subjects, enabling the legal system to adjudicate on the basis of rights-focused claims. Therefore, in the new Islamic republican governance, emerging social reform efforts often wrestled with diverse philosophies, recognizing women either as legally equal entities with rights or as mothers and wives safeguarded by their societal status.[26]

After the Iran-Iraq War (1980–88) and Khomeini's death, discussions on statehood, law, and rights began to emerge in new public forums. The Khatami presidency (1997–2005) encouraged these discussions. Women actively engaged in them across various platforms, challenging official stances on their roles and status.[27] Mohammad Khatami's election, fueled by women's unprecedented participation, led to a shift in Iran from focusing on women's status to focusing on their individual rights. Khatami's overarching goals of reinforcing the state's legal structures allowed women to be recognized not just as wives and mothers but as individual citizens with rights. However, Mahmoud Ahmadinejad's victories in the 2005 and contested 2009 presidential elections signaled a change in discourse, reasserting women's roles as wives and mothers. Despite perceptions that Ahmadinejad's elections reversed Khatami-era reforms, the rule of law, especially regarding the proposed amendments to the Family Protection Law, has continued to make progress since being revisited by the Legal and Judicial Commission.[28]

The Family Protection Bill, first introduced under the Principlist government of Ahmadinejad in 2007 by the country's judiciary, initially appeared to propose regressive measures toward family law. However, closer scrutiny reveals that the judiciary had its own agenda for proposing the Family Protection Bill. Primarily, the bill was a step toward continuing the judicialization of issues related to family.[29] Additionally, the judiciary had devoted considerable time and energy to pass the bill with the aim of reforming the dysfunctional family law system. The 2007 Family Protection Bill, as detailed in its introductory section, is set forth as a "component of a comprehensive family law that fits within the broader civil law reform initiative."[30] This suggests that the judiciary's primary focus was on the procedural aspects of family law, with the goal of introducing innovative solutions for prevailing issues. Through the introduction of this bill, the judiciary expressed its commitment to safeguarding and fortifying the family structure.

The 2007 bill reflected the endeavors of the Guardianship Council members, who were tasked with scrutinizing legislation, to address inconsistencies found in certain clauses of the earlier Family Protection Law. The members of the Guardianship Council specifically aimed to rectify shortcomings in the earlier family law that had led to uncertainty among judges, coupled with the law's vagueness and its disconnection from contemporary issues. The goal of the new bill was to solve the existing problems in family law, settle the ambiguities and vacuum in the family law, minimize the length of court proceedings in family disputes, and streamline family law and affairs.[31] To achieve these targets, the following recommendations were made in the new bill by Parliament's Legal and Judicial Commission:

1. Establish exclusive family courts.

2. Promote the participation of female judges and ensure their active engagement in all stages of proceedings, from trials to the confirmation of judgments.

3. Create family counseling centers.

4. Streamline the courts' decisions regarding issues such as custody rights, visitation rights, and child support.

5. Enhance communication efficiency by informing the family court and delivering documents via mail, courier, and email.

6. Allow women the choice to seek legal recourse from their place of residence without the need to appear in person in a courtroom.

7. Provide mothers the option to request child support.

8. Permit couples to apply for a mutual consent divorce without a mandatory court appearance, provided they have obtained a certificate from the family counseling center.

The amendments to the Family Protection Bill introduced by the Legal and Judicial Committee in 2007 clearly showed an intention to streamline and improve the procedural aspects of family law rather than a desire to overhaul the substantive content of the law related to remarriage, polygyny, and other similar issues. Drawing heavily from the 1967 Family Protection Law and the Civil Code, the initial changes seemed to emphasize the facilitation of legal processes and the incorporation of modern practices, such as remote communication for legal proceedings. However, subsequent intervention by the conservative government proved contentious, causing significant friction between lawmakers and entities like IIZ. The challenges highlighted the complexities of navigating traditional norms and progressive aspirations in the realm of family law.

In its original form, the Family Protection Bill of 2007, prepared by the Legal and Judicial Commission, marked the third attempt to codify an iteration of Iranian family law that would supplant previous codifications. The controversy over certain articles came at a moment of heightened tension after the government's interference and subsequent amendments to the proposed bill. Over eight years, heated debates ensued regarding the bill's provisions. In addition, the government's interference jeopardized the inventive solutions proposed by the judiciary to reform the family law.

The bill was originally formulated by the judiciary to set procedural guidelines for family courts. However, under Ahmadinejad's conservative administration, various articles were modified, leading to major disputes over the following provisions:

- Article 22 eliminated the obligation to record *mut 'a* (temporary marriages), effectively stripping legal safeguards for women in such unions and children conceived during these temporary marriages.
- Article 23 authorized polygynous unions when a man demonstrated his financial ability to maintain multiple families. No explicit parameters were set to ensure a man's financial stability before entering into a polygynous relationship. Furthermore, the permission of the first wife to enter into a polygynous marriage was no longer required.
- Article 25 allowed the Ministry of Finance to impose taxes on women's *mahr* (marriage gift) if it surpassed 110 gold coins. This article significantly affects women who leverage *mahr* during divorce negotiations, limiting their negotiation power for certain rights.

It was the insertion of these controversial provisions that raised serious concern among women's rights activists. Women from different ideological and political backgrounds decided to unite to oppose the bill and in the process received support from reformist political and religious authorities.[32] IIZ was a leading voice that spoke out against these measures. Article 23 proved to be the most contentious in the bill as it legalized polygyny irrespective of the first wife's consent. This was in contrast to the previous family law, in which the husband's remarriage was subject to the written consent of the first wife.

When asked about Parliament's suggested modification, the former vice president for women and family affairs and legal analyst of the IIZ Coalition, Shahindokht Molaverdi, told me, "I am not against the Family

Protection Bill. However, I disagree with the later amendments added by Parliament. I personally believe the initial bill prepared by the judiciary was an attempt to regulate the legal procedure for families, as it was a solid effort to frame family disputes in a systematic manner."[33] It was the intervention by the government that sparked concern among IIZ activists.

The subsequent section explores the legal, social, and religious rationales presented by these activists to express their opposition toward the revised bill, especially concerning Article 23. The struggle exemplifies the persistent activism of the women in the IIZ Coalition, who relentlessly opposed policies that threatened to set back women's rights in Iran by several decades.

## IIZ OPPOSES POLYGYNOUS MARRIAGES

Undeterred by any attempt to marginalize women's voices, IIZ was particularly vocal in their criticism of the controversial articles proposed by the Principlist government in power. For instance, Article 23 blatantly ignored the 1982 Marriage Contract Amendments by replacing the consent of the first wife with the consent of the court, thus making it increasingly convenient for men to enter into polygynous marriages. Article 23 also broke with the Family Protection Law of 1967 by dismissing other restrictions previously imposed on polygynous marriages. Traditionally, entering into a polygynous marriage had been contingent upon consent of the first wife and the man's financial capabilities. But according to the new bill, neither the consent of the first wife nor proof of financial solvency would be required for a man to enter into a polygynous marriage. As IIZ's secretary stressed, "Not only is the wife's consent not required for remarriage, but the new bill does not impose any penalty for those who violate the law."[34]

As part of its public awareness campaign, IIZ held several press conferences to address the controversial article.[35] They criticized the Family Protection Bill for presenting a problematic view of women and failing to address and resolve the existing legal flaws, despite Parliament's initial assurances to the contrary. IIZ viewed the amendments to the bill as an exploitative move by the parliamentarians, who appeared to prioritize men's desires over Qur'anic principles that emphasize the importance of family unity and the well-being of all family members.[36]

Drawing on the family paradigm model, IIZ's argument was rooted in a deep concern for the integrity of the family unit. Prior to the introduction of the new bill by the parliament in 2007, a man could pursue a polygynous union if he satisfied at least one of the following conditions: (1) the first wife's consent; (2) the first wife's inability to engage in intimate relations; (3) *nushūz*, or the first wife's defiance and noncooperation toward her husband; (4) the wife's affliction with issues such as mental disorders, communicable illnesses, or any other chronic disease that hinders marital harmony; (5) the wife being found guilty of a crime; (6) the wife's engagement in substance abuse; (7) the wife's desertion of family duties and responsibilities; (8) the wife's inability to bear children; or (9) extended absence of the wife from the marital residence. Women's rights activists were critical of these conditions, arguing that although they were meant to restrict men's access to polygynous marriages, they remained vague and open to a wide range of interpretations by judges. Specifically, some of the prerequisites for entering into polygynous relationships were ambiguous and could not be verified without field investigation and detailed review. For instance, a wife's *nushūz* would be an issue that could not be verified easily.

Exacerbating the matter, Article 23, introduced by the Family Protection Bill in 2007, suggested amendments to the polygyny laws that required men to obtain a wife's consent before marrying additional spouses. This article would permit a husband to marry a second wife after a judge had verified his financial ability to support multiple wives and to maintain equal treatment among them. However, the article lacked explicit parameters regarding the financial adequacy needed for supporting multiple wives and did not define the meaning of equal treatment among them.[37]

According to the secretary of the IIZ Coalition, the Family Protection Bill "completely ignored the first wife's rights and lacked assurance that a man would carry out his responsibilities as a husband and a father after getting a second wife." The secretary also highlighted the absence of "legal enforcement that guarantees the first wife's financial rights, including mahr and *ujrat al-mithl* [wages in kind]."[38] IIZ condemned such oversights as violations against the ethos of *ḥusn* (goodness) and the fundamental principle of dignity and respect that are integral to the family paradigm model. They recommend that Parliament prioritize revisions to the bill to compel a husband to honor his financial, emotional, and child-rearing responsibilities. Drawing on sociological findings, IIZ suggests that children from polygynous unions are more susceptible to depression and delinquency. Consequently, IIZ posits that men who shirk their responsibilities to their wives and children ultimately impose an undue burden on the broader society.

Additionally, IIZ issued a public statement in which they listed the legal, religious, and social reasons behind their demand for major revisions to Article 23. The press published IIZ's bold statement, which gradually garnered the support of reformist 'ulama' and other women's rights activists. In that statement, which is grounded in the principles of the family paradigm model, IIZ presents ten reasons for disagreeing with Article 23.

The first reason is related to the article's unjust nature. While justice is a fundamental principle in Shi'i Islam, IIZ maintains that the proposed article fails to address it. The conditions for remarriage articulated in Article 23 do not guarantee justice, which should include not only treating one's wives equally but also being fully committed to one's family. Hence, a man's commitment to justice at home should translate into respect toward his first wife and children. The Qur'an alludes to this point in verse 4:3: "If you fear that you will not act based on justice, then take only one [wife]." Thus justice is the most important issue that legislators must take into account. Since justice is a Qur'anic criterion for remarriage, a man's ability to carry out justice must be proven to a judge who is a *mujtahid*.

The second justification for opposing Article 23 is its deliberate undermining of the first wife's consent as a mandatory condition for remarriage. If justice is to prevail, the first wife's consent should be a necessary prerequisite for a man to enter into polygynous marriages, and her consent must trump other prerequisites. The first wife's approval can be an indication of whether the man acts in a just manner with his family. In addition, the court must ensure that a woman's satisfaction and consent are legitimate and that she has not been coerced into giving consent. IIZ argues that one of the fundamental issues in family relations is consultation. Given that the Qur'an suggests consulting with one's family on all matters, how is it that the family law allows a husband to remarry without the first wife's consent? How is loosening restrictions on men's ability to remarry compatible with Qur'anic teachings? If the first wife's consent is given less importance than other conditions in the bill, a husband might use those other conditions to justify entering a polygynous marriage without seeking his spouse's approval.[39] IIZ is adamant that the article in question subverts the Qur'anic ethos by undermining the first wife's dignity and her right to consent.

The third argument IIZ levels against Article 23 centers on the compensation the first wife receives for her contributions to the household. Customarily, the wife makes financial and nonfinancial contributions toward her family throughout the marriage, and thus should be compensated for all of the contributions she has made. IIZ emphasizes that without the contributions of the first wife, the husband would not be able to climb the economic and social ladder and build a successful life. However, Article 23 does not take this important contribution into account. Traditionally, women bring *jihāz* (trousseau) and spend their own money for their family without demanding *mahr* from their husbands. Additionally, most of the responsibilities regarding nursing and raising the children fall on women's shoulders. The newly proposed bill needs to ensure that in addition to alimony and *mahr,* women's other financial rights and needs are met before the husband is allowed to remarry.

Another issue with Article 23 is that frequently the financial well-being of the first wife and their children isn't secured before a man decides to remarry. Legislators must ensure that the financial stability of the first wife and their children is established before granting approval for the husband's subsequent marriage. There must be mechanisms to ensure the husband's assets are sufficiently documented and allocated for the first family's benefit, thus safeguarding their financial security and justice. The court should enforce these provisions, especially in cases where the first wife consents to the husband's remarriage, to ensure that her financial needs and those of the children are adequately safeguarded.

IIZ further argues that the Family Protection Bill violates the principle of *la ḍarar* (avoidance of harmful behavior) as highlighted in the family paradigm model, by overlooking the first wife and the children's spiritual and emotional needs and rights after the father's remarriage. A study conducted by IIZ found polygynous family structures to be harmful to children. Children from a man's first marriage often suffer from these arrangements, as they must come to terms with their fathers becoming part-time caregivers. These children also lack confidence in their own ability to have a stable family life in the future. Moreover, IIZ questions the role an absentee father can play in meeting the children's emotional and educational needs. The bill does not, and essentially cannot, guarantee that the children's material and nonmaterial needs will be met after their father remarries.

The next point of opposition to the article arises from the fact that the first wife's right to divorce is not addressed in the bill. If the first wife decides she no longer wants to continue to be part of a polygynous marriage, the Family Protection Bill does not grant her the right to file for divorce. IIZ maintains that the law must support women who allow their husbands to remarry and must guarantee the first wife's financial rights in case of a divorce. If men are given the right to remarry, women must also be afforded the right to file for divorce in cases where they no longer wish to be part of such marital arrangements.

The seventh criticism of Article 23 is related to the absence of repercussions for men who remarry without meeting the necessary preconditions. Previously, men who remarried without obtaining permission from the court had faced penalties. However, the revised bill removed the enforcement of any penalty, paving the way to polygynous marriages. IIZ underscores the importance of reintroducing these legal consequences, emphasizing that a truly just Family Protection Bill should hold individuals accountable for bypassing set regulations.

IIZ further criticizes Article 23 because of its failure to provide family counseling before approving a remarriage. Some of the conditions introduced in the bill that allow men to remarry are a direct consequence of the husband's transgressions. For example, the wife's *nushūz* (disobedience) or addiction may be caused by the husband's mistreatment and neglect of his family. IIZ strongly encourages the courts to prioritize the family's welfare, rather than enabling men to sidestep their duties and challenges by entering into another marriage. Instead of permitting a husband unbridled freedom to remarry amid marital conflicts, the courts should see to it that the couple's issues can be addressed and resolved through family counseling centers.

Moreover, IIZ argues, in circumstances where the wife is imprisoned, the husband should bail her out of prison instead of bailing out of his responsibilities toward the family. One of the conditions that allows men to enter into a polygynous marriage is related to circumstances where the first wife has been sentenced to at least one year in prison and the husband is financially incapable of bailing her out. IIZ challenges the reasoning that permits a man who can't even afford his wife's bail to be deemed financially capable of sustaining two households.[40] According to official statistics, a significant number of female prisoners, particularly those incarcerated because of financial disputes, are serving prison sentences because of financial problems caused by their husbands. IIZ expresses major reservations about whether it is ethically acceptable to permit the husband to remarry in such cases. Influenced by the principle of *ḥusn* (good intentions), they advise that spouses offer each other mutual support. It is specifically advised that should the current wife be incarcerated because of financial issues, the husband should not contemplate entering into a second marriage.

The tenth and final critique of Article 23 concerns its inconsistency with the Iranian Civil Code, which mandates the protection of family sanctity above all. Further, Article 40 of the code prohibits any person from exercising their rights to the detriment of others' rights or interests. The Civil Code emphasizes couples' duty to behave in an appropriate manner (Article 1103) and collaborate to reinforce familial bonds and promote their children's development (Article 1104). In harmony with these provisions, Qur'anic teachings and jurisprudential rulings underscore the importance of virtuous behavior and avoidance of harm, encapsulating the principle of *la ḍarar* (no harm).[41] IIZ maintains that upholding *la ḍarar* is imperative for all Muslims, ensuring that their actions do not inflict harm upon their family.

IIZ's compelling arguments faced resistance from the bill's proponents, who argued that the critique contradicted Islamic precepts. Responding to this, IIZ countered by accusing the bill's supporters of deviating from true Islamic values, positioning their stance as a safeguard of Islamic tenets. Highlighting the disfavor toward polygynous marriages in Iranian society and *'urf*, IIZ asserted that measures to curtail polygyny were necessary. They fortified their stance by referencing the Qur'anic verse that advises that a man should marry only one wife if he fears he cannot treat multiple wives equitably. IIZ's condemnation of the bill called into question the rationale of polygyny advocates who claim to uphold Islamic standards.

## SOCIOLEGAL CRITIQUE OF POLYGYNY

The issue of polygyny, as authorized by Article 23 of the Family Protection Bill, falls within the legal court's jurisdiction. In these cases, the judge is tasked with verifying that the husband has adequate financial resources to support two families and is committed to equal treatment of both wives. IIZ's argument, rooted in a sociolegal critique, posits that this contentious article jeopardizes family security and societal well-being, as it contravenes the *'urf* and *maṣlaḥa* (public interest) and also violates principles enshrined in the family paradigm model.

Supporters of Article 23 assert its alignment with shari'a, citing the Qur'anic allowance for polygyny (4:3) as justification. They argue that polygyny can help lower divorce rates and provide marital prospects for women who may face difficulties in finding partners for age, health, or social reasons. By offering such women the option to become a co-wife, proponents believe polygyny upholds financial and social security, thus contributing to the stability of the family unit.[42]

IIZ challenged this view, arguing that it overlooked the historic and societal circumstances that had led to the acceptance of polygyny in Islam. IIZ emphasized that in contrast to seventh-century Arabian customs, today it is incumbent upon the nation-state to provide support to disadvantaged women and families. Given the societal context of modern-day Iran, polygyny no longer serves its initial purpose and is instead often exploited by married men for personal desires, rather than to offer security to women. IIZ contended that if Article 23 was passed, it would undermine the idea that advancing justice in society is a central premise of Islamic law. To protect societal interest and promote justice, IIZ argued, it is imperative to adhere to Islamic principles that help safeguard and strengthen the institution of the family. However, they maintained that legalizing and encouraging polygynous marriages ultimately undermines the family unit.

Members of the IIZ asserted that contemporary Iranian women no longer identify with traditional gender roles reinforced in the legal system. Women are active in the workforce and society, and the traditional perception of women is no longer aligned with the realities of a modern society. Acknowledging the fallibility of Islamic family law, IIZ insisted on the necessity to challenge unjust rules established under the guise of religion. Thus all laws should be subject to public debate and must be adapted to societal and cultural norms. Religious authorities and institutions that insist on maintaining the traditional jurisprudential and legal system are failing both Islam and its followers. Jurists' obliviousness to the unfolding transformation in women's situations has driven women toward reaction and resistance. IIZ stated that religious authorities and institutions can no longer blame Western hegemonic powers as being behind the rise of social vices and immorality in Iran. Most of the current anomalies are a direct result of reaction to the gendered view of women as subordinate to men. The implementation of discriminatory laws, such as polygyny, has only led to greater feelings of agitation and alienation among women. Consequently, women are distancing themselves from religion and are becoming increasingly opposed to it. In IIZ's view, legislators can no longer deny such problems by blaming the West, hiding behind religion, or accusing the opposition of being anti-Islamic.

This stance is exemplified by their critique of the conditions for remarriage as outlined in Article 23.

Within Article 23, two conditions for a man to remarry are his ability to provide for two families and his commitment to carrying out justice among his wives. However, IIZ's legal research highlighted that judicial discretion in these matters is highly subjective, leading to inconsistencies in the application of the law. Through interviews with judges, IIZ's research committee uncovered a lack of consensus on the interpretation of "justice," and in some cases, judges expressed unfamiliarity with such an analysis. The findings of IIZ suggest that these ambiguities in legal interpretation not only undermine the very justice they are supposed to uphold but also potentially cause greater societal harm.

The IIZ Coalition emphasized that proponents of Article 23 needed to identify the age demographic of men who claim to have the financial capacity for polygynous marriage. Given that a primary objective of the current legislation is to encourage the younger generation to marry, it is notable that a rising percentage of Iranian youth are grappling with unemployment and find it hard to sustain even a single household. Therefore, most of the individuals who remarry and benefit from this article are middle-aged men who also have children from their first marriage: they have reached financial stability and can "afford to remarry." IIZ contended that this particular category of men tend to lust after younger women and offer financial support in return for youthful companionship. Coalition members posited that the first wife often finds herself compelled to consent and tolerate the husband's polygynous relationship because she lacks financial resources and the social support to pursue divorce. To prove its point, IIZ extensively examined the lived experience and real-life struggles of first wives in an attempt to highlight the injustices perpetuated by the Family Protection Bill.

An additional argument put forth by IIZ, anchored in sociolegal research, cited statistics demonstrating an increase in infidelity among women whose husbands were involved in polygynous marriages. IIZ argued that this trend, and the increase in crimes of "killing polygynous husbands," stemmed from a system that deprived women of legal and social solutions against disloyal partners. If Islam views the family as a sacred unit, then justice demands that this sanctity be preserved equally for everyone involved, including women and children. IIZ activists claimed that encouraging men to enter into polygynous marriages led to greater emotional distress for women and children as well as to harmful social disorders. Furthermore, statistics revealed that over the course of three decades, polygyny emerged as a central reason for the breakdown of the family unit in Iran.

## REVISING THE FAMILY PROTECTION BILL

The proposed changes to the Family Protection Law, which negatively affected women, were met with determined resistance from women's rights activists. Organizations such as IIZ helped raise public awareness, and subsequently the contentious Article 23 was placed on hold, with a final decision deferred until Parliament's Legal and Judicial Committee could conduct further analysis. This was seen as a significant win for women's rights organizations like IIZ, who had tirelessly worked to raise public awareness on this issue. After a brief period of calm, the bill found its way back to the Parliament floor in 2009. The proposed amendments to it included changes in the legal procedures related to Article 22 (on temporary marriage), Article 23 (on polygyny), and Article 25 (on dowry).

Despite thorough criticisms and demonstrations, fundamental legal issues raised by IIZ, like the need for the first wife's approval before remarriage and the husband's obligation to act justly, were overlooked once more. While Article 23's failure to hold men accountable for breaking the law was a primary catalyst for the protests, Parliament's Legal and Judicial Committee decided to ignore the issues highlighted by proponents of women's rights. The law failed to hold men liable if they did not seek the permission of the court before remarrying or if they failed to be just toward their spouses. Members of IIZ had insisted that the bill grant the first wife the right to divorce, which the Legal and Judicial Committee also did not honor. During discussions, the IIZ secretary emphasized that in numerous polygynous marriages the primary wife remains with her husband because of economic dependence, underscoring the necessity of securing financial support for the first wife compelled to accept such a circumstance.[43]

IIZ also held the women involved in the Center for Women and Family Affairs responsible for not speaking up against these discriminatory bills. Because of the fragility of women's religious and political authority, a significant majority of female politicians in office are reluctant to challenge the status quo. Most women who have reached high-ranking positions prioritize maintaining their positions over taking bold stances and supporting women's issues. Consequently these women are willing to comply with some of the discriminatory proposals put forth by male parliamentarians. IIZ demanded that women in such positions prohibit Parliament from passing bills that disrespect women and break up families. In an interview the secretary of IIZ asked, "Why is the Center for Women and Family Affairs silent about a bill that not only weakens the family but also overlooks men's commitment and responsibilities as husbands and fathers? Are they blind to the fact that the so-called Family Protection Bill disrupts the security and peace of the family? When exactly is this Center planning on taking action? As women, we have a right to know what this Center has done regarding these controversial bills in the past few years."[44]

The limited advocacy from the Center for Women and Family Affairs underscored a critical point: mere female representation is not sufficient to ensure that women's rights are protected and promoted. For this reason IIZ has pushed for greater representation in leadership and decision-making positions among women who are vocal about advancing women's rights and has long been training women to assume such positions. These faith-based activists insist on the presence of female *mujtahidas*[45] on Parliament's Legal and Judicial Committee. IIZ asserts that having a female *mujtahida* on the committee could emphasize the importance of fortifying the family unit. Her presence might underscore the Qur'an's inclination toward monogamy and its emphasis on preserving the dignity of women. Furthermore, *mujtahidas* could underscore the principle of *maṣlaḥa,* the valuing of societal interests over individual ones, and bring attention to the Qur'anic tenet of love and compassion within the family. IIZ believes that Parliament's Legal and Judicial Committee is ignoring both the family paradigm model and Islamic principles such as justice and compassion, which ought to form the bedrock of an Islamic family.

IIZ points out that Articles 22, 23, and 24 of the Family Protection Bill have a direct impact on the future of women and families. The secretary of IIZ stresses that not only religious and legal experts but also sociologists and psychologists should serve on Parliament's Legal and Judicial Committee. A significant concern often overlooked is that decisions affecting women are made without their presence or input in the decision-making process. Moreover, these decisions are often made devoid of insights from comprehensive social, legal, and scientific research, which are essential to understanding the full implications of discriminatory laws on women and society at large.

The secretary of IIZ stated, "The Family Protection Bill should be enacted only after the controversial Articles (22, 23, and 25) are either amended or removed. These contentious articles have to be reconsidered in a committee that specializes in family affairs. The findings of the committee should then be presented to Parliament as a separate bill."[46] Members of IIZ assert that expert opinions should be grounded in comprehensive facts and should incorporate the perspectives of women. This approach advocated for amendment in the Family Protection Bill that would genuinely safeguard and fortify the family unit.

In response to IIZ's request to amend the bill, the head of Parliament's Legal and Judicial Committee, Farhad Tajari, stated, "The bill was not prepared overnight; therefore we cannot simply put it aside." IIZ responded, "We, too, believe that initially a lot of thought went into the Family Protection Bill; however, these three articles (22, 23, and 25) that were added to the bill by the government are not compatible with the stated purpose of the Family Protection Bill and were in fact added to the bill overnight; therefore it is imperative to remove these controversial articles." IIZ further declared that "originally, the Family Protection Bill outlined general legal protocols. However, the inclusion of the three new articles threatens the very foundation of the family. Therefore, it is vital that the bill be passed without these three contentious articles. In the revised bill, the inherent dignity of every family member should be respected and acknowledged. Additionally, the bill ought to guarantee the financial security of the first wife, regardless of whether she chooses to remain in or exit the marriage."[47] After facing rigorous opposition and pressure from IIZ and other women's rights groups, the three controversial articles were sent back to the Legal and Judicial Commission for further consideration.

The secretary of IIZ further stated, "IIZ has consulted with experts about the effect of these articles on families, and the findings have been presented to Parliament's Legal and Judicial Committee."[48] After holding two separate sessions to discuss the aforementioned objections, the Judicial and Legal Committee decided to make further amendments to Article 23. Ultimately a clause was added to the article that granted the first wife the right of divorce in case of the husband's remarriage. This amendment represented a significant step toward addressing some of the concerns raised by IIZ, yet the organization continued to push for more comprehensive reform.

In 2010, a group of former female MPs, including the late Maryam Behroozi and notable IIZ affiliates, visited Parliament to express their concerns about the bill's shortcomings. Behroozi made several recommendations for the improvement of Article 23. In a letter to Parliament's

Judicial and Legal Commission, Behroozi drew attention to IIZ's demands and recommendations. Grounded in the family paradigm model, the letter reads as follows:

> I hereby request that members of the Legal and Judicial Commission consider adding the following clauses to Articles 23:
>
> Clause 1) A man seeking a polygynous marriage must present specific reasons and supply the necessary legal documentation to a special authorization court.
>
> Clause 2) The special authorization court should be composed of a *mujtahid*, a magistrate, and a female judge.
>
> Clause 3) Before pursuing a polygynous marriage, the husband must fulfill all financial obligations to his first wife, including *mahr*, her financial share, alimony, and providing her with separate living accommodations.
>
> Clause 4) All cases should be referred to family counseling centers before the court reaches a decision.
>
> Clause 5) Penalties should be imposed on those who engage in polygynous marriages without meeting the established criteria, affecting the man, the second wife, and the marriage officiant.[49]

Finally, after three years of political debate, countless reviews, and protests, Parliament decided to modify Article 23 of the Family Protection Bill so that the first wife's permission was once again included as one of the preconditions of polygynous marriages. In the revised version of the bill, before a man could enter into a polygynous marriage he was required to obtain the consent of his first wife or fulfill one of nine other specified conditions to remarry.[50] Furthermore, the first wife was once again granted the right to file for divorce in case the husband's remarriage caused unbearable *'usr wa ḥaraj* (difficulty and hardship).

While legal experts viewed these changes as a step in the right direction for women, it is clear that the new amendment did not give women new rights, as women already possessed these rights under the 1967 Family Protection Law. Furthermore, according to Article 1130 of the Civil Code, if continuing a marriage causes difficulty for the wife, she can appeal to the judge and request a divorce. When a husband remarries without the wife's consent or does not treat the two spouses equally, the marriage contract gives the first wife the right to file for divorce. IIZ advocated for additional amendments, proposing that the first wife be granted an unequivocal right to divorce in the event of her husband's remarriage.[51] However, these recommendations were not taken into consideration in the amended version of the bill. Considering that the mindset of most members of the Commission is rooted in traditional

Islamic jurisprudence, divorce is cautiously prescribed only in cases where the wife faces unbearable pain and excessive hardship. Nonetheless, changes made to the bill may be interpreted as a temporary retreat by Parliament in the face of increasing pressure from the public.

The controversies surrounding Article 23 of the Family Protection Bill wreaked such havoc that several other changes made by Parliament went unnoticed. Among these were the elimination of the special family court, which was initially proposed to handle such issues as domestic violence, *nushūz* (disobedience), and *tamkīn* (obedience). Additionally, Article 22 eliminated the requirement to register temporary marriages, unless previously agreed upon or in case of pregnancy. Without such regulatory measures in place, women and children born into temporary marriages have no access to legal recourse. The bill proposed government-approved standard sums for *mahr,* and Article 25 imposed tax on *mahr,* further limiting women's financial independence.

Despite all the controversy and changes the Family Protection Bill underwent, Parliament passed the amendments to the Family Protection Act on February 2014. The details of the bill were published in a state-sponsored newspaper after the Guardianship Council's approval. After thorough examination IIZ identified key differences between the amended 2014 Family Protection Bill and its earlier version proposed in 2007. One was that the new Family Protection Bill increased the number of female judges. According to Article 2, judicial decisions should take place in the presence of the presiding judge as well as a consulting female judge. The new bill mandated judges to consult a female family counseling judge before issuing a verdict. It also provided guidance to judges on how to handle modern family law issues, including sex change and artificial insemination, so they could meet societal demands.

The Family Protection Bill also aimed to establish family counseling centers. According to the bill, in cases of consensual divorce, the court was required to refer the matter to a family counseling center, which would provide mediation for the couple. Another modification introduced in the new bill was related to establishing engagement centers that would focus on engaged couples who were in the process of separation. Although the creation of engagement centers was not explicitly mentioned in the bill, the first clause of Article 4 pointed out that a couple's engagement and its dissolution would be among the issues that needed to be addressed in family court.

Establishing a cap for *mahr* was another contentious change in the revised Family Protection Bill. Article 25 of the 2014 bill set the allowable *mahr* limit at 110 gold coins. Even when the *mahr* exceeded this amount, the husband would be obliged to pay only the amount of 110 coins unless evidence demonstrated his capacity to settle the entire sum. The article further stated that the judiciary should establish a new standard rate for *mahr* every three years. Should the husband neglect to provide the *mahr* when asked (within the prescribed limits), he might face imprisonment. Additionally, the bill required compliance with guidelines that dictate the current standard *mahr* rate.

IIZ notably highlighted the relaxation of regulations pertaining to the registration of temporary marriages. Within the Shi'i tradition, a man and woman can enter into a temporary marriage that is contracted for a fixed period.[52] Although Article 21 of the Family Protection Bill emphasized the centrality of permanent marriages, temporary marriage was considered as an accepted practice by religious and civil law. This type of marriage had to be registered under one of the following three conditions: (1) pregnancy of the temporary wife, (2) agreement of both parties to register the marriage, and (3) inclusion of registration as a precondition in the marriage contract. If the couple did not meet these conditions, the registration of temporary marriages would not be necessary.

Another point highlighted by IIZ was that the 2014 bill restricted the presence of children in family courts during divorce proceedings. According to Article 46 of the revised law, the presence of children under the age of fifteen in family trials was prohibited, except in special cases as ordered by the court. The rationale behind this prohibition was to shield children from potentially harmful and distressing courtroom environments. The Family Protection Bill also facilitated resolving family disputes through petitioning family courts. According to Article 8, lawsuits had to be submitted through a formal petition, as the courts would no longer accept verbal appeals in family disputes.

The 2014 bill further stipulated penalties for the neglect of legal obligations in the following areas:

1. According to Articles 40 and 54, if the child's guardian neglects their duties or denies the other parent visitation rights, they will be subjected to financial penalty.

2. According to Article 49, individuals who neglect to register temporary marriages will be subject to either a monetary fine or imprisonment. This penalty also extends to men who do not register the termination of the temporary marriage.

3. According to Article 50, anyone facilitating the marriage of a girl under the age of thirteen or a boy younger than fifteen without obtaining court approval will be subject to imprisonment. Moreover, if such a marriage leads to injury or a lasting medical condition for either party, the individual responsible will not only face jail time but also be required to pay *diya* (financial compensation).[53]

4. According to Article 51, if a foreign Muslim man marries an Iranian woman without the permission of an Islamic court, as mentioned in Article 1060 of the Civil Code, he will be sentenced to time in prison.

5. According to Article 52, any individual who falsely denies a marital relationship or wrongfully claims to be married will be subjected to imprisonment and may also incur a monetary fine.

6. According to Article 53, a man who fails to provide his first wife with alimony or *mahr* upon request will face imprisonment.

Though a number of significant changes were implemented in the amended 2014 Family Protection Bill, IIZ found these modifications to be far from sufficient. The initial impetus for the new version of Family Protection Bill was to address shortcomings in the laws governing family and to make them compatible with the social norms of modern-day Iran. Although IIZ recognized the positive changes enacted in the 2014 version of the bill, these faith-based activists maintained that further improvements were needed if the bill was to reflect the realities of Iranian society. Members of the Coalition stressed the importance of implementing women's jurisprudence and judicial justice as effective methods toward achieving gender justice in society. Considering that judicial justice is a fundamental pillar of an Islamic society, they argued for the integration of ethical injunctions into the judicial structure. Furthermore, these faith-based activists advocated for the family paradigm model, informed by women's jurisprudence, as a practical and valuable blueprint for promoting gender justice within the existing family law framework.

# CHAPTER 4

# Islamic Family Law and Gender Politics

*Legal Provisions of Family Formation*

Expanding on the analysis of the partial amendments to the Family Protection Bill, this chapter transitions toward a more comprehensive examination of Iranian family law, delving into the Civil Codes of Marriage and Family and Shiʿi *fiqh*. As encapsulated in the Iranian Civil Code, family law presides over all aspects relating to marriage, divorce, and custody for Muslims, forming an integral part of a sophisticated system of Islamic jurisprudence. Embedded deeply within the religious, social, and familial fabric of Iranian society, this legal framework stands as the primary focus of this chapter and the subsequent one. This investigation highlights the complexities of family law, while also laying out IIZ's call for ongoing reform. The chapter emphasizes the legal and theological foundations of Shiʿi family law in Iran, including a study of the prerequisites for an Islamic marriage, such as the protocols of proposal and engagement. It ventures into the legal stipulations surrounding the minimum age for marriage and the involvement of legal guardians in sanctioning marriages for minors. In addition, it provides deeper understanding of the traditional Islamic marriage contract and dowry, concurrently underscoring the reform proposals advanced by IIZ.

In recent years, Islamic Family Law (IFL) has emerged as an intensely contested domain grappling with a variety of dynamic legal conundrums. These debates have engaged a range of actors, including the state, ʿulamaʾ, and female activists. IFL, implemented in most predominantly Muslim countries, has resisted European influence, thereby transforming into a symbol of Muslim identity for followers of the religion. In Iran, IFL has evolved into a contested ground upon which competing interpretations by the state, religious authorities, and female activists intersect, sometimes in collaboration but often in contention.

The societal upheaval in the aftermath of the 1979 Revolution led to the repeal or modification of many laws deemed un-Islamic. This instigated significant legal and judicial changes, one of which was the replacement of the Civil Code with an Islamic Civil Code, thereby significantly transforming women's status within the family realm. The preexisting 1967 family law was replaced with a legal system in line with Twelver Shi'ism, irrevocably changing the trajectory of Iranian civil law, particularly family law, and deeply affecting Iranian society. Despite these changes, persistent reform attempts have been initiated by women's rights activists like IIZ. Meanwhile, progress has been slow and fraught with challenges, stemming primarily from tensions between tradition and modernity, state and religion, and the inherent complexities of the Iranian legal system.

The Family Protection Bill, introduced in 2007, underwent significant improvements, due in no small part to the efforts of women's activism. Motivated by these improvements, IIZ embarked on an ambitious campaign to propose modifications to all discriminatory elements within Iranian family law overlooked by the bill. The ensuing analysis centers on the legal foundation of family law in Iran, with particular emphasis on family formation, and evaluates IIZ's advocacy for comprehensive reform in this area.

Shi'i *fiqh*, which includes both traditional and modern juristic perspectives, is an important source informing the Civil Code and women's legal status within the family unit. Legal manuals compiled by eminent scholars Muhaqqiq al-Hilli and Shahid al-Awwal and Shahid al-Thani, focusing on moral duties as well as legal issues, are often referred to in civil and family courts, forming the foundational texts for traditional Shi'i *fiqh*.[1] In the context of contemporary Shi'i *fiqh*, Ayatollah Khomeini's book *Tawdih al-Masa'il* holds sway and is frequently referenced by judges and legislators.[2] Its influence over the Civil Code is such that, in a controversial move, the Guardian Council ruled that propositions contradicting Ayatollah Khomeini's perspective would not be passed into law. The Guardian Council's adoption of this contentious stance has elicited considerable critique among traditional Shi'i jurists. The dominance of Khomeini's writings and the uncritical acceptance of his position on family law can be attributed more to his sociopolitical clout than to his religious authority.[3]

In this chapter, a comprehensive exploration is undertaken to analyze the significant elements of the modern Civil Code, with a particular focus on its implications for family formation. This examination involves a thorough consideration of both traditional and modern legal discourses as presented in the scholarly contributions of Muhaqqiq Al-Hilli, Shahid al-Thani, Ayatollah Khomeini, and other influential jurists. The inquiry aims to contextualize the critical aspects of family law, with a specific focus on aspects related to family formation. This involves exploring preconditions for marriage, the marriage contract, and *mahr* (dower), as well as both permanent and temporary marriage arrangements. Through an examination of both traditional and modern legal discourses surrounding family law, the chapter discerns the extent to which modern religious discourse, as utilized by IIZ, is entrenched in Islamic tradition or subordinates it. The proposed reforms advanced by IIZ provide a further focus of study, highlighting the influence these faith-based activists have in shaping both policy and practice.

## MARRIAGE PRECONDITIONS: PROPOSAL AND ENGAGEMENT

Family formation is one of the most central components of Islamic law. According to several sayings attributed to Prophet Muhammad, marriage is "half of religion," as it fulfills a moral imperative. Particular conditions and processes are required to ensure both Islamic and cultural legitimacy of a marriage. This gives rise to crucial questions such as: What is the process of a proper marriage proposal and the selection of a lifelong partner? What constitutes the legal age for marriage, and what role do legal guardians play in the marriage process?

In both Islamic and Iranian tradition, a marriage proposal is understood to be an explicit act extended from a man to a woman. In this context traditionalist jurists argue that when the Qur'an and hadith refer to a marriage proposal, they are explicitly addressing men.[4] The Iranian Civil Code recognizes the social customs related to a marriage proposal and the ensuing engagement. Whereas the traditional Shi'i *fiqh* highlights the gendered aspect of proposals, the Civil Code does not impose such restrictions. In fact, the late president Akbar Hashemi Rafsanjani (d. 2017) encouraged women to propose to men they were interested in marrying. Although this idea is not socially popular, it offers women agency to choose their partner.

Men are allowed to propose to women only when there are no legal impediments to the marriage.[5] Therefore it is forbidden to propose to women who are married or are in the *'idda*[6] period, during which they remain celibate awaiting their divorce. On the basis of the consensus of Sunni jurists, a man should not propose to a woman who has already accepted a proposal.[7] However, Shi'i jurists differ in their approaches to the issue. A number of prominent Shi'i 'ulama' and jurists, such as Shahid al-Awwal,[8] argue that a proposal to a woman who has accepted the proposal of another man is not permissible because it might cause hardship and conflict between the suitors. Other scholars, like Shahid al-Thani, assert that proposing to a woman who has already accepted a proposal by another man, although not encouraged, is not prohibited.[9] These jurists base their argument on the fact that a proposal is not legally binding and both parties have the right to reject or change their mind during the engagement period. However, because of conventional norms, proposing to a woman who has already accepted a proposal is deemed objectionable by the majority of jurists.

The Civil Code, on the other hand, differs from traditional Shi'i *fiqh* in that it does not explicitly state that a Muslim man is prohibited from proposing to a woman who has already received and/or accepted a proposal. A proposal does not necessarily amount to marriage even if all or part of the *mahr* is awarded to the woman prior to the marriage.[10] According to the Iranian Civil Code, if the marriage has not been officiated or if the proposal is annulled, the parties involved will need to be compensated for the gifts they have exchanged during the engagement period.[11] Legally, the engaged partners are under no obligation to provide justification for the annulment of their engagement, so long as they return presents that were customarily exchanged during the engagement period. Therefore, pursuing legal recourse for emotional distress caused by the dissolution of engagement or a verbal agreement of marriage lacks legal ground in court.

In accordance with Shi'i *fiqh,* during the engagement the parties involved can request proof of health and income, among other things. The Civil Code similarly allows both individuals to request a doctor's certificate indicating that the other has not contracted a contagious disease.[12] Customary norms discourage individuals from making such requests, as it is viewed as impertinent and intrusive. However, because of the rise of children born with the blood disease thalassemia, in 1996 the Iranian Ministry of Health approved a mandatory blood test to ensure that couples do not suffer from a serious genetic disorder prior to marriage.[13] This requirement is considered to be a civic duty, and if the notary or couple fail to comply, although their marriage will not be annulled, they will face financial penalty.

In a traditional proposal ceremony, the couple have not seen each other. The idea of "seeing" one's partner before marriage has become a contested issue in societies where men and women are advised to maintain modesty in their gaze and attire. Shiʻi scholars have cited contradictory hadiths concerning it. Al-Muhaqqiq al-Hilli, for instance, asserts that a man and woman are permitted to see only the hands and face of the other before marriage.[14] Other Shiʻi scholars state that it is acceptable for potential spouses to view each other's hair and body. One such scholar is Shiʻi jurist Sheikh Murtada al-Ansari, who argues that it is particularly important for a woman to look at a man's body to ensure that she is satisfied with her choice, considering that women are not given the same right and leverage as men to dissolve the marriage.[15] Despite these differing positions, the culturally acceptable practice is for couples to see the parts of the body that are customarily visible, such as the face and hands. The issue is complex because, by traditional norms, the bride would have been normally seen by the in-laws prior to the engagement ceremony. However, contemporary practices often deviate from this, with most couples choosing their own partners. Only after this initial mutual agreement do families typically become involved.

Traditionally, the age of consent for entering into a marriage contract was set at puberty. In Shiʻi *fiqh*, the age of puberty is set at nine years old for girls and fifteen years old for boys. Individuals who have not reached the age of maturity, set at eighteen, may not contract their own marriage; however, their legal guardians can initiate a marriage contract on their behalf. In the period leading up to the legal amendments of 1982, the legally prescribed marriage age for girls was set at fifteen, with the age for boys being eighteen. Exceptions were accepted in situations where judges allowed for the marriage of underage individuals. However, such exceptions were not extended to girls under the age of thirteen or boys under the age of fifteen. This ruling was later overturned after the establishment of the Islamic Republic because it was viewed to be in conflict with the notion of puberty in Shiʻi *fiqh*. The current legal age for marriage is set at thirteen for girls and fifteen for boys.

While traditional Shiʻi legal texts do not specify the age for legal maturity, there is consensus that the legal maturity of individuals can be based on when a person reaches puberty and on their ability to make sound judgments (*rushd*). In the Civil Code, however, the age of legal maturity has been set at eighteen, and if an individual who is fifteen years of age or older seeks to demonstrate their maturity, they need to prove it to the court.[16] As we will see, neither traditional *fiqh* nor contemporary legal thought considers maturity a precondition for marriage. Although it is argued that obtaining the permission of the legal guardians before marriage can safeguard the minor from potential harm, in reality it is much more complicated, particularly when dealing with unfit guardians.

While Shiʿi scholars differ in their opinions on the minimum age of marriage, there is agreement on an age limit set for the consummation of marriage. Al-Muhaqqiq al-Hilli posits that girls are ready to consummate marriage upon reaching puberty, traditionally deemed to be at nine for girls and fifteen for boys—a stance that incites disagreement among many activists, including those of the IIZ Coalition. Regardless, marriage before puberty is allowed if permission has been obtained from the child's guardians and the child's interests are taken into consideration. Such a marriage can move forward only when official permission from the child's guardians and the court is obtained.[17] It is common practice to wait until a girl reaches puberty before the marriage is consummated, even if she has entered into a legally binding union. Therefore, the start of a young girl's official married life is dependent on her reaching the age of puberty.

According to Shiʿi *fiqh,* the *walī* (guardian) of a minor can make decisions in line with the child's interest. The term *walī* is not defined in the Iranian Civil Code; however, in traditional Shiʿi *fiqh* it is used to refer to the father and the paternal grandfather of a minor. A minority of Shiʿi jurists believe that the term can also be extended to the mother and the maternal grandparents.[18] According to traditional Shiʿi *fiqh,* both the father and the paternal grandfather have the right to contract a marriage on behalf of minor girls or mature virgins. However, jurists have not reached a consensus on the role of the paternal grandfather in the absence of the father. The majority of scholars, such as al-Muhaqqiq al-Hilli, argue that the grandfather continues to possess the right to consent to the marriage even in the absence of the father.[19] Concurrently, the Civil Code grants both the father and the grandfather permission to authorize the marriage.

Shiʿi jurists have reached consensus regarding the guardian's role in contracting marriage for minors; however, they have not reached an agreement as to whether the child can annul the marriage contract once they reach the age of puberty. While some jurists permit boys to annul the marriage contract, they do not extend the same right to girls. The legal reasoning behind this position is that boys are responsible for *nafaqa* (financial maintenance of a wife) and *mahr* (the "dower" that a man must pay for his wife-to-be) once they reach the age of maturity, while girls are not burdened by such obligations. Furthermore, when a marriage is contracted on behalf of a minor girl, the responsibility of her natural guardian is to ensure that her interests are protected in the marriage. Other Shi'i scholars draw upon prophetic hadiths to support the claim that minors, irrespective of their gender, should possess the right to nullify their marriage contract once they reach puberty.[20] Although Shi'i *fiqh* allows legal guardians of a girl to contract a marriage for her before she reaches puberty, there are loopholes that can affect the practice. For instance, a young girl whose marriage has been arranged by someone other than her immediate guardians can appeal for an annulment of the marriage contract once she reaches puberty.[21]

Traditional *fiqh* allows girls and boys who are not virgins and have reached the legal age of maturity to arrange their own marriage.[22] However, opinions vary as to whether a *wali* should have any say in the marriage of a virgin girl who has reached the age of maturity. In his commentary on the Qur'an, *Al-Tibyan fi Tafsir al-Qur'an*, Shi'i *faqih* Sheikh al-Tusi maintains that once a girl reaches *bulūgh* (maturity) she can contract her marriage without the consent of the *wali*.[23] Other Shi'i scholars assert that the *wali* of a virgin girl has the right to contract her marriage regardless of her age.[24] Furthermore, there is a perspective among scholars that emphasizes the necessity of a mutual agreement between the girl and her *wali* to validate the marriage contract.[25] Ayatollah Khomeini agrees with the latter position, stating that an adult virgin should have the consent of her *wali* as a mandatory caution (*ihtiyāt*).[26] Such a ruling generally applies to virgin girls and women. Therefore, if a woman was previously married but got divorced prior to the consummation of marriage, she too would need the approval of her *wali* before formalizing a new marriage contract.

The majority of Shi'i jurists, like their Sunni counterparts, have proclaimed that although a mature woman can contract her own marriage, in the case of a virgin girl the permission of the *wali* is required for the marriage contract to be considered legal. However, Shi'i *fiqh* sets limits on the necessity of the *wali*'s consent for marriage of a mature virgin girl. If, for instance, the *wali* does not have a reasonable cause for denying or refusing to give his opinion on the marriage, his consent is no longer deemed necessary. The Civil Code (1043) endorses a similar legal position. To comply with Shiʿi *fiqh,* the Iranian Civil Code allows women to obtain permission from the Civil Court in order to get married. If a woman intends to marry without the consent of her *walī,* she needs to provide information about the person she intends to marry in addition to the terms of the nuptial agreement. The court will then notify her *walī* of the particulars of the case. If the court does not hear back from the *walī* regarding the reason for their refusal within two weeks, it will issue permission for marriage. These differing views regarding marriage prerequisites are reflective of the plurality of views that exist in Shiʿi *fiqh* in relation to family law. As we will see, members of IIZ have strategically used these diverse opinions to argue for women's right to choose their partner within the Shiʿi legal framework.

Alongside the conventional method of contracting a marriage through a *walī,* the Civil Code permits parties to designate a legal representative to contract the marriage. This representative is granted power of attorney, comparable to that of a *walī,* and is charged with the task of legitimizing the marriage contract.[27] In accordance with the Civil Code, the appointed individual is authorized to select a spouse and sign a legally binding agreement under the conditions specified by the client.[28] Per Article 1073, the marriage's validity is contingent upon the client's approval should the representative fail to meet the client's requests. This individual also has the capacity to officiate the wedding and agree to the proposal on the couple's behalf. Any actions by the representative that do not align with the client's best interests may lead to the annulment of the contract.[29] Furthermore, the Civil Code stipulates that the parties need not be physically present to declare their consent. Echoing this perspective, Ayatollah Khomeini supports the concept of marriage contracted through a representative, with the caveat that both parties provide their consent afterwards.

The couple must give their consent for the *nikāḥ* (marriage contract) to be recognized. Legally, *nikāḥ* is considered a civil law contract that involves *iʿjāb* (the offer of marriage), *qabūl* (acceptance of marriage), and *mahr.*[30] Given the contractual nature of Islamic marriages, lawmakers have included additional steps to validate the marital union. The signing of the contract is not sufficient for the marriage to be Islamically recognized. The couple must verbally declare their offer and acceptance in front of witnesses. As per Article 1070, even if one party exhibits hesitation in approving the marriage contract, it remains valid unless the hesitation is so profound that the individual's intention to proceed with the *nikāḥ* is questioned.

The legal recognition of a marriage in the Civil Code is finalized by a contract, which requires the consent of both parties involved. However, with regard to minors, Khomeini allows a child's *walī* to finalize the marriage without acquiring the child's consent. By drawing on the concept of *jabr* (coercion),[31] Khomeini denies the child the right to terminate the marriage upon reaching puberty.[32] Khomeini's opinion contradicts the Civil Code, which explicitly states that if the minimum age for marriage is not met, the marriage contract will be annulled.

While obtaining the permission of the *walī* for marriage of an underage girl is mandatory, the issue of acquiring the girl's consent for marriage poses legal complications. Consent of girls who have not reached the age of legal maturity is disputed, as they are not considered capable of providing mature opinions on such matters. Other cultural factors such as silence during marriage officiation, which can be interpreted as a sign of consent, add further complexity to the matter.[33] In Iranian culture, the bride is customarily silent when the wedding vows are being declared. During the marriage ceremony, the officiant initially inquires about the woman's consent, but the bride offers her consent only upon the third request. By taking into account Iranian cultural norms, the Civil Code states that the consent of the marrying individuals is a necessary condition for the marriage contract to be legally binding. In such a scenario, should there be any hesitation on the part of either the woman or the man, it is advisable to delay the ceremony until mutual consent can be fully established.[34] Khomeini also takes a decisive stance on this issue and reiterates that the marriage contract is valid only if both parties announce their consent and agree to the terms of the marriage. Navigating the complexities of consent and age of marriage within Iranian society presents a significant challenge. Influences from diverse cultural and social practices can contribute to the way these rulings are implemented. Women's rights groups such as IIZ have raised concern over the lack of progress and uniformity on issues pertaining to consent and age of marriage.

## CONSENT AND AGE OF MARRIAGE: IIZ'S CRITICAL INSIGHTS AND SUGGESTED REFORMS

Issues of consent and age of marriage have led to intense debates between women's rights activists and the state. IIZ members contend that despite some progress in women's legal status, marriage laws are still out of touch with the realities of women's lives. These religious activists are critical of regulations that limit women's agency in determining the terms of their own marriages. While acknowledging the potentially constructive role of the *walī* in marriage arrangements, IIZ members draw attention to the rights afforded to women in Islam in relation to giving their consent for marriage. The faith-based activists cite various Qur'anic verses and prophetic hadiths that emphasize the centrality of women's consent concerning the legitimacy of marriage. IIZ members have delved into reinterpreting sacred scripture to promote gender-inclusive policies concerning women's consent. Through the adoption of women's jurisprudence, these faith-based activists repudiate laws that allow the *walī* to marry an underage girl without her consent. They also question the gendered aspect of *walī*, which is limited to the father and the paternal grandfather. They argue that "the status of *walī* should also be extended to women, particularly the mother. A mother ought to possess rights equal to those of the father and paternal grandfather in initiating a marital contract for her children."[35]

IIZ also contends that while the *walī's* role in marriage was originally meant to safeguard girls, it has perpetuated a gender hierarchy that is outdated in contemporary societies. These religious activists challenge the relevance and usefulness of the concept of *walī* in contemporary societies, given the shift in power structure where the modern state assumes the role of guardian, responsible for protecting its citizens. IIZ believes that the profound changes in today's sociopolitical landscape call for a reevaluation of rulings that may have been appropriate for traditional societies but are no longer viable for modern systems of governance and societal norms.

Pivoting toward more specific concerns, women's rights activists have been vocal critics of child marriages. They argue that it is fundamentally irrational for a minor who has not reached the age of legal maturity to shoulder the complex responsibilities associated with managing a family. Official statistics reveal that over 33,000 girls under fifteen were married between 2006 and 2013. Other disturbing statistics indicate that in 2012, 1,537 girls below the age of ten and nearly 30,000 girls between the ages of ten and fourteen entered into legally binding marriages.[36] Further, the legal endorsement of early marriages has led to higher rates of divorce among couples who consummated their marriage before the age of maturity. By highlighting the lived experience of young women who enter into child marriages, IIZ activists challenge policies that are detrimental to women's physical, psychological, and spiritual well-being. Through the support of influential female religious authorities, IIZ eventually succeeded in raising the minimum age of marriage for girls from nine to thirteen. Although that may be considered a small victory, IIZ continues to raise awareness about the physical and mental health risks of early marriage.

The Family Protection Bill (FPB) of 2007, introduced by Ahmadinejad's conservative administration, failed to address concerns about early and forced marriages. IIZ activists also seemed to sideline this matter, possibly because of their primary focus on the contentious Article 23, which eased the conditions for men to practice polygyny. The current Iranian family law permits the *walī* to arrange marriages for girls who are underage. According to IIZ, the enactment of this legislation could potentially promote violence against these underage girls.[37] In response to the criticisms, some of the orthodox defenders of the law point to protective measures taken to prevent violence against young girls. According to the Civil Code, if a man enters into a marital union with an underage girl, he will be sentenced to anywhere between six months to two years in prison. If the marriage contradicts Article 1041[38] and results in the wife's injury, the husband will be sentenced from two to five years in prison, in addition to paying *diya* (financial compensation) to the wife. IIZ argues that such protective measures are not sufficient to safeguard underage girls. As a rule, underage girls should not be placed in a compromising position that might be harmful to their mental and physical well-being.

To enhance the well-being of women and children and reduce potential harm to young girls, IIZ recommends raising the minimum marriage age to eighteen, aligning it with the legal age of maturity. In their effort to influence the decision of Parliament's Judicial and Legal Committee, these faith-based activists have presented numerous findings informed by social science and legal research on the adverse effects of early marriages, citing associated physical, psychological, and emotional risks. The Coalition has also pointed out that early marriage could prevent or limit young girls' prospects of pursuing their education. Acknowledging cultural and religious diversity throughout Iran, IIZ recommends that while the minimum age for marriage needs to be raised to eighteen, in cases where the minor's guardian wants to contract a girl's marriage, they should seek the court's permission and the judge must evaluate the girl's level of maturity and decide accordingly. Aligning their efforts with the female *mujtahida* Zohreh Sefati, IIZ, and other women's rights advocates successfully pushed for legal reform that effectively influenced the Guardian Council to raise the legal marriage age for girls to thirteen and limited the *walī's* role in facilitating marriages for underage girls.[39] These advancements, among others, will be further examined later in the chapter.

## THE MARRIAGE CONTRACT

With the couple's consent and the *walī's* approval secured, the process progresses to the finalization of the marriage contract and determination of the *mahr*. For a marriage contract to be legally binding, it must include a specific amount of dower. Once the couple give their consent and the marriage contract is signed, the marriage becomes official and legally binding. No further procedure, such as consummation of marriage or celebration of the marriage union, is necessary to prove the validity of the marriage. While traditional *fiqh* recommends public announcement and celebration of the marriage, contemporary law does not require couples to publicly announce their union.

Current state law mandates that all marriages be reported to the Ministry of Justice in order to be documented in the public registry. Any marriage contract that falls outside this framework is regarded as customary rather than an official marriage. According to the Civil Code, it is essential to register a marriage once the contract has been signed, and failure to do so puts the couple at risk of being penalized. Such mandates by the state have received pushback from the Guardian Council because they contradict Islamic law.[40] By traditional Shiʻi law, a marriage is recognized when both individuals acknowledge its validity, and registering a marriage is not necessary for its legitimacy. Registering a marriage restricts a man's ability to enter into a polygynous marriage, as he needs to obtain approval from the court.

According to the Civil Code, the presence of a witness is not mandatory at the time a marriage is officiated. Medieval Shiʻi scholars highlighted the importance of having witnesses present during the conclusion of a marriage contract. This was to safeguard the rights of children and to prevent any unfair practices concerning inheritance. However, al-Muhaqqiq al-Hilli stated that the presence of witnesses and the public announcement of the marriage were not obligatory, which implies that private marriages were considered to be binding.[41] Such a view corresponds with the perspectives of contemporary jurists and the Civil Code, which does not require any witnesses to be present at the time of contracting a marriage. However, the same does not hold true for divorce, as the presence of a witness is mandatory for a divorce to be considered valid.[42] Accordingly, Shiʿi *fiqh* and the Civil Code consider marriages that have not been disclosed to the public as acceptable. However, on the basis of Iranian custom, the presence of witnesses and a wedding ceremony are required for the marriage to be considered valid.

To uphold the sanctity of marriage, there are distinct criteria for those eligible to conduct an Islamic marriage. Notably, the individual officiating the *nikāḥ* must be of sound mind, of legal age, and competent in making decisions.[43] The majority of Shiʿi jurists assert that for a marriage contract to be valid, the individual officiating must conduct it in Arabic.[44] Yet some jurists display more leniency on this issue,[45] a perspective that is also echoed in the Civil Code.

Such leniency is necessary in a culturally diverse country such as Iran, where a myriad of cultural and tribal practices also affect the ways a marriage is contracted. People have at times utilized and modified aspects of religious law for purposes other than their original intent.[46] There are practices taking place in remote regions of Iran that are contradictory to the positions held by both traditional and contemporary jurists such as Ayatollah Khomeini and Ayatollah Sistani. For instance, the presence of the bride during the officiation of the marriage depends on regional customs. The variations in cultural norms across communities often affect the decisions and rulings of jurists.

The marriage contract has undergone several alterations throughout its history. A notable change has been the inclusion of specific clauses or stipulations within the contract. While some Shiʿi jurists authorize the inclusion of mutually accepted stipulations, others oppose including stipulations that encroach on the husband's marital rights. To ensure that the stipulations are binding, jurists link the stipulations to the payment of *mahr*. Therefore, if the man refuses to honor the stipulation specified in the marriage contract, the woman can invoke her right to *mahr* and request immediate payment.[47]

Marriage laws in post-Revolution Iran have undergone significant changes. The amendments that were introduced to the family law in 1982 permitted both men and women to insert mutually agreed-upon stipulations into the marriage contract. In a way, Khomeini broke with traditionalist jurists by allowing women to insert stipulations into their contract.[48] Moving forward, it will become evident how IIZ has encouraged women to take advantage of this opportunity and stipulate their rights in the contract. The Iranian Civil Code also allows the inclusion of stipulations in the marriage contract so long as they are compatible with the objectives of the marriage. According to Article 1119, individuals entering into a marital union can incorporate any condition in the marriage contract as long as it does not contradict the nature of the marriage. For instance, within the contract, a woman can stipulate that if her husband engages in polygyny, is absent for a set duration, fails to provide *nafaqa*, or behaves abusively, she will be granted the right to divorce by being given full power of attorney.

Shi'i jurists have varying views regarding stipulations that limit men's Islamic rights in the marriage contract. Some jurists, including al-Hilli, argue that stipulations limiting a man's rights, including to sexual intercourse, polygynous marriages, and having his wife join him on travels, are invalid and can annul the marriage.[49] While stipulations have been added as protective measures for women, they cannot override the nature of the marriage as understood in Shi'i *fiqh*. But jurists such as Khomeini believe that although such stipulations are not recommended, the marriage itself is not void.[50] Others state that such stipulations are acceptable; however, if the husband violates the terms of the marriage contract by entering into a polygynous relationship, the second marriage does not become automatically annulled.[51]

Women also have the option to include a provision in the marriage contract granting them the right to initiate divorce. In these instances, the husband can transfer the rights of divorce to his wife by granting her full power of attorney (*wakīl*). This arrangement allows a wife to seek a divorce without needing to provide a justification, particularly if this right is explicitly stated in the marriage contract. This is a notable departure from standard marriage contracts, which require the wife to demonstrate her husband's deficiencies in order to be granted a divorce, aligning with both the Shi'i legal principles and the Civil Code.

The Civil Code, adding another layer to the complexity, permits the inclusion of the couple's qualifications and traits within the marriage contract.[52] This legal provision opens the door for an individual to annul a marriage on the grounds that their partner does not meet the specific qualifications or traits agreed upon in the contract. Furthermore, any stipulations deemed unfounded and unattainable are void, which can lead to the termination of the marriage contract.

The Civil Code has established clear regulations for marriage contracts, expressly nullifying those with conditional terms.[53] For instance, if an individual makes the marriage conditions dependent on a future event, the contract will be considered void. Similarly, including a provision in the marriage contract that gives either party the right to terminate the contract will render the contract as void.[54] Therefore, the couple cannot make provisions such as the right to terminate the contract within a specified period of time. According to the Civil Code and the interpretations of contemporary jurists, while a conditional *nikāḥ* (marriage contract) does not invalidate the marriage, it does void the stipulated condition. This perspective diverges from that of the majority of medieval jurists, who believed that a conditional *nikāḥ* compromised the validity of the marriage altogether.

Shi'i jurists concur on the matter of conditional marriage contracts, emphasizing that a marriage contract shouldn't be equated to a standard contract because of its profound spiritual and religious significance. Thus a conditional *nikāḥ* is deemed unacceptable. These jurists further reason that the annulment of *nikāḥ* has legal and social implications for women. This is mainly why a man is obligated to pay half of the *mahr* if he divorces his wife even prior to the consummation of the marriage. To safeguard women from the potential adverse effects of conditional contracts, both medieval and contemporary jurists have unanimously argued against them.

## *MAHR* (DOWER) AND *JIHĀZ* (TROUSSEAU)

One of the important elements in a marriage is *mahr,* which jurists view as a fundamental condition of the marriage contract. The two types of transactions recognized in the Iranian legal system are known as *mahr* (marriage gift) and *jihāz* (trousseau). *Mahr* and *jihāz* are considered to be the woman's exclusive property, and under no circumstances can the husband or male relatives take possession of these assets. *Jihāz* is any property that the wife brings to the husband's house at the time of the marriage, and it is considered to be the financial property of the woman in the Iranian legal system. The wife has complete ownership of these assets, while the husband can have no claims to them. In civil law, a legal definition of *jihāz* has not been provided, subsequently leading to complications in family courts. Aside from the cultural and customary differences, the allocation and restitution of *mahr* must follow specific legal procedures. Reclaiming the *jihāz,* on the other hand, typically occurs when disagreement arises between a couple or members of their families.

In many Iranian families, it is customary for women to bring their own properties and household furniture to the marital home. This tradition carries a variety of socioeconomic implications, especially when considering the husband's duty to provide financially for the family. In the traditional division of labor, a woman who does not have income is responsible only for maintaining the house. Therefore, to contribute financially and support her husband, it is customary for the wife to bring her own *jihāz* into the marital home. In fact, the tradition of providing *jihāz* signifies goodwill and symbolizes the collaborative spirit between the two families. Bringing *jihāz* in no way signals giving up ownership of assets or the sharing of the wife's property with the husband. The wife's rights over her possessions will remain intact, though the husband can benefit from and use these properties.

Despite popular belief and customary practices, neither legal nor religious mandates require a woman and her family to provide *jihāz* for the marital home. This is further underscored by the fact that a wife can formally request her husband to purchase household appliances for their shared residence. Although the practice is uncommon, a woman can donate the *jihāz* to another person or return it to her parental home. It is, however, customary for a woman to use these possessions to support her new family. In the event of divorce, it is the court that decides whether the household items remain in the possession of the husband or are returned to the wife. To settle disagreements, the arbitration court is responsible for determining the value of the woman's assets. When there is no proof of purchase, the man and woman will claim items that are customarily considered to be their property.

Another pivotal component in matrimonial transactions is *mahr*, a term originating from Arabic. Although the word *mahr* is not directly mentioned in the Qur'an, the concept of dower is used several times.[55] *Mahr* is the sum a man is obliged to pay his wife upon the officiation of the marriage, and it can be claimed immediately after the marriage contract is finalized. The amount of *mahr* has to be accepted by both sides involved in the marriage. Both modern and medieval jurists view the payment of *mahr* as a fundamental condition of the marriage contract. Among Shi'i jurists, there exist two schools of thought regarding the amount and value of *mahr*. The majority of jurists believe that since the amount of *mahr* has never been explicitly defined in jurisprudence, the couple can determine its amount as long as it is possessable and has monetary value. However, a minority of jurists have discouraged women from requesting high amounts of *mahr*. These jurists have sought to prohibit *mahr* that exceeds 500 Dirham, basing their argument on a hadith attributed to Imam Ja'far al-Sadiq, the sixth Shi'i imam.[56]

According to Article 1082 of the Civil Code, the wife is entitled to *mahr* immediately after the marriage contract has been signed. By Iranian custom, however, *mahr* is dispensed in two payments: the first before the consummation of marriage, and the second upon divorce or the death of the husband.[57] Customarily, a portion of *mahr* is used to assist with the purchase of *jihāz*. Although a minority of Shi'i jurists believe that a woman is entitled to half of the *mahr* prior to the consummation of the marriage, the majority of jurists argue that a woman is entitled to full *mahr* after the marriage contract has been finalized, albeit conditional.[58] Despite the different interpretations, a consensus was reached among premodern jurists that allowed women to have access to full *mahr* prior to the consummation of the marriage. This was based on a Qur'anic verse (4:4) that says a woman can have access to the *mahr* immediately after the officiation of marriage. However, if a separation occurs before the marriage is consummated, the woman is expected to return half of the *mahr* in accordance with Article 1082 of the Civil Code. According to medieval Shi'i jurists, if the husband dies before the consummation of marriage, the wife is entitled to the full *mahr*.[59] However, in his book *Tahrir al-Wasilah*, Khomeini states that if a man dies or leaves before the consummation of marriage, the woman is entitled to half the *mahr*.[60] While the Civil Code doesn't explicitly speak on this matter, Article 1082 suggests an alignment with the views of medieval jurists, who believe that women should receive the full *mahr* if the husband dies or departs before consummation of the marriage.

According to Article 1083 of the Civil Code, "A duration of time or installments can be fixed for the payment of *mahr*, as a whole or in parts." Unlike medieval jurists, contemporary legal scholars have argued that there is no obligation to pay the *mahr* all at once. Men have the option to specify in the marriage contract how they will pay the entire *mahr* over a predetermined timeline. This may mean that an initial portion of the *mahr* is paid at the start of the marriage and the remainder subsequently. According to Article 1092, if a husband chooses to end the marriage before its consummation, he must pay half of the agreed *mahr*. Should he have already provided more than this half, he is entitled to ask for the extra amount to be returned.

A marriage contract that does not specify an exact amount of *mahr* is still considered a valid contract. In these scenarios, the man commits to paying a proper *mahr* (*mahr al-mithl*), which is considered the right of the woman.[61] *Mahr al-mithl* applies to situations where the husband and wife consummate their marriage before specifying the *mahr* in the marriage contract and the husband divorces his wife. This could put the husband in a predicament, as the legal *mahr* is a mutually agreed amount between both parties, while the specific amount for proper *mahr* varies for each individual. *Mahr al-mithl* is calculated according to the socioeconomic status and character of the woman. The courts that determine *mahr al-mithl* take into account various factors to ensure that a fair amount of *mahr* is awarded to the woman. For instance, Shiʻi jurists have taken into consideration the women's lineage, family, education, age, virginity, and reputation in order to determine the amount of *mahr al-mithl*.[62]

The Civil Code, in accordance with the opinions of medieval jurists, does not specify a set amount of *mahr al-mithl*.[63] Consequently Article 1091 states that *mahr al-mithl* should be based on the status of the woman and her family and other conditions, including regional customs. In situations where the *mahr* is not brought up in the marital contract and the husband divorces his wife before consummating the marriage, the wife is entitled to *mahr al-mutʻa* (a reasonable marriage portion).[64] Conversely, if the man divorces his wife after consummating the marriage, the wife is entitled to *mahr al-mithl*. The status of the man, including his financial standing, will be considered when deciding the amount of *mahr al-mutʻa*.[65] Unlike *mahr al-mithl*, where a woman's status is the determining factor when deciding the amount of *mahr*, in the case of *mahr al-mutʻa* the man's status determines the amount of *mahr*. According to traditional jurists, the payment of *mahr al-mutʻa* is mandatory. These jurists base their ruling on a Qurʼanic verse (2:236) and the tradition of the Prophet and imams.[66] According to Shiʻi tradition and the Civil Code, a woman is entitled to *mahr al-mutʻa* if divorced before marriage consummation. After consummation, she is entitled to *mahr al-mithl*.

The *mahr* amount is considerably different for temporary marriages as compared to permanent ones. A temporary marriage is a Shiʻi practice where a man and woman come together as husband and wife for a specified duration. Unlike a permanent marriage, the absence of *mahr* for a temporary marriage will render the contract void.[67] Thus *mahr* changes depending on the type of marriage the couple agrees upon. Such a distinction can be attributed to the nature of temporary marriages. A temporary marriage has been compared to a contractual lease by some jurists. In this analogy, *mahr* is provided in exchange for renting a women's body, emphasizing its crucial role in temporary marriage.[68] Much as in a permanent marriage, in a temporary marriage the woman can receive the *mahr* in full once the marriage is officiated. In a temporary marriage, if the woman is *nāshiza* (disobedient) after consummating the marriage, the *mahr* will be proportionately reduced depending on the duration of her disobedience. The reason, as noted by traditional imami scholars, is the nature of these marriages, where *mahr* is viewed as compensation for the temporary wife's *tamkīn* (obedience).[69]

Most jurists advise against a *mahr* agreement that is conditional or abstract in temporary and permanent marriages. Traditional Shi'i jurists uphold the idea that the *mahr* can incorporate anything of value, including a commitment to offer the wife educational opportunities, such as teaching her to read and write.[70] The Civil Code tends to have more strict guidelines regarding the definition of *mahr*. Article 1078 of the Civil Code maintains that anything that can be referred to as property and be owned by an individual can be considered as *mahr*. The inclusion of an invalid clause would not render the marriage contract void, and the proper *mahr* would continue to be legally binding. Modern jurists stand firm on this issue and state that the wife can even refuse to consummate the marriage until she receives the *mahr* from her husband.[71]

According to Article 1085 of the Civil Code, if the husband does not fulfill his obligations and fails to pay the *mahr* upon demand, the woman can refrain from upholding her responsibilities toward the husband. In such circumstances, both traditionalist jurists and the Civil Code assert that if the husband does not offer his wife the agreed-upon *mahr*, the wife can refuse to consummate the marriage and the husband remains responsible for paying *nafaqa*.[72] Should the husband continue to refuse payment of the *mahr*, he can be fined or even imprisoned. A widely accepted view among both contemporary and medieval jurists is that if a wife chooses to consummate the marriage before receiving the *mahr*, she cannot later decline sexual relations. In the same vein, if it is agreed upon that the *mahr* will be paid in installments, the wife is still obligated to fulfill her marital responsibilities.

The Shi'i and Sunni regulations regarding *mahr* share considerable similarities. The majority of Shi'i jurists view marriage as analogous to a contractual agreement, and *mahr* as compensation for consummating the marriage.[73] Many jurists suggest that the husband provide a part of the *mahr* before the marriage is consummated, with the remaining amount to be given after the consummation.[74] A number of traditional jurists are of the view that failure to pay the complete *mahr* can invalidate the marriage.[75] The logic behind such a strict stance is that *mahr* is received in return for the consummation of marriage. However, the law does not support the opinions of traditionalist jurists who interpret *mahr* as a payment for sexual relations. The distinction arises from the provision that women are entitled to half of the *mahr* if the marriage ends before it is consummated. This is because *mahr* falls under the law of contract and transaction. Thus the law does not draw a direct correlation between *mahr* and sexual relations, seeing *mahr* as more than just a contractual obligation. IIZ contends that it is demeaning and legally unsound to view *mahr* solely as payment for sexual intercourse. Even if the amount of *mahr* is not clearly defined, the marriage agreement remains legally valid, differentiating it from standard financial agreements.[76]

Following the 1979 Revolution, the nation underwent a significant cultural transformation, which also influenced the suggested *mahr* amounts in marriage arrangements. During that period in Iran, the *mahr* amounts established were notably lower than in previous times. As a result, in the event of a divorce, a wife's entitlement to *mahr* often had little financial significance. In 1997, legislation was introduced to adjust *mahr* amounts for inflation. This was done to ensure that the value of the *mahr* remained consistent with its original intended value, thereby offering financial protection to the wife.[77] In contemporary Iranian society, the *mahr* amount is often set higher than what the husband can immediately afford. Culturally, the husband is not expected to provide the *mahr* at the time of marriage.[78] Nowadays, as IIZ argues, *mahr* has turned into a source of financial support for women, which contradicts its original purpose. Men are required to pay *mahr* upon demand, and if they refuse, they will be held legally accountable. In such situations, the wife can file a lawsuit against the husband over his refusal to pay *mahr*. According to Article 1129 of the Civil Code, if a husband declines to pay the *mahr*, it can serve as a basis for divorce. In recent decades, the *mahr* has turned into a valuable negotiating tool for women in divorce settlements.[79] For instance, when a man wants a unilateral divorce, the woman has the right to claim her *mahr*. This can either deter the man from formally initiating the divorce or, at a minimum, offer the wife some financial security after separation. A common reason women seldom ask for their *mahr* during the marriage is to retain it as a bargaining tool if the relationship deteriorates, potentially forgoing the *mahr* in return for a divorce or child custody.[80] Often the sheer intimidation of a wife's claim for *mahr* is sufficient to persuade the man to agree to the separation.[81]

Since *mahr* is among the limited rights granted to women, they employ it as a negotiation tool to offset for the rights they lack. Thus it is not surprising that the amount of *mahr* has increased significantly in recent years. IIZ observes that in Iran, *mahr* functions similarly to an insurance policy for women. The notable rise in *mahr* amounts has led to modifications in the 2014 Family Protection Bill, which now imposes a maximum limit on the *mahr* that can be received. The new FPB established a ceiling of 110 gold coins to control the excessively high *mahr* figures. Under Article 25 of the FPB, even if the *mahr* is set at a value less than or equivalent to 110 gold coins, the husband may not face penalties if he fails to pay beyond the specified value unless it can be proven that he has the financial means to pay the entire *mahr* amount. This becomes particularly important when considering that in 2013 alone, twenty thousand men were imprisoned for their inability to pay *mahr*.[82] It is noteworthy that such regulations go against Article 1080 of the Civil Code and traditional Shiʻi *fiqh*, both of which grant full agency to couples to determine the amount of *mahr* without any pressure or coercion from the state.

## IIZ'S APPROACH TO THE MARRIAGE CONTRACT

The state's recent attempts to further modify the laws in favor of men have been met with resistance from women's rights activists. Women's organizations such as IIZ have highlighted the incompatibility between contemporary societal values and traditional norms pertaining to marriage. IIZ emphasizes that marriage should no longer be viewed as a mere transaction in modern societies, but rather recognized as an act of companionship and love, as underscored in their family paradigm model. The IIZ Coalition argues that the sanctity of marriage needs to be preserved by refraining from viewing it as a contractual agreement where *mahr* is offered in exchange for sexual intercourse. By relying on women's jurisprudence, these faith-based activists question the notion that *mahr* provides exclusive sexual access for the husband. IIZ's position is in line with traditional Shiʻi teachings that do not consider *mahr* to be an exchange for the consummation of marriage. Grounding their interpretation in women's lived experiences, these religious activists argue that with companionship being a primary reason for modern marriages, the traditional view of *mahr* should be reconsidered. IIZ highlights evolving perceptions of marriage, advocating for legal rulings to mirror this change and viewing marriage as a covenant of love and compassion between partners.

Another subject that has caught the attention of IIZ is the legal change, after the 1979 Revolution, that allowed men and women to insert conditions into the marriage contract. This amendment to family law has influenced the scope of women's roles within the marriage and the duties of men toward their wives. While IIZ acknowledges the advantages for women in incorporating provisions into the marriage contract, the Coalition also reminds the judiciary that the burden of requesting these conditions ultimately falls on the woman. Often women find themselves in a vulnerable position, hesitant out of fear that the requested conditions will foster an atmosphere of mistrust and jeopardize the marriage. Relying on women's lived experience, IIZ advises lawmakers to include prewritten stipulations in the marriage contract, thereby releasing women from this responsibility and shifting it from her or her *wali* to the state. But until the law catches up with women's demands, IIZ urges that women across Iran exercise their rights and contest entrenched hierarchical norms by placing stipulations in the marriage contract themselves.

Without strong legal protections, women frequently turn to practical tactics for their safety. Raising the *mahr* amount is one such strategy. In response, conservative factions proposed changes to the Family Protection Bill during Ahmadinejad's administration. The amended Article 25 set a limit of 110 gold coins for *mahr* in an attempt to curb the exorbitant amounts of *mahr* women had been requesting in their marriage contracts. IIZ contends that with women's restricted rights, the *mahr* becomes one of the few bargaining instruments and safeguards they have in the event of a divorce. Women frequently employ *mahr* as a negotiation strategy to deter or seek a divorce or to secure the custody of their children. IIZ activists believe that any attempt to cap the amount of *mahr* is bound to have adverse effects on the lives of women, especially those with limited economic support outside the marriage. Therefore, rather than setting a limit on the *mahr* to address concerns about high *mahr*, the government should improve women's legal standing, eliminating the need for them to resort to such protective strategies.

## PERMANENT AND TEMPORARY MARRIAGE

Two different types of marriage are recognized within Shi'i jurisprudence: temporary and permanent. Although the Family Protection Law states that marriage is primarily understood as a contract between one man and one woman, it legally permits men to simultaneously marry four wives and even more temporary wives, which has caused concern among IIZ activists. Medieval Shi'i jurists differentiate *mut'a* (temporary marriages) from permanent ones. They maintain that *mut'a* primarily serves the purpose of sexual fulfillment, whereas permanent marriages encompass both procreation and intimate pleasure.[83]

Temporary marriages, whereby a man and a woman agree to be in a temporary union, can be traced back to pre-Islamic Arabia. Typically, this type of marriage would take place between a man and a woman who were not virgins. A *mahr* would be offered to the woman for the time the couple spent together, and the marriage would be terminated upon the expiration of the contract. The practice continued during the time of Prophet Muhammad and after his death during the time of the first caliph. Muslim jurists, however, were unable to reach a consensus as to whether *mut'a* should continue to be practiced after the Prophet.[84] Ultimately, the second caliph, 'Umar ibn al-Khattab, banned this practice, and after a period of indecisiveness the majority of Sunni Muslims outlawed it.[85] However, temporary marriages continued among the followers of Shi'i Islam.

Historically, the registration of temporary marriages in Iran was not a requirement. Although Shi'i jurists recommended the presence of witnesses, it was by no means a requisite.[86] The 1967 Family Protection Law did not address this issue either. The goal was to discourage this type of marriage without legally prohibiting it. However, following the 1979 Revolution, the Special Civil Court decided to legally authorize temporary marriages.[87] Iran's Civil Code requires temporary marriages to be registered if they meet certain conditions. According to Article 21 of the 2014 Family Protection Bill, temporary marriages must be registered under three specific circumstances: when the wife is pregnant, when both parties mutually consent to register the marriage, and if the marriage contract contains predefined terms and conditions. The primary intent behind this is to safeguard women, especially during pregnancy, and to curb potential misuse of temporary marriages. While the Civil Code recognizes *mut'a* as a legitimate form of marriage, subsequent laws do not specify the need for registering such marriages in the absence of the previously mentioned conditions.

While Shi'i *fiqh* recognizes temporary marriages, Sunni *fiqh* no longer adheres to this type of marriage. In the context of permanent marriage, a man can have up to four wives in both Shi'i and Sunni *madhāhib* (schools of thought). But contrary to the norm in a number of Muslim-majority countries, Iranian men have not been keen on having more than one permanent wife. Instead, there is a noticeable inclination toward engaging in *mut'a* marriages. Iran is one of a handful of Muslim-majority nations that legitimizes *mut'a* in its legal system.[88] On the basis of Shi'i *fiqh*, both permanent and temporary marriages are deemed as legitimate ways to engage in sexual intercourse. In modern-day Iran, temporary marriage is perceived and rationalized as a means to address and regulate sexual desires. It not only provides a way for individuals to fulfill their sexual needs but also establishes boundaries and duties for those participating in this type of union.

*Mut'a*, which means "enjoyment," is a type of marriage where the couple may not necessarily have the intention of establishing a permanent life together. There are two different types of temporary marriages: sexual and nonsexual *mut'a*. The intent behind nonsexual *mut'a* is to foster permissible interaction between men and women. This type of platonic *mut'a* contract creates a space for men and women to interact freely without ignoring religious laws.[89] Because of religious mandates on gender separation, regular interactions between men and women who need to work together can pose challenges. Contracting a nonsexual *mut'a* presents a culturally legitimate means to interact with the opposite sex, especially for those who are keen on following such religious guidelines.[90] Khomeini supported this type of *mut'a* by stating that such a contract is valid if it does not involve sexual gratification. For this form of *mut'a* to be valid, the contract needs to explicitly underline the nonsexual nature of the relationship.[91] It is important to point out that Iranians today rarely resort to platonic *mut'a* for daily interactions between men and women.

Although temporary marriage is recognized in the Iranian Civil Code, there exists a broad cultural and ethical ambivalence toward this practice as reflected in the stance of IIZ. There are no set limits on the number of temporary marriages allowed for men, and they can renew them at will. Jurists have not reached a consensus on whether a virgin girl can enter into a temporary marriage without the consent of her *wali*. However, there is a consensus that in the case of nonvirgin women, there is no need to attain permission from the *wali*. While a number of jurists assert that the father's permission is a prerequisite for the validity of a temporary marriage, others believe that a woman is capable of deciding whether to enter into a temporary marriage so long as her actions do not humiliate her family.[92] The argument for limiting temporary marriages draws from a hadith by Imam 'Ali ibn Musa al-Rida: "A virgin may not be married temporarily without her father's permission."[93] Even in situations where the *walī* of a virgin girl permits her to enter into a temporary marriage, the girl is strongly discouraged from engaging in sexual intercourse. The reservations stem from a hadith attributed to Imam Jaʿfar al-Sadiq, implying that such an act could potentially tarnish the reputation of the girl's family.[94]

Ambiguities surrounding the duration of temporary marriages present potential issues that could result in the annulment of the contract. Jurists have yet to reach a consensus on this issue and still grapple with ambiguities concerning the duration of temporary marriages. A number of jurists believe that if a temporary marriage doesn't have a specified duration, it becomes permanent.[95] However, others contend that if the marriage term isn't clearly defined, the marriage may be invalid, emphasizing that the duration is fundamental to the concept of a temporary marriage.[96] Similarly, in accordance with the Civil Code, it is imperative that the duration of the temporary marriage be determined.[97] In situations where there is ambiguity concerning the duration of the marriage, the problem can be resolved by confirming the details with the couple involved. In case of a dispute between the couple about the type and duration of the marriage, it will be viewed as a permanent union by default unless proven otherwise by either party. If one of the parties presents credible proof, then the marriage is deemed temporary.

When the specified duration of a temporary marriage ends, the relationship terminates without requiring a formal divorce. At this point, the couple can choose to renew their contract or transition into a permanent marriage. In the event that the couple decides to change the contract into a permanent marriage, they need to perform a new *nikāh*. The rights and duties of couples in temporary and permanent marriages overlap and diverge in different areas. The two forms of marriage differ in aspects such as the wife's entitlement to maintenance and her marital duties. Differences also extend to the woman's *mahr* and her rights of inheritance from her spouse. The Civil Code also maintains that provisions that apply to temporary marriages regarding *mahr* and inheritance are the same as those of permanent marriages.[98]

The majority of Shiʿi jurists consider temporary marriages as an arrangement where the *mahr* is regarded as a form of compensation for the time the husband spends with his temporary wife.[99] In line with the opinions of imami jurists, a temporary marriage has to include a specified amount of *mahr*. Thus the absence of *mahr* in a temporary marriage will render the contract void.[100] Much like permanent marriages, in a temporary union the woman can have access to her *mahr* immediately after the *nikāḥ*. If the temporary marriage is annulled before the consummation of marriage, the woman can receive half of the *mahr*. The woman will not receive the full amount of the *mahr* if she initiates the annulment of the temporary marriage.[101] In similar fashion, if the husband decides to annul the *mutʿa* prior to consummating the marriage, he is obliged to pay the woman half of the *mahr*. Khomeini also maintains that the husband should not be apart from his temporary wife for more than four months.[102] Such commitment is not required by the Civil Code unless it is mentioned in the marriage contract. Much as in permanent marriages, in a temporary marriage the couple can add stipulations to the marriage contract. The death of the husband in a temporary marriage will not lead to loss of the *mahr*; the same holds if the husband does not consummate the marriage throughout the union.[103]

While women who are in permanent marriages have high social standing and economic privileges, the same are not extended to women in temporary marriages. A temporary wife, even if she is expecting a child, is not entitled to *nafaqa*. She is, however, entitled to *mahr* as indicated in the contract. When a temporary marriage is contracted, both partners take on minimal responsibility toward one another. In this type of marriage, the husband has full sexual access to his wife and in return the temporary wife receives *mahr*. The legal obligations of a temporary wife toward her husband are less confining than the obligations of a permanent wife.[104] These include the freedom to leave the house without her spouse's permission and engage in work outside the home, provided she remains sexually available to her husband.[105] Similar to permanent marriages, upon the termination of the contract, women in temporary marriages are also required to observe *ʿidda*. The historical rationale behind this practice is to ensure the identification of the child's father in the event of the woman's pregnancy.[106]

In temporary marriages, the couple do not inherit from each other unless such a condition is stipulated in the marriage contract. While in the Civil Code the temporary wife can benefit from mutual inheritance, Khomeini is of the belief that the individuals partaking in a *mutʿa* should not inherit from each other.[107] Whereas a woman in a temporary marriage may not be eligible for inheritance from the husband, a child born into a temporary marriage will receive inheritance from the father. In Shiʿi *fiqh*, it is the legal protection afforded to women and children in temporary marriages that distinguishes this arrangement from prostitution.[108] However, culturally, the child born into a temporary marriage in

Iran is perceived to be illegitimate and is often marginalized. Another cultural difference between a temporary and permanent marriage is the terminology used to refer to the woman. In a permanent marriage she is culturally referred to as *zawja* (wife), while in a temporary marriage she is called *ṣīgha* (contractual partner).[109] Such categorization is an indicator of the difference in the status of women who enter into temporary marriages. *Mutʿa* is a tradition that places religious beliefs and the prevailing social and culture norms in direct opposition to each other.[110]

Among points of contention for IIZ regarding *mutʿa* is that there is no official stance on whether a man needs his first wife's permission to enter into a temporary marriage. Culturally men have been contracting such marriages without seeking the consent of their first wives, and they have rarely faced repercussions. As a result, the country is witnessing one of the highest divorce rates in the region in recent years. The Family Protection Law requires men to declare their marital status at the time of contracting a marriage. The declaration is incorporated into the marriage agreement, and if it is found to be untrue, the man may be subjected to legal and monetary consequences. It is noteworthy that in 1984 the Guardian Council expressed their opposition to these minor restrictions placed on men, arguing that they were contradictory to the Shiʿi tradition.[111] However, that did not stop legislatures from requiring men to proclaim their marital status when entering into a marriage. For instance, if a man neglects to mention that he is already married, the second wife could take legal action on charges of treachery. If found guilty, the husband could be imprisoned for up to two years.[112]

The modern nation-state's interest in regulating marriage has led to the reevaluation of traditional Shiʿi *fiqh* as evidenced in the Civil Code.[113] The state has taken the initiative to revisit *mutʿa* in response to the changing needs of society. In this reframing, the Islamic Republic endorses *mutʿa* as a valid expression of intimacy for couples, promoting it as a preferable alternative to celibacy and as a more favorable option than Western-style dating. The issue of temporary marriage gained prominence during the eight-year Iran-Iraq War (1980–88), which resulted in the death of numerous Iranian men. As a result, many war widows were left behind, and it was within this period that the government legally sanctioned temporary marriage. In 1990, President Hashemi Rafsanjani's endorsement of temporary marriage startled everyone, not least the hardliners within Iran. Rafsanjani believed that temporary marriage was an ethically and legally acceptable way to fulfill the inherent sexual needs of youth.[114] Decades after Rafsanjani's assertion, sociopolitical upheavals in Iran once again brought this controversial topic to the public attention. Despite a resurgence of interest in temporary marriages, it is still difficult to verify the extent to which temporary marriage is practiced in Iran, as there are no legal obligations to register this type of marriage.

Today, among the most recognized and widely discussed forms of *mut'a* in Iran are trial marriages and *izdivāj-i sifīd* (white marriages). In a trial marriage, the couple agree to live together without consummating the marriage. This allows a young couple to marry temporarily while protecting the girl's virginity.[115] In some traditional families, this type of marriage is considered acceptable for a virgin girl with the condition that the marriage not be consummated. This period is typically known as engagement, during which a couple can become personally acquainted with one another. The second type of marriage that is becoming increasingly popular among Iran's urban youth is known as white marriage. In this type of marriage, unmarried partners live together without any contracts or preset conditions. The purpose of white marriages is to have an informal relationship that includes sexual intercourse without facing legal repercussions.[116]

## IIZ REFORMS: REIMAGINING THE MARRIAGE PARADIGM IN IRAN

For nearly four decades since the 1979 Revolution in Iran, women, the state, and jurists have been engaged in an intense debate on how to effectively regulate the practice of marriage. IIZ emphasizes the sanctity of marriage by viewing it as both a contractual and a covenantal relationship, as outlined in their family paradigm model. While there is no explicit reference to the sanctity of marriage in the Iranian Civil Code, the Iranian Constitution refers to the family as the fundamental unit of an Islamic society.[117] Hence, every law, regulation, and policy must work to engender an environment that supports the formation and preservation of the family unit. The state's involvement in the institution of marriage expands this contract from merely a legal agreement between two individuals. In this role, the state is simultaneously responsible for safeguarding the family unit and upholding the rights of women in public and private spheres, in harmony with Islamic principles and Article 21 of the Constitution.[118]

IIZ considers temporary marriages as one of the most contentious issues in the Shi'i practice of marriage. While couples who enter into temporary marriages are motivated by a wide range of factors, there is mounting evidence that such arrangements tend to exploit women. Studies have shown that women who are involved in temporary marriages tend to become emotionally invested in the relationship in hopes of forming a more permanent union. Members of IIZ assert that "such practices should be prohibited except in extraordinary circumstances. *Mut'a* should be limited to single men who are looking for a companionship that has the potential to lead to marriage."[119]

The registration of temporary marriages is another controversial issue for IIZ members. According to the Family Protection Bill, couples involved in a temporary marriage are not required to register their marriage unless the wife becomes pregnant or registration is previously stipulated in the marriage contract. IIZ points out the benefits and drawbacks of such a policy. The Coalition argues that the requirement to register temporary marriages can break the taboo of this practice and normalize immorality in society. If these marriages go unregistered, proving their existence becomes challenging, especially if one party denies the union. Therefore, the legal recognition of temporary marriages is vital to uphold the rights of women in these contracts, ensuring that they receive state protection.

The state advocates for *mut'a* as a substitute for contemporary dating, catering to the sexual needs of a younger generation that appears less inclined toward marriage. Nevertheless, IIZ challenges this perspective and questions whether promoting temporary marriages is the appropriate response to the increasing average age of marriage, a trend largely influenced by unemployment. The Coalition urges the government to focus on its economic policies and tackle unemployment instead of advocating *mut'a*. Although IIZ recognizes that *mut'a* can bring a degree of sexual freedom and autonomy for women, it questions whether this is the right solution to such a complex phenomenon.

Additionally, it is predominantly affluent married men who engage in *mut'a*, with the needs of women in these relationships often receiving scant attention. By Islamic law, a wife has the right to sexual gratification and affection, which is compromised when a man enters into multiple temporary marriages. IIZ asserts that in modern times such a practice is an insult to women's dignity. By incorporating women's narratives and lived experience into their debates, these faith-based activists urge religious and political leaders to limit such controversial practices. Basing their reasoning on women's jurisprudence, IIZ argues that the Qur'anic verses addressing *mut'a* were context-specific and thus no longer applicable to modern society, where marriage is understood to be based on companionship and trust.

These faith-based activists similarly raise concerns over the advocacy of polygyny. Modern legislation aimed at governing polygynous marriages focuses on registration procedures and requires the court's permission to authorize such unions. In earlier discussions, it was noted that the Family Protection Bill of 2007 initially approved polygynous marriages without requiring the consent of the first wife. The bill based the condition for polygynous marriages on the man's financial stability. In the most recent amendment to the Family Protection Law, the husband's remarriage[120] is contingent on the first wife's consent or on the husband's meeting nine preconditions mandatory for such a union.

Women's rights activists are concerned that a lack of punitive measures facing men in polygynous relationships undermines both the sanctity of the family and the dignity of women. IIZ argues that a husband's remarriage without the first wife's consent goes against the Islamic principle of justice. Basing their argument on women's jurisprudence, members of IIZ argue that "the husband's remarriage without the permission of the first wife should be considered illegal."[121] IIZ believes that entering into polygynous marriages should be allowed only in cases where the wife is unable to engage in sexual relations because of a chronic illness. Even in these extreme circumstances, the consent of the first wife should be a necessary measure for a man to enter into a polygynous marriage.

IIZ's study into the varied interpretations of the Qur'anic verse concerning polygyny indicates that this verse emerged from a distinct historical and situational context. This was a time when wars had reduced the male population, leaving many women in need of added protection.[122] Contrary to the societal norms in seventh-century Arabia, the modern nation-state should be in charge of supporting disadvantaged and marginalized women and families. In contemporary Iranian society, polygyny no longer serves its intended purpose and is systematically abused by married men who are more interested in seeking sexual pleasure than in offering protection to women. The majority of men who are involved in polygynous relationships are middle-aged affluent men who become involved with younger women. IIZ members note that it is extremely problematic that religious and political institutions are legitimizing men's affairs without much consideration for the welfare of the first wife. Such relationships put the first wife and children in a disadvantageous and precarious position. Drawing upon the family paradigm model, IIZ reminds lawmakers that the Islamic vision of marriage is centered on the union of two individuals who come together in love and compassion (Qur'an 30:21). As such, the legal basis of marriage should reflect the needs of women in modern society, and laws should be informed by Qur'anic verses that consider marriage as companionship and compassionate living.

These women's rights activists reject polygyny and temporary marriages on psychological grounds as well. Highlighting women's lived experiences, they argue that polygynous marriages and temporary relationships are detrimental to the nuclear family and can cause irreversible emotional distress for women and children. IIZ also references Islam's great emphasis on the family and the Constitution's declaration that the family is the foundation of a healthy society. These activists argue that it is rather contradictory to adopt laws that threaten the foundation of the nuclear family, especially when a law favoring polygyny goes against the prevailing norms of Iranian society.

IIZ is critical of the manner in which temporary marriage and permanent marriage are viewed among traditionalist jurists. Informed by women's jurisprudence, these activists challenge the conventional view that *mut'a* is merely a way to meet the sexual needs of men and *nikāh* is a means of reproduction. In contemporary Iran, where the public perception of marriage is undergoing fundamental and historically unprecedented changes, marriage is no longer viewed as an institution for the sole purpose of procreation. In modern times, permanent marriages have surpassed their traditional function and are grounded in companionship and sexual fulfillment as well as reproduction. While *mut'a* and polygyny are legally acceptable within the Shi'i tradition, they remain socially taboo. The ongoing discrepancy between the official legal code of the country and societal customs presents a persistent challenge. IIZ is taking a proactive stance, pushing for changes in both the legal and religious frameworks to address and rectify these controversial practices.

CHAPTER 5

# Navigating Islamic Family Law

*Life after Marriage and Rights after Divorce*

Continuing the analysis of family law and the significant impact of IIZ, this chapter delves into the complex intersections of legal and theological tenets in Shi'i family law, with a particular focus on women's lives after marriage and divorce. With a detailed exploration of Shi'i *fiqh* and the Civil Code, this chapter unveils the distinct roles and responsibilities that each individual assumes within the family unit. It specifically focuses on the nature of responsibilities within marriage, the dissolution of marital bonds, and legal guardianship and custody of children.

Further examination is conducted into various types of divorce, including *ṭalāq* (unilateral divorce), *khul'* (woman-initiated divorce), *mubāra'a* (divorce by consent), and *tafrīq/faskh* (judicial divorce), as outlined in the Shi'i legal tradition and the Civil Code. The study also assesses the consequences of these forms of divorce for women, examining the legal, ethical, social, and economic challenges they frequently encounter post-divorce. Furthermore, the exploration extends to traditional Islamic concepts of *ḥiḍāna* (custodianship) and *wilāya* (guardianship), examining their influence on family relations with respect to custody and remarriage. A nuanced perspective on Islamic family law is provided, incorporating aspects of classical and modern Shi'i *fiqh,* drawing on the works of prominent and influential jurists such as al-Muhaqqiq al-Hilli, Shahid al-Thani, and Ayatollah Khomeini. The analysis then juxtaposes these viewpoints with the Civil Codes of Marriage and Family.

This chapter seeks to broaden the conversation around Islamic marriage and divorce by exploring their sociolegal implications and introducing the reforms suggested by IIZ as potential interventions. It also closely examines IIZ's commitment to reinterpreting Islamic family law, emphasizing the integration of women's jurisprudence into their initiatives. Subsequent sections offer an analysis of family law regulations in the Civil Code and bylaws, and delve into both traditional and contemporary juristic arguments, setting the stage for understanding IIZ's position and evaluating the scope of their call for comprehensive reform in Iranian family law. The reforms recommended by IIZ are examined in view of the pivotal role these faith-based activists play in guiding policy and practice. In keeping with the broader objectives of this study, the discussion untangles the complex interplay of legal, religious, and societal narratives that shape family law in Iran, underscoring the important role of faith-based activism in instigating reform.

## MUTUAL DUTIES OF HUSBAND AND WIFE

Both the Islamic tradition and IIZ highlight the Qur'anic principles of mercy and compassion as essential to building a successful relationship.[1] According to the Qur'an a sign of a God-conscious marriage is when the couple have reached a state of tranquility in their relationship. The Qur'an (4:19) also highlights the importance of being kind and just toward one's partner. These verses are supported by a hadith attributed to Prophet Muhmmad stating that the noblest among believers are those who have good manners and are kind toward others, and the most honorable are the ones who behave kindly toward their wives.[2] In another hadith, the Prophet stresses that the greatest jihad for a woman is to carry out her responsibilities toward her husband.[3]

In addition to acting kindly toward one another, a couple should also cooperate for the welfare of the family and work in partnership to educate their children.[4] Although raising children and caring for their well-being is not considered the wife's legal responsibility, traditionally the mother plays an active role in nurturing the children and fostering their growth. Such actions are classified as ethical mandates as opposed to legal ones. Therefore a woman who refuses to raise or nurture her child is not considered disobedient. From the Islamic viewpoint, the father is entrusted with the responsibility of fulfilling his duties as the child's guardian.

For couples to maintain a healthy relationship and create a nurturing environment for the family, they are required to live together for the duration of the marriage. The emphasis that jurists place on a couple living together is rooted in the belief that the central premise of a marriage is to build an emotional and intimate connection that is strengthened by cohabitation. This principle is so pivotal that Islamic courts may implement various measures to encourage couples to reside together. Additionally, a husband who prevents his wife from living in the marital home is required to provide another place of residence for her. However, if a wife leaves the couple's home and refrains from carrying out her responsibilities toward her husband, she will lose the right of *nafaqa* (maintenance). Article 1114 of the Civil Code stipulates that a wife is to reside in the house provided by her husband unless she has specified in the marriage contract her right to decide the couple's living arrangements. If such a provision exists, she can choose the residence and is not bound by her husband's preferences.

The inheritance rights between a husband and wife are joint, yet they are not evenly distributed.[5] Articles 913, 927, and 938 of the Civil Code maintain that a wife whose husband is deceased may inherit one-quarter of his estate. However, if the couple have children, the wife's share of the estate is reduced to one-eighth. On the other hand, a surviving husband still receives one-fourth of his wife's estate even if they have children. If the couple do not have children, the husband inherits the entire estate. Among other inequitable provisions is Article 907, which states that male heirs inherit twice as much as female heirs in the family. Such disparity is based on the belief that men are responsible to financially provide for the entire family. While a woman is not burdened with the same responsibility, she is entitled to the entirety of both her own wealth and her husband's assets throughout the marriage.

## HUSBAND'S DUTIES AND RIGHTS IN MARRIAGE

From an Islamic perspective, husbands and wives play a complementary role in terms of rights and responsibilities toward each other. The responsibility of providing for the family rests squarely on the shoulders of the husband in permanent marriages. This includes the cost of maintenance such as dwelling, clothing, food, furniture, and hiring of a domestic worker if the woman requests one.[6] Such actions are supported by the Qur'an and hadith, which require men to provide for the family and meet the various needs of the wife.[7] Providing maintenance for the wife trumps the needs of other members of the family, including the children. Thus the husband is required to meet the needs of his wife in line with cultural expectations. In return, the woman must be obedient and be sexually available to her husband.

While the wife has rights to *nafaqa*, she is not required to perform household duties or nurse the children.[8] If the wife chooses to perform such tasks, she can demand financial compensation from her husband. According to contemporary law, if the wife chooses to carry out these tasks, the husband should compensate her. However, according to traditional Shiʻi *fiqh*, men are not legally compelled to reimburse their wives for carrying out household chores.[9] A wife's right to *nafaqa* is contingent on her obedience and sexual availability. A disobedient wife (*nāshiza*) forfeits her *nafaqa* rights unless there is a plausible reason for her defiance. For instance, if the wife refrains from having sex with her husband because of health issues or religious obligations, she will not be prevented from receiving *nafaqa*.

Many scholars assert that if a husband alleges his wife is disobedient and she denies it, the burden of proof falls on the husband. If he cannot prove her disobedience, the wife retains her right to financial support. Other ʻulama' put the onus of proof on the wife's shoulders.[10] In cases where there is a considerable age gap, with the wife being much younger than the husband, and she is accused of being *nāshiza*, the husband may not be required to provide financial support because of her young age.[11] Conversely, when the wife is significantly older than the husband, on the basis of the opinion of the majority of ʻulama', the husband is bound to provide *nafaqa*, regardless of his own age.[12]

Even if women are active in the workforce and have their own earnings, the Civil Code places the responsibility of family provision primarily on the husband. If the husband fails to provide *nafaqa*, he must reimburse his wife for the period during which he faced financial difficulties and she took on the role of family provider. However, should the wife decide to forgo the outstanding sum, the husband is released from the obligation of these missed payments. In instances where the husband becomes *nāshiz* (disobedient) by failing to provide maintenance for his family, the court can compel him to pay.[13] In such circumstances, the judge will be the one deciding the amount of the *nafaqa* and will enforce measures for the husband to reimburse the wife. The amount of maintenance determined by the jurist is expected to reflect the couple's social standing. In such a scenario, the judge acts as the mediator for the wife, ensuring she is granted a fair amount of *nafaqa*. The husband's inability or refusal to offer maintenance because of poverty or because of persistent absence is considered to be *nushūz* (disobedience). In such instances, the woman can evoke 'usr wa ḥaraj (difficulty and hardship) as grounds for divorce. Should the husband fail to meet his responsibilities, the judge will support a legal separation if the wife decides to initiate a divorce.[14]

Besides receiving maintenance, the wife is entitled to receive *mahr* as specified in the marriage contract. She can demand her *mahr* and may refuse to perform her marital responsibilities until it is provided.[15] Consistent with cultural norms, women initially request a small portion of the *mahr* at the start of the marriage. The larger portion of the *mahr* is usually used by women as a negotiating tool in case the husband is in a state of *nushūz*. In such instances, the wife can resort to the law to receive her full *mahr*. Unlike *mahr,* which is owed to the wife immediately after the marriage, *nafaqa* becomes payable upon the wife's obedience and sexual availability.[16] The wife has full authority on how to manage her assets, and the husband does not have a say on how she should spend her *nafaqa* or *mahr*.

The association of *nafaqa* with *tamkīn* has been a point of contention, especially as it pertains to sexual relations. Shi'i jurists are of the opinion that if the wife declares her readiness to engage in sexual relations with her husband, she is eligible to receive *nafaqa*. Her entitlement to *nafaqa* remains, even if the husband is not prepared to consummate the marriage, as long as she has declared her readiness for marital intimacy.[17] The right to *nafaqa* is a constant, as long as the wife is not in a state of defiance.[18] A husband who fails or refuses to provide *nafaqa* does not have the right to engage in sexual relations with his wife. In the same vein, a wife who refuses to follow her husband's reasonable requests, particularly in relation to sexual intercourse, no longer has claim to *nafaqa*.[19]

In Islam, marital intimacy is seen as a mutual right. Once the marriage is formalized, engaging in sexual relations becomes permissible, and neither spouse has the authority to refuse the other without a justifiable reason.[20] In traditional *fiqh,* the wife is granted the right to demand sexual intercourse and reproduction. According to medieval Shi'i jurists, the husband is not allowed to postpone the consummation of marriage for more than four months. This is also reflected in Khomeini's position regarding the husband's sexual responsibilities toward his wife.[21] Early withdrawal (coitus interruptus) is also unlawful, unless it is performed with the consent of the wife. Although it may not be grounds for divorce, the wife is entitled to financial compensation if any of her rights are violated. According to Article 1130 of the Civil Code, there are circumstances where a woman can legally hold her husband accountable for his sexual incapability or infertility. Given that one of the central purposes of marriage is to procreate, any barrier that prevents the couple from procreating is considered an obstacle to the marriage. If the husband is unable to have children, the law allows the wife to look for an alternative medical solution or to file for divorce.

## WIFE'S DUTIES AND RIGHTS IN MARRIAGE

While the specifics of the rights and responsibilities of each partner can be negotiated and stipulated in the marriage contract, the primary obligation of the wife is to show obedience to her husband in exchange for maintenance,[22] a concept that IIZ finds problematic. Traditional *fiqh* states that the wife's *tamkīn* consists of accepting her husband's requests for sex, not leaving the house without his permission, and accompanying him on journeys at his request.[23] If the wife does not carry out these marital responsibilities without a justifiable cause, she will not be entitled to *nafaqa*.[24] Because the wife receives *nafaqa,* she is required to comply with her husband's sexual needs and is not in a position to decline sex without a valid justification. Reasons to decline sex include menstruation or fear of contracting a sexually transmitted disease from the husband.[25] Aside from these reasons, a compliant wife should permit her husband to have access to her body. Traditionally, refusing sexual intercourse is classified as *nushūz* on the wife's part and can temporarily interrupt *nafaqa.*

Another obligation of the wife is to reside with her husband at his chosen place of residence. The law permits the husband to select the place of residence unless this right has previously been secured for the wife in the marriage contract.[26] Additionally, the wife will be considered as disobedient if she leaves the couple's home against the husband's will. Though the wife is expected to live in the residence provided by the husband, she may opt to live in a separate dwelling in certain situations. These circumstances include the threat of bodily or financial harm, or any situation that compromises the dignity of the wife.[27] If situations occur where the wife cannot stay in their shared home, the husband remains obligated to provide maintenance while she lives elsewhere until he arranges a suitable home for them.[28] This provision offered to women is based on the principle of *la ḍarar* (legal harm/hardship), which is based on Qur'anic verses that advise men to facilitate a comfortable life for their wives and be kind to them.[29]

A wife's responsibilities in a marriage entail more than being sexually available and living under the same roof as her husband. A woman's duty toward her husband also has bearing on her right to work and travel. Unless a woman's right to work has been explicitly stated in the marriage contract, the husband has the power to prevent her from working in vocations that would harm the well-being or dignity of the family.[30] If the wife refuses her husband's request, she will be considered disobedient and will forfeit her right to *nafaqa*. If a woman is employed prior to the marriage with the understanding that she will continue to work after the marital union, the husband cannot prevent her from working. This results in discrepancy between the Constitution,[31] which grants individuals the freedom to choose their occupation, and the Civil Code, which gives the husband unilateral rights to prohibit his wife from working in careers that are in conflict with the family's interests.

In addition to being able to prevent his wife from working in certain occupations, the husband can restrict his wife's mobility, an issue contested by IIZ. According to Article 18 of the Passport Law, women must obtain their husband's consent before they are permitted to travel abroad. Article 19 of the same law states that men can impose travel bans on their spouses.[32] However, there are limits to a man's ability to restrict his wife's movement, particularly in cases where the woman wishes to go on a religious pilgrimage. According to Shi'i jurists, a husband's permission is not required for a woman to travel to Mecca in order to perform hajj (pilgrimage); in fact, the man is required to provide *nafaqa* even if he is not traveling with her. This ruling also extends to traveling for necessary reasons such as seeking medical treatment.[33] Other jurists maintain that if a woman chooses to travel to a nonreligious or nonmandatory destination without the husband's permission, she is in violation of her responsibilities and the husband is no longer obligated to pay *nafaqa*.[34]

Even though *nushūz* is the violation of the rights of one partner by the other, IIZ argues that contemporary jurists have primarily linked this concept to a woman's disobedience toward her husband. Traditionally, jurists discussed men's *nushūz* as well. While medieval jurists' texts contain multiple references to men's *nushūz*, when a man does not fulfill his legal duties the law does not provide the wife with rights to discipline or coerce the husband into compliance. The husband's failure to perform his marital duties can only serve as grounds for divorce. In case of the wife's *nushūz*, however, the husband can resort to the court and request a *nushūz* warrant to compel his wife to submit to his request. Additionally, the husband will be exempted from paying *nafaqa* to the *nāshiza* wife.

## FROM DEPENDENCY TO PARTNERSHIP: IIZ'S QUEST
## FOR REFORMATION IN FAMILY LAWS

The reductive framing of *nushūz* as a woman's disobedience toward her husband has widened the existing disparity between the rights of men and women within the family structure. As a result, IIZ has intensified its efforts to problematize such framing with the intention of reforming family law in Iran. IIZ members have urged policymakers to reevaluate the way they conceptualize the relationship between a husband and a wife. Traditionally, Shi'i 'ulama' viewed the marital relationship as a dependency of the wife on the husband. Such policies have led to systematic limitations on women's mobility and a reduction in their autonomy. At the same time, placing the exclusive responsibility of *nafaqa* and the financial sustenance of the family on men can create significant stress, especially during challenging economic conditions.

Although family laws in Iran have been partially amended since the 1979 Revolution, the changes have not been systemic. For instance, according to Khomeini, if a woman is working to support herself because of the husband's inability to provide financially, she is no longer required to *tamkīn* (be obedient).[35] This statement implies that women who are financially supporting their families do not have to comply with their husband's demands. Iranian women have been financially contributing to their households either through paid labor such as employment (30 percent) or unpaid labor, including the supervision and care of children. From an Islamic standpoint, men are required to compensate women for any household work, although this obligation often remains unfulfilled in reality. IIZ argues that women's domestic work should be assigned economic value. This perspective posits that women, by virtue of their financial contributions to the household, should not have to be obedient to their husbands.[36] Drawing from this argument, IIZ pushes for legal changes, though these reforms have yet to come to fruition.

These religious activists have attempted to redefine the rights of working women within the family unit. More specifically, IIZ members maintain that women's increased participation in the workforce is not reflected in current family law.[37] IIZ claims that "lawmakers seem to be overlooking the growing economic independence of women. Recognizing women's financial contributions to the family might require a change in their legal status."[38] In order to eliminate existing legal gaps, it is imperative to legally recognize women's financial contributions to the welfare of the family. Such legal recognition would directly affect the dynamics of family relationships, including the issue of women's obedience and financial security.

By relying on women's jurisprudence, IIZ argues that the duties of a husband and wife toward each other go beyond *nafaqa* and *tamkīn*. Citing the Civil Code, IIZ asserts that a prosperous marriage emerges from compassionate partnership, emphasizing that reciprocal collaboration is essential to stability of the family unit.[39] According to Article 1104 of the Civil Code, a couple must help one another in family affairs and work to strengthen family ties. IIZ further draws upon its family paradigm model to argue that a couple's relationship should be based on mutual respect and dignity. It contends that the connection between *tamkīn* and *nafaqa* must be reconsidered and supplanted by the Qur'anic principles of love (*mawadda*) and compassion (*raḥma*).[40]

According to IIZ, the modern Iranian family no longer consents to the traditional gender hierarchy and the authority of the husband over his family. Yet contemporary family law is firmly rooted in a traditional understanding of a woman's role in the marriage and has not accounted for socioeconomic and cultural changes affecting Iranian families. Members of IIZ have called for major revisions of existing laws in an effort to make women's legal standing more compatible with their social reality. In line with the views of IIZ, some scholars contend that advocacy for a broad reassessment of male authority within the family sphere is not aimed at absolving men of their financial duties toward their families. Instead, it seeks to recognize and appreciate women's contributions through unpaid household labor.[41] Members of IIZ have highlighted that acknowledging women's unpaid labor can decrease male dominance in financial matters within the family and reduce their overarching authority over women.

These religious activists believe that one of the controversial constructs that lends itself to male domination is the *nafaqa/tamkīn* binary. According to Shi'i law, the wife is entitled to *nafaqa* only if she complies with her husband's sexual demands. Accordingly, the wife cannot decline sex without a justifiable reason. In this context, the charge of marital rape would not hold in court unless the wife could prove that she had a valid reason for declining sex.[42] IIZ argues that the concept of marital rape should be classified as sexual coercion and extended to instances where one partner, usually the wife, is forced to have sex against her will. IIZ posits that forcing a woman to have sex is in itself an act of *shuzūz* (sexual perversion) and that such acts are contrary to the essence of justice that is central to Islam. By utilizing women's jurisprudence, these activists argue that *shuzūz* is prohibited in Islam and is grounds for divorce. The issue of marital rape continues to be a sensitive topic in women's rights circles. While activists advocate for legal consequences for such acts, they face strong opposition from conservative legislators and 'ulama'.

IIZ raises concerns about a prevalent sexual double standard that exists between men and women. Although Shi'i 'ulama' recognize women's inalienable rights to sexual satisfaction and reproduction, research conducted by IIZ reveals women's sexual dissatisfaction to be one of the main reasons for divorce among Iranian couples. IIZ points out that the primary reasons for sexual dissatisfaction among Iranian couples are limited sexual knowledge and marital disputes. In many marriages, there is an unequal power distribution, with men often holding the dominant role. This dominance extends into the couple's intimate life, leading to increasing dissatisfaction among women. Additionally, women's growing engagement with social media has heightened their expectations for sexual fulfillment from their partners. IIZ believes that the root of this dissatisfaction lies in the broader sexual inequality women experience. To address this, IIZ emphasizes the need for women's empowerment and increased cultural awareness and education.

Another point of contention highlighted by IIZ is women's unequal rights in relation to property distribution in Islamic law. While Shi'i *fiqh* views itself as favorable to women in matters of inheritance, it still has stipulations that prevent a widow from inheriting real estate from her late husband.[43] After objections from women's rights groups such as IIZ, the law was revised to permit a widow to inherit the monetary equivalent of her late husband's estate. Continued advocacy from women's rights groups led Parliament members to pass a bill allowing women to inherit one-eighth of their husband's movable assets and one-eighth of his immovable assets, such as land. Despite these minor changes in property distribution, IIZ has persisted in advocating for additional reforms to further women's rights in the realm of inheritance laws.

Members of the IIZ Coalition recognize that inheritance laws constitute a subdivision of an interrelated and complex legal system that regulates property distribution among individuals. The justification for the inequality in inheritance between men and women, as rationalized by jurists, is that women have financial rights such as *mahr* and maintenance, where they fare better than men.[44] In this context, women's right to *mahr* and *nafaqa* are viewed as reparation for the comparatively smaller inheritance share. Thus *mahr* and *nafaqa* should be understood in relation to Islamic law regarding inheritance.

IIZ members are well aware of the legal and social complexities related to *mahr* and *nafaqa* as potentially powerful tools adopted by women to cope with shortcomings in family law. Furthermore, the economic disparity and lack of job opportunities faced by women compel them to endure inequitable legal rulings in exchange for financial support from their husbands. These nuances are often sidelined by the demand for absolute equality in the realm of family. Members of IIZ have carefully addressed the imbalances in family law, understanding that demanding complete legal equality might compromise women's entitlements to *nafaqa* and *mahr*. These provisions are beneficial when women are unable to financially support themselves. Considering the reality faced by many Iranian women, IIZ has taken the pragmatic approach of demanding a reevaluation of the relationship between *tamkīn* and *nafaqa* instead of denying women their right to *nafaqa* or *mahr*. Additionally, these religious activists contend that jurists have overlooked the reality that not all women may find marriage a viable option. This underscores the need for comprehensive legal provisions addressing the needs of unmarried women.

Another area of concern highlighted by IIZ is the husband's power to prevent his wife from working or traveling unless it has been stipulated in the marriage contract. While this view is supported by traditional Shi'i *fiqh* and the Civil Code, it goes against the Constitution, which allows individuals the freedom to work and travel. Drawing attention to these inconsistencies in the law, IIZ points out that the mere existence of such contradictory laws is an indication of the need for major reform. As a result of pressure from women's rights organizations, the law for working women has been modified. The new version of the law stipulates that a competent court must approve a husband's decision to prohibit his wife from working in vocations that are in conflict with the family's values.[45] While minor modifications have been made to the law relating to women's employment, the law for traveling is still in need of reform. According to Article 18 of the Passport Law, men have the power to prevent their wives from leaving the country. Considering that women need written permission from their husbands or guardians to be issued a passport, they inadvertently live in a constant state of fear that they may be barred from working or traveling. IIZ believes that similar to men, women should be able to travel and obtain a passport without their partner's permission.

The belief that a husband has the authority to determine if his wife can work or travel, as well as choose her place of residence, originates from a Qur'anic verse mentioning that men have a *qawāma* (charge) over women.[46] The concept of *qawāma* is traditionally interpreted as men's authority over women, which reinforces a paternalistic view in gender relations. Basing their argument on women's jurisprudence, IIZ asserts that men's role as protectors of women is not a license for male dominance. The Coalition encourages jurists, policymakers, and legislators to integrate women's narratives and lived experiences into family law to better reflect women's societal realities. In their effort to explicate patriarchal influences and gender hierarchy, IIZ members employ women's jurisprudence to offer a more inclusive interpretive lens when reinterpreting sacred scriptures. Members of IIZ advocate an interpretation of *qawwāmūn* that rejects an understanding anchored in dominance, focusing instead on safeguarding the well-being of the wife and family. Consistent with other Muslim women's organizations, IIZ understands the concept of *qawwāmūn* to mean that men are tasked with providing physical and financial protection for women, considering women's role in procreation.

## DISSOLUTION OF MARRIAGE

Marriage is a crucial part of the social fabric of society; however, marital bliss can sometimes take a negative turn, affecting the dynamics within this fundamental institution. According to Islamic teachings, ending an unhealthy marriage is preferable to staying in an emotionally destructive and abusive relationship.[47] Although divorce is generally discouraged, there are provisions for both men and women to annul the marriage if reconciliation is no longer an option. Several verses in the Qur'an allude to this issue and discuss the option of divorce under particular circumstances.[48] In Shi'i jurisprudence and the Civil Code, divorce pertains solely to permanent marriages. In the case of a temporary marriage, the wife is relieved of her marital duties once the specified duration in the marriage contract comes to an end or if the husband decides to forgo the remaining period.[49]

Traditionally, Shi'i jurisprudence recognizes two types of divorce: revocable and irrevocable. With a revocable divorce, the husband has the option to reinstate the marital relationship without necessitating a new marriage contract. This can be done as long as he revokes the divorce within the *'idda* (postdivorce waiting) period. During this *'idda* period, the wife is prohibited from marrying someone else.[50] In an irrevocable divorce, the husband does not have the right of return (*rujū'*) to his wife. Unlike in revocable divorce, the man cannot resume sexual relations with his wife without a new marriage contract. *Mubāra'a* (consensual divorce), divorce initiated before the marriage is consummated, cases of a woman's inability to conceive,[51] and *khul'* (women's divorce)[52] are all classified as irrevocable types of divorce. Another example of irrevocable divorce is known as triple divorce, in which a man declares the divorce formula three times. In such situations, the couple cannot remarry unless the wife has entered into a legally binding marriage with another man and later separates from him.

In an irrevocable divorce, the woman is not entitled to *nafaqa* during *'idda* unless she is pregnant. She also does not need to be obedient toward her husband and is free to do as she wills. Furthermore, the couple cannot inherit from one another during the period of *'idda*. However, in a revocable divorce the husband retains the choice to rescind the divorce before the conclusion of the *'idda* period.[53] This means he can choose to reconcile and resume marital relations without needing a new marriage contract before the *'idda* duration ends. In such divorces, the husband has the option to renounce the divorce prior to the termination of *'idda*. After a separation, reconciliation with the wife can be signified either through an explicit declaration of intent or through an action that indicates the husband's wish to renew the marital bond. The act of returning to one's wife in this context is known as *rujū'*. The intention for *rujū'* can be conveyed either through words or through resumption of marital relations, emphasizing the critical role of timing. Imam Ja'far al-Sadiq elucidated that if a husband resumes intimate relations with his wife during the *'idda* period, it is recognized as *rujū'*. Conversely, if such relations are resumed after the *'idda* period has lapsed, it is considered *zinā'* (adultery) and is subject to legal consequences.[54]

The Islamic courts have intentionally made the divorce process long and complicated so as to afford the couple ample opportunity to reconsider their decision to separate and engage in new efforts to make the marriage work. Despite the laws that are essentially designed to preserve the family structure, the recent years have seen a significant surge in divorce rates in Iran. The sudden evolution from a traditional to a modern society has unsettled the family structure in Iran, and the prevailing laws appear only to prolong the divorce process rather than to deter divorce initiation. The sharp increase in divorce rates, particularly in the middle and upper social strata, has been attributed to infidelity, sexual dissatisfaction, an increase in women's awareness of their rights, high levels of unemployment, high rates of addiction, women's refusal to be restricted, women's education, women's increasing participation in the workforce, and depression and anxiety about the future.[55] Currently, one in every four marriages in Iran ends in divorce, which is a cause of great concern for both authorities and women's rights activists such as IIZ.

## Ṭalāq (Unilateral Divorce)

One of the most common types of divorce is *ṭalāq*, where the man initiates divorce proceedings by choosing to part ways with his wife. In the process of *ṭalāq*, both parties must adhere to specific legal procedures to ensure that the separation is legally binding. An integral part of this procedure is the utterance of the formal divorce declaration. According to the majority of the ʿulamaʾ, the divorce formula must be stated accurately for the divorce to be valid, otherwise it will not be effective. It is recommended that the divorce formula be stated in Arabic unless the person is unable to recite it in Arabic.[56]

It is not acceptable for a man to recite the divorce formula while his wife is menstruating or during the convalescent period after childbirth.[57] The husband can move ahead with the divorce if the wife is pregnant or the divorce takes place before the consummation of marriage. According to Article 1141 of the Civil Code, it is not appropriate for a man to divorce his wife between two menstrual cycles during which intercourse has taken place. The protocol is in place to rule out the possibility of pregnancy, except in cases where the wife is already pregnant or unable to conceive. In a hadith reported from Imam al-Baqir, a man may divorce his wife if (1) she is pregnant; (2) they have not engaged in sexual relations; (3) they have been living separately; or (4) she is unable to conceive because of either infertility or menopause.[58] The logic behind such a provision is to determine the paternity of the child should the wife be pregnant during the period of *ʿidda*.

Shiʿi *fiqh* and the Civil Code stipulate that the pronouncement of divorce must occur before two male witnesses of integrity who can impartially attest to the event.[59] These witnesses must be not only men of good character, committed to justice, but also free from serious infractions.[60] If the witnesses do not possess these qualities, the divorce will not be considered valid. For the divorce to be acceptable, two witnesses who are acquainted with the couple should be present. While Iranian law mandates that witnesses be male, various hadiths suggest that two female witnesses can be equivalent to one male witness. However, these hadiths are considered to be less credible; as a result, Shi'i jurists err on the side of caution and recommend two male witnesses for the finalization of divorce.[61]

For a divorce to be legally valid, the man initiating the divorce process should meet specific criteria. He must possess free will, be of legal age and sound mind, and display a clear intention to end the marriage.[62] Showing signs of maturity is also an essential quality of the divorcer; otherwise the divorce will not be recognized.[63] According to the Civil Code, a person should have free will when deciding to annul their marriage. Thus, if an individual is forced or threatened to divorce their partner, the annulment is void.[64] Intention and comprehension of the implications of divorce also hold paramount importance. Shi'i jurists assert that for a divorce to be valid, it must be pronounced intentionally and without anger, with both clarity and precision in the declaration. Additionally, Shi'i legal scholars concur that conditional divorces lack legal standing, invalidated by their very nature of being contingent.[65]

A legal representative is also authorized to finalize the divorce on behalf of the couple.[66] When a husband and wife reside in the same city, it is recommended for the husband to begin the divorce proceedings rather than a legal representative.[67] However, under specific conditions, women too can have equivalent authority to conclude the divorce. According to traditional *fiqh,* a husband can grant his wife the right to act as a legal representative and file for divorce on his behalf. While there are some opposing views that discourage women from taking on this role, Shi'i jurisprudence and the Civil Code empower women with the legal authority to initiate divorce proceedings.[68]

In traditional Shi'i *fiqh,* men are not required to provide any justification for *ṭalāq.* However, the intention to divorce needs to be clear, as does the utterance of the word *ṭalāq.* According to Shi'i tradition and the Civil Code, the husband can initiate *ṭalāq* at any time or place.[69] While for marriage consent from both sides is required, in the event of divorce a man's simple declaration of his wish to divorce is sufficient to terminate the marriage. Shi'i *fiqh* does not require the husband to inform the woman or seek her consent for the divorce. Women are not afforded the same rights to unilateral divorce unless the husband delegates the right of divorce to the wife in the marriage contract. However, granting women the right to file for divorce in the marriage contract is not without its limitations, as women are permitted to file only for a revocable divorce.

Considering that in modern times *ṭalāq* is under the jurisdiction of the court, the Iranian Special Civil Court requires men to register their divorce. To ensure the validity of *ṭalāq*, the man must either have the approval of his wife or obtain authorization from a judge. Moreover, contracts issued shortly after the 1979 Revolution enabled divorced women to claim half of the family assets unless the divorce was consensual or the woman was at fault.[70] Women do have the option of including the right of divorce in their marriage contract. Khomeini's implicit support of women's right to divorce strengthened women's legal standing to some extent.[71] A law was enacted in 1980 that empowered women to seek divorce under specific circumstances. Situations where these conditions apply involve cases of the husband's violent conduct, his failure to provide financial support, or his engagement in dishonorable occupations. These reforms have led to an increasing involvement of the state and the courts in the divorce procedure, all the while partially limiting men's monopoly on divorce.

In contrast to the past, when divorce was regarded as a private act, today the state has taken on the responsibility of overseeing divorces. Following the amendments to family law in 1992, a man must approach the court to secure a divorce certificate. In this context, a man is allowed to register the divorce only after he has paid the *mahr* and *nafaqa* in full. Subsequent revisions to the law enable the court to assign financial value to any work performed by the wife throughout the marriage, including domestic duties and childcare responsibilities. The court can compel the husband to compensate the spouse for *ujrat al-mithl* (wages in kind), which provides a level of financial protection for women.[72] This compensation is relevant only when the wife did not start the divorce proceedings or was not found at fault for the marriage's termination.[73] Should the couple fail to agree on the sum of *ujrat al-mithl,* the judge holds the power to suggest a settlement amount.[74] The marriage is formally dissolved once the husband has settled the *mahr* and given back the woman's assets. In addition, to curtail men's rights to divorce, the law can penalize men who do not perform their marital duties. For instance, according to Article 642 of the Islamic Penal Code, if a man who is financially stable refuses to pay *nafaqa,* the court can sentence him to up to five months in prison.

It is important to note the contradiction these legal provisions pose to traditional Shiʻi legal thought. While Shiʻi jurisprudence does not permit the court to outright reject a husband-initiated divorce case, the court does retain the ability to postpone delivering a decision. A man's right to unilateral divorce can be delayed and regulated through the enforcement of legal arbitration.[75] Judges in special civil courts can

mandate an arbitration process where each spouse is allocated a mediator. The mediators must then present a report to the court outlining
their efforts to reunite the couple within a two-month period.[76] The
logic behind this mandate is to delay the divorce and provide an opportunity for the couple to reconcile. If reconciliation efforts are not successful, the court then issues an authorization to the husband to divorce
his wife. If the woman does not agree to the divorce, the court has the
power to restrict the husband's unilateral right to divorce.

The 2014 amended Family Protection Bill brought forth alterations,
especially regarding the role of the couple's arbitrator in family disputes. As per Article 27 of the bill, the involvement of arbitrators in
consensual divorce cases is not mandatory. In scenarios where women
file for divorce, judges often attempt to reunite the couple by either
referring them to arbitrators or compelling the husband to write an
affidavit. Through this affidavit, the husband can grant his wife the
authority to divorce if he does not meet his obligations.[77] If arbitration
is unsuccessful, the court will issue a divorce, citing irreconcilable differences. In circumstances where the couple decide to reconcile, the divorce
will be declared void and annulled.

### Khul' *(Woman-Initiated Divorce)*

Within the Islamic legal tradition, the right of divorce is not exclusively
held by men but is a shared right available to all. Consequently, IIZ
activists advocate for women and lawmakers to emphasize the right of
the women to divorce. Women possess the ability to file for divorce by
resorting to *khul'* (dethroning) or *mubāra'a* (divorce by consent). *Khul'*
is recognized as a woman-initiated divorce where the wife provides a
financial settlement to the husband in order to be granted divorce. The
husband's consent for a *khul'* divorce is necessary and legally required
in the event of a complete collapse of the marriage. To prevent impul-
sive decisions, legal scholars mandate that the wife present credible evidence explaining why she cannot continue living with her husband.
From the jurists' perspective, safeguarding women's rights in a *khul'*
divorce is paramount. In line with this view, the legal system strives to
ratify any infringement on women's rights.

*Khul'* divorce is supported by verses from the Qur'an and the imami
tradition.[78] Surat al-Baqara (2:229) sets the parameters for *khul'*
divorce: "Divorce can happen twice, and [each time] wives [can] either
be kept on in an acceptable manner or released in a good way. It is not

lawful for you to take back anything that you have given [your wives], except where both fear that they cannot maintain [the marriage] within the bounds set by God: if you [arbiters] suspect that the couple may not be able to do this, then there will be no blame on either of them if the woman opts to give something for her release. These are the bounds set by God: do not overstep them. It is those who overstep God's bounds who are doing wrong."

As indicated, the husband's consent is necessary for a *khul'* divorce to take effect. If the husband is hesitant about divorce, the wife has the option to propose a *khul'* arrangement, in which she offers him financial compensation in exchange for a divorce.[79] The compensation may include the *mahr* or its monetary equivalent or any other negotiated amount.[80] Most Shi'i legal scholars hold the view that in a *khul'* divorce the husband should accept only an amount equal to the *mahr* he has given to the wife during their marriage as compensation. The financial compensation that a woman offers in a *khul'* divorce is called *fidya*. *Fidya*, much like *mahr*, is expected to be of value. According to Imam Ja'far al-Sadiq, the amount of *fidya* can be the same as women's *mahr* or even a larger or smaller sum.[81] A woman can initiate the *khul'* divorce or she can appoint a legal representative to assume the responsibility on her behalf and offer the *fidya* to her husband in exchange for his approval to divorce.

Similar to *talāq*, in a *khul'*, the person who is filing for divorce should be of sound mind, of legal age, and in control of their faculties. The presence of two just witnesses is also mandatory for a *khul'* divorce.[82] *Khul'* cannot be filed during the woman's menstrual cycle, during the convalescent period after childbirth, or before the consummation of marriage. While *khul'* is generally seen as an irreversible divorce, there are certain conditions where it can be retracted. If a woman chooses to reconcile with her husband before the completion of the *'idda* period, the *khul'* can become revocable.

A situation that could lead to a *khul'* divorce is when the wife's dissatisfaction with her husband intensifies to the point that she no longer wishes to remain with him. This discontent might arise from his looks, demeanor, or engagement in actions she finds intolerable, like entering into a polygamous relationship. A number of Shi'i 'ulama' believe that a mere dislike of the husband is not sufficient grounds for a *khul'* divorce. Aversion toward the husband should be so intense that if the wife continues in the marital union she will become *nāshiza* (disobedient) or commit a sin.[83] However, if the husband is abusive or if he does not fulfill his responsibilities, the wife can file for divorce. In such a situation, the divorce cannot be classified as *khul‘*, and it becomes forbidden for the husband to receive monetary compensation as a prerequisite for divorcing his wife.[84]

## Mubāra'a *(Divorce by Consent)*

When both the husband and wife are inclined to split, considering a *mubāra'a* divorce is a practical alternative. *Mubāra'a* is a mutually decided-upon divorce where both sides choose to relinquish all financial and emotional obligations toward the other. Fundamentally, *mubāra'a* mirrors *khul‘* with a few distinctions. In *mubāra'a*, divorce transpires when the aversion between husband and wife is mutual and they both desire separation. In this type of divorce, the compensation for divorce offered by the wife should not be more than the *mahr* amount. This contrasts with *khul‘*, where the amount of compensation can surpass the *mahr*.[85] *Mubāra'a* divorce is classified as an irrevocable separation. However, if the wife chooses to reunite with her husband before the completion of the *'idda* period, reconciliation is possible. The husband's privilege of *rujū‘* in this form of divorce is restricted, and reunion is permissible only if the wife initiates the request for it.

Shi'i 'ulama' hold varied views regarding *mubāra'a*. Some jurists believe that the husband should retain any remaining *mahr,* while others argue that he should receive the entire *mahr* amount as compensation.[86] According to the Civil Code, the compensation expected in a *mubāra'a* divorce cannot exceed the amount of *mahr* specified in the marriage contract.[87] Considering that the husband already possesses the right to divorce his wife at any time, *mubāra'a* divorce arises only when the husband is reluctant to grant a divorce or is financially incapable of paying *mahr* and compensating his wife for "wages in kind" (*ujrat al-mithl*).[88]

In situations where the couple has reached an agreement on all matters concerning their separation, they are no longer bound by conventional court procedures and can advance with filing for divorce. When either party hesitates to finalize the divorce or when the parties can't agree on the terms of separation, the matter is taken to the court. According to the 2014 Family Protection Bill, if the spouses are interested in a consensual divorce, the court must send their case to a family counseling center before issuing its final decision. The couple is expected to undergo counseling for a specified period, and then if they still wish to carry through with the divorce they can file a petition. The family counseling center will proceed to identify areas of agreement and inform the court to help determine the most suitable course of action.

## Tafrīq/Faskh *(Judicial Divorce)*

In Iranian courts, the judicial dissolution of marriage has traditionally been employed when addressing women's divorce requests. However, some jurists propose that the right to *tafrīq/faskh* should also be extended to the husband. In a judicial divorce, a judge can dissolve a marriage at the request of the wife. Conditions that warrant *tafrīq* include the husband's infertility, chronic absence, abusive behavior, inability to provide *nafaqa,* serious health issues, or contagious diseases that could endanger the health and well-being of the wife.

In Shiʻi jurisprudence, the husband can grant the wife the authority to divorce, provided it is specified in the marriage contract. The set conditions should be consistent with the essence of the marital bond. For instance, the wife may reserve the right to divorce on account of any number of conditions, including if the husband marries another woman, remains absent for a certain period of time, fails to provide *nafaqa,* or treats her with such severity that cohabitation becomes intolerable (ʻ*usr wa ḥaraj*). The Civil Code gives the judge the authority to compel a husband to divorce his wife if she can prove that living together would induce undue hardship.[89] Similarly, a woman who is dealing with an absentee husband can apply for a judicial dissolution of the marriage.[90] In cases where the wife is dealing with an absentee or missing husband, the law requires a waiting period of approximately four years before she is granted divorce.

Another type of divorce, called *faskh,* occurs when a marriage is invalidated because of a flaw in the marriage contract or a significant issue between the couple.[91] In these situations, both the wife and the husband are accorded equal opportunity to request the termination of the marriage. If the request for the annulment is made prior to the consummation of the marriage, the woman is not allowed to keep the *mahr.* If the marriage has already been consummated, the woman can claim half of the *mahr.* The couple can also request an annulment of marriage if an impediment to sexual intercourse presents itself on either side. In such instances, both sides have the right to request an annulment of the marriage.[92]

Obstacles to a strong marital bond leading to *faskh* can include the husband's mental health issues,[93] inability to conceive, or sexual inadequacy.[94] If the wife was unaware of these issues beforehand, she has the right to request an annulment if any of these challenges arise.[95] A husband also has the right to seek *faskh* if his wife suffers from mental health issues,[96] uterine prolapse, leprosy, blindness, or any significant physical disability.[97] The man's right to annulment is valid if he was not informed of these issues at the time of the marriage. If both sides were informed of any of the aforementioned problems prior to the marriage, they will not have any legal grounds to request an annulment.[98] The wife or her legal representative can submit a preliminary application to a court presenting evidence of the husband's flaws. In such circumstances, the judge has the authority to compel the man to divorce his wife.[99] More recently, the courts can rule to annul the marriage on the basis of mistreatment of the wife or lack of compatibility. The judicial dissolution of marriage can also happen when the husband declares the divorce formula. Nevertheless, in situations where this is not feasible, the marriage can be annulled through court order.

## 'IDDA: DURATION OF PROBATION

By Islamic law, a divorced woman is obligated to observe a probation period known as 'idda. A woman who is observing 'idda is not allowed to remarry, and restrictions can be imposed on her movement.[100] The word 'idda is derived from 'adad in Arabic, which translates as "number." In *fiqh* terminology, 'idda is defined as the stipulated period women must observe before the divorce is finalized. This notion of 'idda is drawn from a Qur'anic verse that requires women to enter a waiting period after divorce: "Divorced women shall keep themselves in waiting for three menstrual cycles and it is unlawful for them, if they believe in Allah and the Last Day, to hide whatever Allah might have created in their wombs. Should their husbands desire reconciliation during this time they are entitled to take them back into wedlock" (2:228).

The 'idda period commences once the divorce declaration is made, regardless of whether the woman is aware of the divorce.[101] The length of the 'idda is determined by factors such as the woman's age and the nature of the marriage. Following a divorce, the 'idda lasts for three consecutive menstrual cycles. For a woman who has been in a temporary marriage, the period of 'idda includes two menstrual cycles,[102] and if she is menopausal, the 'idda is reduced to forty-five days. According to Qur'an and hadith, a widow will have to wait approximately four months and ten days from the time she is notified of her husband's passing before she can remarry.[103] Similarly, the period of 'idda is elongated for a pregnant woman until she gives birth.[104]

In relation to revocable divorce, the husband retains the prerogative to retract the divorce before the conclusion of the 'idda period. In such instances, the presence of witnesses is not required for the divorce to be legally binding.[105] The husband can resume (rujū') the marriage after a divorce either by making a clear statement of his intention or through an action that indicates his desire to reconcile and return to the marital relationship.[106] The rationale for rujū' is to offer the husband a chance to reflect and possibly reconcile with his wife, especially considering his enhanced rights to divorce. In an irrevocable divorce, rujū' is no longer an option for either party.

In a revocable separation, unlike an irrevocable divorce, if a partner dies during the 'idda period, the surviving partner can inherit from the deceased. However, if a partner dies after the 'idda period or if the separation is irrevocable, neither party can inherit from the other. In circumstances where the husband is missing or absent for more than four years and his whereabouts are unknown, a woman can request a judicial divorce. In such instances, the women must observe 'idda, starting from the date the judicial divorce is granted.[107]

A woman is entitled to nafaqa throughout 'idda and is not allowed to remarry during that period. She is entitled to nafaqa because of the potential for reconciliation between the couple. However, there are exceptions where the man isn't required to provide nafaqa, such as in cases of divorce due to nushūz, marriage termination, or irrevocable divorce. But if the wife is pregnant, she should receive nafaqa until the child's birth.[108] Apart from these exceptions, the man is legally obligated to pay nafaqa throughout the divorce proceedings and for ninety days following the finalization of the divorce. In case of temporary marriages, the woman is not entitled to nafaqa during 'idda unless it has been stipulated in the marriage contract.[109] In situations where a woman becomes pregnant, the 'idda period will be automatically extended until the child is born. The rationale behind such strict regulations during 'idda is to ensure that the child's paternity is unquestionable.

The husband is obligated to offer both a place of residence and nafaqa to his wife during the 'idda period. The choice of residence is determined by the agreement of both parties. Should a consensus fail to be reached, the court assumes responsibility to determine the residence after consulting with close relatives. In the absence of relatives, the court will intervene and find a suitable dwelling for the woman.[110] A divorced woman receiving *nafaqa* during the *'idda* period is prohibited from relocating without the husband's consent. If the woman does not remain in the specified place of residence during *'idda,* she forfeits her right to maintenance. A widow or divorcée who forgoes her rights to *nafaqa* during *'idda* can leave her place of residence in order to financially support herself.

CUSTODIANSHIP AND GUARDIANSHIP

Upon the completion of divorce proceedings, settling child custody often becomes the most contentious issue. The Civil Code, in line with traditional Shi'i *fiqh,* distinguishes between *ḥiḍāna* (custodianship) and *wilāya* (guardianship). The custodian is in charge of the child's well-being and upbringing, while the guardian manages the child's financial and civil affairs. Typically, the child's physical custody is taken on by the mother or close maternal relatives, while the guardianship is legally assigned to the father or other paternal male guardians. To transcend these binaries, IIZ advocates for equal contributions from both parents for the well-being of their children, addressing and opposing the conventional gender biases found in existing laws.

Parents have the authority to establish limits for their children and can implement appropriate disciplinary actions when necessary.[111] Should a parent cause harm to the child, they may face penalties. If one of the parents is awarded legal custody, they cannot refuse this obligation. If they do not follow through with their responsibility, the court can transfer the custody of the child to a guardian, a close relative, or the public prosecutor. The responsibility of the parents extends to taking necessary steps to secure quality education for their children.[112] When it comes to infants, the mother is not legally required to nurse the child except in the absence of suitable nutrition.[113] Although Khomeini, along with other Shi'i jurists, encourages women to breastfeed their children,[114] a woman has the right to refuse. In such cases, the man can hire a wet nurse to breastfeed the child.[115] Should the mother choose to breastfeed her child, she is entitled to receive compensation.

According to Shi'i law, children need to be under the protection and supervision of their parents until they reach the age of majority, which is around the time of puberty. According to the Civil Code, the age of majority is nine for girls and fifteen for boys, while the age of maturity is set at eighteen for both genders.[116] In legal terms, the responsibility for children concludes when they attain the age of majority. However, in Iranian culture parents typically care for their children until they achieve maturity. After reaching the age of majority, children can choose which parent they want to reside with following a divorce. In the event that both parents and the child are undecided, the court will deliver the final verdict.

The Family Protection Law of 1967 recognized mothers as guardians, putting them on equal footing with paternal grandfathers in matters of guardianship. However, this law was revoked following the 1979 Islamic Revolution.[117] As per recent legal provisions, the Civil Code permits mothers to retain custody of boys until the age of two and girls until the age of seven.[118] In 2002, following an amendment to Article 1169,[119] a mother's physical custody of her son was extended from two years to seven years. In addition, the courts have been vested with the power to grant custody of children over age seven to the mother if the father is proven to be unfit. The revised legal position contrasts with the traditional views held by most Shi'i 'ulama', who advocate that boys should stay under the mother's care until they are two, and girls until they reach the age of seven.

A mother has the right to retain custody of her children until they reach the age of seven; however, she must also reside in close proximity to the children's legal guardian to enable him to perform his guardianship responsibilities effectively. Should the mother relocate in a way that impedes the father's ability to carry out his duties, she may jeopardize her custodial rights. The parent granted custodianship cannot move outside of the residence designated for the child unless the consent of both parents is obtained.[120] Moreover, a mother who has custody of her children will not be reprimanded or lose custody if she has a full-time job and consequently leaves the children in day care centers during her work hours.

The law stipulates that the parent who does not have physical custody of the child must be granted visitation rights. If disagreement exists about visitation rights, the court can intervene and determine an appropriate time and place for visitation.[121] If a child is with a custodial parent, they cannot be removed unless there are valid reasons.[122] If the mother with custody is diagnosed with a mental illness or gets remarried, the child's custody will be transferred to the father.[123] If the parent who has legal custody passes away, the surviving parent will be left with the responsibility of raising the child.[124]

The Islamic Republic of Iran emphasizes the vital importance of mothers in raising children. However, contemporary guardianship laws do not fully embody this perspective. Following a divorce or the death of her partner, a mother's custodial rights to her children can be notably affected.[125] If the husband dies, the woman is granted custody of her children. However, a woman can assume guardianship roles only if the father or paternal grandfather of the child is no longer alive. If a mother is deemed mentally unfit or decides to remarry, she forfeits her custodial rights. This puts many mothers in a challenging situation where they must decide between their children and their fundamental right to find companionship. However, if the mother's subsequent marriage dissolves or her health conditions ameliorate, she can regain custody.[126]

In 1986, the custody law underwent further revisions. During the Iran-Iraq War (1980–88) many Iranian men lost their lives, resulting in many war widows.[127] Confronted with the tragic loss of their spouses, these widows were determined not to let their children be taken under the custody of their paternal grandfathers.[128] In response to sustained advocacy from these women, Khomeini requested amendment of the custody law to address these concerns. The revised article allowed a war widow to retain custody of her child after her husband's death or even after she remarried. However, the children's paternal family continued to hold their status as the legal guardians. The law's adaptive change is a testament to its responsiveness in critical situations (*ḍarūra*), underscoring its capacity to evolve to support women's rights.

When it comes to child support following a divorce, the father, being the legal guardian, is responsible for the child's financial needs, even if the mother has legal custody. Any inheritance or money the child receives should be used to cover their expenses. If the child's assets do not meet the necessary costs, the financial responsibility falls on the father.[129] If the father refuses to financially support his child, the courts can intervene and impose penalties. If the father is deceased or deemed incapable or unfit to carry out his guardianship duties, the role is passed on to the paternal grandfather or next of kin. If the *walī* is absent or incapable of providing support, the mother assumes this responsibility. In case the mother is incapable of providing for the child, the obligation to care for the child will be left to the maternal grandfather or grandmother.[130] Recent amendments have placed some restrictions on the influence of unfit guardians. If the child's natural guardian is incapacitated or incapable of carrying out his responsibilities, the court has the power to appoint another guardian.[131]

Under Shiʻi law and the Civil Code, the guardianship (*wilāya*) of the father or paternal grandfather is unequivocal. On the other hand, the mother's role in caring (*ḥiḍāna*) for her children, whether it is about custody or visitation rights, is limited and open to discussion. Matters related to the child's property, civil, and financial aspects come under the jurisdiction of the natural guardian or the child's legal representative.[132] The properties of a man who dies come under the control of his father. The paternal grandfather reclaims the guardianship role even when the children are in their mother's custody. This tradition stems from the age-old perception of women being less proficient in dealing with financial matters—a presumption challenged by IIZ.[133]

A woman is not permitted to assume guardianship responsibilities unless this is explicitly stated in the guardian's will or ordered by the court. If the appointed guardian of the child proves incapable of managing the child's assets, the court assigns a financial trustee to aid the guardian.[134] The court also reserves the right to appoint the mother as her children's guardian if she remains unmarried. When a mother undertakes guardianship duties and chooses to remarry, she is obliged to inform the court. However, this action will not necessarily lead to the mother's loss of guardianship. Guardianship remains compulsory until the child reaches the legal age of maturity.

## BREAKING BARRIERS IN DIVORCE RIGHTS: IIZ'S CALL FOR REFORM

IIZ has been proactive in advocating for changes to existing divorce laws, aiming to limit men's unchecked divorce rights and expand the divorce avenues available to women. It has sought to streamline the processes for women seeking *faskh* (judicial divorce) and *khul'* (women-initiated divorce). While the conditions under which women can opt for *faskh* and *khul'* are currently limited, IIZ has lobbied to widen the circumstances where women can apply for these types of divorces. These religious activists believe that the criteria for these divorces should also encompass irreparable differences and cases of psychological abuse.

IIZ has highlighted that while a *khul'* divorce offers women an exit from abusive marriages, the associated compensatory obligation can be formidable, particularly for women from less wealthy backgrounds. For example, a woman might be discouraged from pursuing a *khul'* divorce because of the excessively high compensation she must pay her husband. In certain cases, obtaining a *khul'* divorce may require the wife to relinquish her custody rights.[135] Further complicating matters is the requirement to secure the husband's full agreement, except in dire situations. To address these issues, IIZ activists aim to reduce men's dominance over *khul'* divorces by eliminating the need for the husband's consent in such cases.

By utilizing women's jurisprudence, IIZ offers an alternative interpretation of sacred texts to challenge biased divorce laws that harm women. IIZ asserts that men have historically misused guardianship laws, necessitating significant reforms. By wielding their status as children's guardians, men often manipulate women's apprehensions about losing their children to keep them in abusive marriages.[136] The matter of guardianship usually puts mothers at a disadvantage in divorce cases, as men exploit their guardianship privileges to restrict or deter their wives from ending the marriage. IIZ advocates for equitable divorce legislation that supports women and shields them from detrimental relationships.

Another point of contention taken up by IIZ activists is female guardianship and a woman's capacity to financially support her children while safeguarding the child's assets. Concerns about property and the child's assets fall under the purview of guardianship, legally assigned to the father or paternal grandfather. Such laws are informed by traditional perceptions that view women as less competent in dealing with financial matters. IIZ points out the apparent inconsistency in Islamic legal customs, where women are recognized as competent to oversee their personal assets and properties gained from inheritance and *mahr*, yet are concurrently deemed incapable of managing similar responsibilities for their children. IIZ advocates argue that this disparity directly contradicts Islamic tenets that regard women as autonomous legal individuals.

Through women's jurisprudence, these faith-based activists counter traditionalist and patriarchal interpretations of sacred scripture that have given rise to gender hierarchy and inequality. IIZ has fiercely rejected hadiths that state women should not be anyone's guardian because they are less intelligent than men. Although some assert the authenticity of these hadiths, IIZ does not recognize them, arguing that their ethics go against the central principle of justice found in the Qur'an. These religious activists emphasize the contrast between the Qur'an's depiction of empowered women like Asiya and the Queen of Sheba and the less favorable portrayals of women in certain hadiths. By underscoring the Qur'anic portrayals of women, these activists push for reforms in policies that hinder women from being guardians of their children.

Despite the efforts of IIZ to improve women's legal position, some laws still do not grant women the same rights as men. For example, under Articles 1251 and 1252 of the Civil Code, when a mother remarries, it is interpreted as her showing lack of interest in custody of her children. However, these activists point out, the Civil Code doesn't explain why being a single mother would make a woman more qualified for guardianship. These religious activists believe that such regulations are in conflict with Article 21 of the Constitution, which bases guardianship on a woman's abilities and qualifications. IIZ campaigns to abolish unfair laws that limit women's choices by potentially taking away their custodial rights if they choose to remarry.

The discriminatory nature of divorce laws that impose restrictions on female-initiated divorces has also sparked intense debate among female activists and lawmakers. For instance, the Civil Code asserts that men can divorce their wives whenever they desire, whereas women seeking divorce are required to provide evidence that staying in the marriage will cause them unbearable difficulty and hardship ('usr wa ḥaraj).[137] Drawing from its family paradigm model, IIZ aims to expand women's rights in areas of custodianship and guardianship while emphasizing the significance of social support in lessening the effects of prejudiced laws on Iranian mothers. A central goal of the IIZ is to change laws that uphold an outdated patriarchal perspective on women as inferior and reliant on men for their well-being. These activists note that such androcentric views of women are increasingly out of touch with current realities and have not been effective in reducing the rising divorce rates in Iran.

IIZ cites sources such as data published by Tehran's City Council, which suggests that Iran has an alarmingly high divorce rate. The percentage of divorces in the capital, Tehran, is significantly higher than in other cities in the country.[138] In the Iranian capital, one in four marriages end in divorce. The most recent data reveals that 82 percent of couples applying for consensual divorce in court receive approval in under fifteen minutes. Most of these divorces involve couples aged twenty to thirty. Beyond official divorce figures, there is a prevalent form of separation among middle-aged couples in Iran called "emotional divorce." Studies by sociologists and psychologists suggest that 30 to 50 percent of couples experience significant emotional detachment in their marriages. Unlike a formal divorce, where couples physically and emotionally part ways, an emotional divorce doesn't involve physical separation. This type of strained marital relationship has detrimental effects on the family structure, especially on children.[139]

In a move to curb the escalating rate of divorce, the head of the Women and Family Affairs Center announced the establishment of a committee of experts to address this phenomenon. Specialists argue that in Iran what makes divorce such an alarming issue is not so much the act of divorce itself as its repercussions for women. Women and children often face the harshest aftermath because of inadequate social support systems. IIZ emphasizes the necessity for the government to establish institutions to assist women and children after a divorce. Moreover, the Coalition contends that the government should explore different strategies to fortify the family structure and consequently lower divorce rates.[140]

Despite numerous setbacks, there have been some advances to financially support women after divorce. In situations where the husband initiates the divorce, the woman is entitled to a significant portion of the man's income. Moreover, a law passed by Parliament mandates that unpaid *mahr* be recalculated in line with inflation.[141] Another notable change that Ayatollah Khomeini brought into effect was to grant Parliament the authority to pass legislation based on the Islamic principles of *ḍarūra* (social necessity) and *maṣlaḥa* (expediency), even if it conflicts with Islamic law. Parliament introduced several measures drawing from Khomeini's decrees to address major challenges facing women. One such measure involved amending the marriage contract to include a stipulation that requires the husband to give half of his income from the duration of the marriage to his wife after divorce, provided the wife is not deemed responsible for the divorce.[142] IIZ has also called upon the concepts of *maṣlaḥa* and *ḍarūra* to modify policies deemed discriminatory under the guise of Islam, aiming to uphold the sanctity of marriage and women's dignity.

IIZ remains steadfast in urging the government to amend prevailing policies that discriminate against women, leveraging women's jurisprudence in their advocacy. Facing opposition from conservative religious and political authorities, these faith-based activists consistently push against entrenched socioreligious boundaries. Historically, in Iran, the growing discontent among women over discriminatory state policies and laws has led the government to rethink and modify some of its practices. This adaptation is seen as a forward step for women, who recognize that if they couch their demands in religious terms and intensify pressure on both religious and political leaders, the Islamic Republic of Iran is prepared to adjust its rules.

# Conclusion

*Women's Involvement in the Production
of Religious Knowledge*

This culminating chapter integrates the complex discourse on female religious authority and the impact of faith-based activism on legal institutions and legislative practices in postrevolutionary Iran. The narrative unfolds through the perspective of female faith-based activists, chronicling the progress and challenges they have encountered in their mission to reclaim their roles as religious authorities and activists. Following the Iranian Revolution, the women's movement underwent a notable transformation in its approach toward gender justice. The increasing participation of women in religious discourse, as a consequence of sociopolitical changes, incited a shift in the power dynamic between women, the state, and ʿulamaʾ.

The active involvement of women in the production of religious knowledge caused a dynamic momentum for reform within religious discourse. Their engagement in faith-based activism challenges the assumptions of secular-liberal feminism, which presumes an inherent conflict between women's agency and faith. Through active engagement with sacred scriptures, these women forge knowledge that brings religious rulings into accord with justice, rationality, and their lived experiences. They draw their scholarship from a diverse range of epistemic traditions, thus challenging conventional Islamic legal frameworks. These activists are paving the way for inclusive interpretations of sacred scripture by implementing women's jurisprudence. Their increasing involvement in knowledge production signals a rising tide for reforming gender relations within the Islamic Republic of Iran.

Informed by a broadened societal presence and unique experiences under both the secular rule of the Pahlavi monarchy and the Islamic Republic, IIZ activists acknowledge the limitations of state interventions in fully securing women's rights. They perceive religion as a more potent legitimizing force for women's rights than the modern nation-state, prompting them to engage with their religious tradition. This shift in perspective has catalyzed a significant expansion in women's roles, propelling them into the public sphere and, importantly, the realms of religious institutions and authority.

Within this newly reshaped religious landscape, women's proactive presence within religious institutions has obligated male 'ulama' to engage with their female counterparts in the interpretation of religious texts. This crucial shift has initiated a democratization of these discourses and has expanded women's authority over the interpretation of sacred scripture. Therefore women are empowered to assert their interpretive authority and offer alternative perspectives on issues that affect them. Penetrating traditionally male-dominated spaces has enabled these activists to centralize women's concerns, pressuring religious authorities to address them. These women's presence within religious institutions has not only endowed the state with a degree of legitimacy but also confronted and contested some long-standing patriarchal policies, marking a significant advance in the pursuit of gender justice.

Faith-based activists, through their unwavering determination, have begun to reclaim their authority and reestablish their positions as religious scholars. Their endeavors have had far-reaching implications for societal development and the pursuit of gender justice in Shi'i Iran. Women's rights advocates, exemplified by the likes of IIZ, have strategically deployed their religious knowledge to navigate and reform the legal and political terrains affecting women. They distinguish their approach to gender justice from both secularist and traditionalist perspectives, though they engage with both. Confronting the restrictions set by traditional power structures, they are showing that women's agency and religion are in fact reconcilable. Their work has catalyzed the emergence of a new generation of women to take a comprehensive, inclusive path toward gender justice.

Informed by this rising tide of reform, this chapter describes women's engagement in the production of Islamic knowledge. It underscores the opportunities and obstacles that female activists have encountered in their quest to reestablish their roles as epistemic authorities. It offers an in-depth exploration of these activists' efforts to reestablish themselves within religious discourse, underlining the continuing disparities in women's rights within Islamic law. The chapter draws attention to the transformative impact that IIZ's approach, grounded in women's jurisprudence, has had on legal reasoning and religious institutions in the Islamic Republic of Iran. In recounting the ongoing strides taken toward gender justice, it offers invaluable insights into the continued struggle for equity in a sociopolitical environment deeply rooted in religious traditions.

## THE PATH TO RELIGIOUS AUTHORITY

Gaining the mantle of religious authority within the Shiʿi tradition has historically posed significant challenges for both men and women. Aspiring individuals are required to undergo intensive training in *hawza* (Islamic seminary), and demonstrate proficiency in Islamic jurisprudence before they are permitted to perform *ijtihād* (make legal rulings). Religious authority is achieved by acquiring and demonstrating extensive understanding of Islamic sciences. By accessing such knowledge and by demonstrating their legal astuteness, the ʿulamaʾ have been able to gain the trust of the masses in matters of faith and to build up influence within scholarly networks and the society at large.[1]

The concept of religious authority has undergone considerable evolution and change throughout Islamic history. ʿUlamaʾ spanning both modern and premodern times have failed to reach a consensus on the question of women's eligibility to become *mujtahida*s. Women, however, have made a significant contribution to religious discourse, specifically through the transmission and preservation of Islamic knowledge. Muslim women's involvement in religious scholarly discourse began in the early years of Islam and continued several centuries afterwards. However, over time, women found it challenging to continue to be involved with institutions dedicated to the teaching and development of Islamic sciences. These religious institutions gradually evolved into bastions of exclusivity, becoming increasingly inaccessible to women. Consequently, women were seldom provided with the same opportunities as their male counterparts to make meaningful contributions to Islamic scholarly discourse.[2]

As Islamic scholar Abdulaziz Sachedina observes, even though women were among transmitters of religious knowledge and though "their narratives were accepted as valid documentation for deducing religious rulings, they rarely participated in the intellectual process that produced decrees that had significant influence upon the personal status of women."[3] The landscape of religious discourses was largely dominated by male 'ulama', who often cast doubt on women's intellectual competency to construct independent legal opinions. This mindset—which still holds sway among traditionalist male 'ulama'—historically contributed to restricting women's access to education and limiting their learning to preliminary Qur'anic texts. Islamic seminaries and theological schools, as hubs of religious knowledge, were frequently off-limits for women. This pattern of exclusion also extended to secular education, resulting in a historical impediment to Muslim women's access to both secular and religious education.[4]

Women's access to religious knowledge increased with the advancement of modernity. The reform movements of the nineteenth century caused a decline in the sociopolitical, legal, and educational dominance of the 'ulama', which subsequently allowed laypeople to break into religious scholarly circles. Women interested in pursuing religious education were among the groups that benefited from these changes in society. Gradually the doors of some seminaries and religious educational institutions opened to female students.[5] Although not all religious institutions embraced women as religious scholars, these sociopolitical changes fostered an increased female presence in the public sphere, especially in schools and universities.

## WOMEN'S ACCESS TO EDUCATIONAL INSTITUTIONS

Before the 1979 Iranian Revolution, women had restricted access to religious institutions. One of the few ways of accessing Islamic knowledge was through small-scale religious schools, known as *maktab*s, offering rudimentary religious education. These schools, which usually operated privately, had numerous branches in larger cities across Iran.[6] While certain 'ulama' sought to institutionalize and centralize *maktab*s and other religious establishments, systemic institutionalization of religious seminaries did not commence until Khomeini came to power.[7]

During Reza Shah's rule (1925–41), women officially gained admittance into secular educational institutions. However, the inauguration of women's seminaries took place only after the establishment of the Islamic Republic of Iran. Jami'at al-Zahra, founded in 1985, was one of the first female religious institutions, amalgamating all the informal religious schools and *maktab*s.[8] This progression was nearly unprecedented, marking one of the few instances in the Muslim world where religious institutions were entirely devoted to women's education. Several decades after the establishment of seminaries for women, the religious education of women became widespread, attracting a significant following among the masses. With the gates of religious institutions now open to women, their access to Islamic sciences and institutions underwent a transformative revolution.[9]

The women who attended these seminaries were often from traditionalist and conservative families. Typically such families had prevented girls from entering educational institutions during the Pahlavi era. This was partly because they felt that mixed-gender spaces were unsafe and inappropriate for women,[10] but even the girls' schools that existed at that time were not attended except by girls from elite families.[11] Women aspiring to pursue religious education received private lessons at home. However, the Revolution sparked a cultural shift, making more women from traditional backgrounds inclined to further their education. Khomeini encouraged this with his concept of "educational jihad," urging women to become literate and educated. Policies enacted after the Revolution made higher education more accessible for women, including institutes of higher religious learning, which began accepting female students. The new enforcement of gender segregation in public institutions and the mandate for veiling in public spaces, justified by the state as ways to protect women's dignity and ensure their safety, did much to alleviate conservative families' concerns. Furthermore, the educational curriculum's new focus on Islamic sciences reassured traditionalists of the alignment between women's education and Islamic teachings.[12] Though these measures placed limitations on secular women, they enabled conservative women to participate more freely in the public spaces.[13] Opportunities extended to traditionalist and conservative women, such as members of IIZ, resulted in their faithful support of Khomeini and loyalty to the Revolution. For them, the Pahlavi era's policy of forced unveiling had manifested an Orientalist view of women as submissive and in need of liberation, a view that IIZ opposes. In contrast, the postrevolutionary state, by increasing access to religious institutions for traditional women, transformed their lives, guaranteeing their participation in religious and political affairs.[14]

More than four decades later, approximately 85 percent of Iranian women are literate, a sharp rise from the prerevolutionary figure of around 30 percent. Additionally, over 67 percent of women are now studying to earn a degree in universities and colleges. This shift owes partly to moderated social interaction between genders, creating a sense of safety for families that could not have envisioned an opportunity for their religious girls to be highly educated or active in the workforce. In this changed sociopolitical climate, traditional families have been more willing to send their daughters to universities and into the workforce. With more women pursuing higher education and becoming more visible in public spaces, demands related to women's rights have become more pronounced.

Moreover, the post-Revolution period has seen an increase in women's participation in religious institutions and their contribution to the production of religious knowledge. The sociopolitical shifts facilitated traditional women's involvement in the public sphere, especially in schools and universities. The educational opportunities provided for women encouraged them to enter public spaces while still adhering to traditional female roles. Balancing domestic responsibilities with an active role in civic life has become the norm. However, it is crucial that a woman's active participation in the public sphere does not compromise her familial responsibilities.[15] In these challenging contexts, women have adeptly navigated traditional roles and modern demands. Access to both Islamic and secular sciences has enabled women to identify the roots of structural injustice and has equipped them to challenge existing inequalities by taking part in religious and political discourse.[16] This integrated approach to education has proved particularly effective for the women of IIZ, who have used it to augment their knowledge and subsequently leverage it to contest discriminatory elements within the system.

Efforts to reinterpret religious doctrines with greater inclusivity for women's rights emerged prominently in the twentieth century, as influential intellectuals like Ali Shariati (d. 1977) and religious authorities like Morteza Motahhari (d. 1979) addressed the subject of women's rights and status in Islam. Shariati and Motahhari laid the groundwork for the conceptual framework that defined "the new Muslim woman." The Western-educated Shariati's modernist positions appealed to both intellectuals and women. In his attempts to embrace a sociological reinterpretation of Islam, Shariati presented Fatima, the daughter of Prophet Mohammad, as an exemplary woman and an ideal role model. A strong woman of faith and virtue, Fatima resisted all forms of injustice and oppression and was an activist in her own right. Shariati's rhetoric attracted a growing demographic of young, educated women, leading them to engage with the Islamic movement.[17] This narrative resonated with many women after the Revolution, some of whom became members of IIZ. According to Monique Girgis, Shariati was intent on showing Iranians that Islam is inherently progressive and that women's liberation is a fundamental component of Islamic teachings.[18]

Morteza Motahhari leaned toward a more traditionalist stance toward women's issues. He supported women's sociopolitical and economic activities, provided that they dressed modestly in public spaces.[19] Motahhari was not a supporter of the 1967 Family Protection Law, believing in different responsibilities and rights for men and women due to inherent physical and psychological differences. Yet he stood against practices harmful to women, deeming such traditions inappropriate for the modern era.[20] Despite his critique of antiquated, discriminatory practices, he did not necessarily favor a Western model. Much like Shariati, he offered a modern and revolutionary image of Muslim women by holding up Fatima and Zaynab as role models. As the second half of the twentieth century progressed, leading into the 1979 Revolution, these feminine archetypes formed a foundation for Islamic feminism and faith-based activism.[21] Members of IIZ have strategically used them to bolster their efforts for women's active participation in sociopolitical discourse.

Gender construction through Shi'i female figures like Fatima and Zaynab has helped traditionalist women exert their agency and reconstitute their status as religious authorities. Allowing women to be enrolled in Islamic religious learning institutions, historically monopolized by men, has in turn enabled them to take active part in the intellectual process. Accredited religious institutions such as the *hawza* have facilitated access to Islamic training for women. In contemporary Iran more than 270 schools provide such training, equipping women with the necessary knowledge to engage in reinterpreting sacred Islamic sources.[22]

The concept of women as religious scholars was relatively new among the masses prior to the establishment of women's *hawza*, but the idea that women too could interpret sacred scriptures gained popularity among traditionalists after the Revolution. Khomeini's legitimization of women's interpretive efforts influenced the way traditionalist men perceived traditionalist women.[23] This in turn changed the power dynamic between women, the state, and 'ulama'. Consequently, women's roles were no longer confined to the private sphere. Women's engagement in the public realm and in particular religious institutions brought their issues to the forefront in traditionally male-dominated spheres, forcing religious authorities to address the "women question." Members of IIZ launched their own initiatives, pressing the 'ulama' to reassess patriarchal interpretations of sacred sources.

With their newly acquired Islamic knowledge, women in the *hawza*, irrespective of their religious or ideological inclinations, contested the conventional understanding of female agency and brought women's issues to the center of clerical discourse. The presence of these women in religious institutions challenged some of the state's patriarchal policies while at the same time offering legitimacy to the state. As Amina Tawasil argues in her study of women in *hawza*, by training these women, the religious establishment could counteract the influx of Western ideas about women's rights and counterbalance the rise of secularist women in positions of power who might conform to the geopolitical agendas of Western powers.[24] Yet traditionalist women, despite their loyalty to revolutionary ideals, do not serve merely as ideological mouthpiece for the state. This is in part because women's Islamic seminaries are funded and supported by *waqf* (religious endowments) and private donors.[25]

The women who study in *hawza* come from various social and economic backgrounds. The *hawza* has given them not only the opportunity to be active in the public sphere but also employment opportunities. Female seminaries established after the Revolution offer a formal degree equivalent to a university degree. With these qualifications, most women take up roles as religious studies teachers in schools and universities. Considering that taking religious studies is mandatory for students in schools and colleges, these educators are in high demand. Women who have reached advanced training teach courses in seminaries, courses previously taught by male 'ulama'. The majority of activities and research groups in these religious institutions are led by women, who are gradually gaining recognition as religious authorities.[26]

The *hawza*, with its strong presence in countries such as Iran and Iraq for over a millennium, requires curricula updates to meet the needs of modern society. Female seminaries, on the other hand, established in the past five decades, have more access to resources and knowledge and are better positioned to respond to the needs of contemporary society. Despite the lackluster curricula in the *hawza*, the participation of women in modern religious institutions has transformed the traditional curriculum. As Keiko Sakurai notes in her research on female religious authority, "In addition to basic seminary studies, such as literature, the Qur'an, *fiqh* (Islamic jurisprudence), *usul al-fiqh* (principles of jurisprudence), *akhlaq* (ethics), *kalam* (theology), and *mantiq* (logic), seminaries teach subjects such as 'introduction to the religions,' 'the political system of Islam,' and 'women in Islam.'"[27] The seminaries have offered women different levels of classes where, in order to qualify as a *mujtahida*, the student must complete advanced courses like *dars-i kharij*, which teaches students Islamic jurisprudence. However, these courses are not regularly available to women.[28] The lack of access to these classes is a systemic failure that makes the process of women becoming *mujtahida*s all the more challenging and time-consuming.

Among the *mujtahid*, the highest level of religious authorities are referred to as *marja' al-taqlid* (source to imitate). These religious scholars, who are a source of emulation for Shi'is, hold the authority to derive legal rulings from sacred texts, issue binding religious edicts, and publish work on religious issues. What sets *marja'* apart from other *mujtahid*s is their role as a source of emulation within the Shi'i community. While all *marja'* are *mujtahid*s, it is only the most distinguished who reach the status of *marja'*, granting them the capacity to significantly influence legal and ethical discourse within Islam. The visibility of *mujtahid*s and the nature of their work have sparked debate on whether women can claim the title of *mujtahida*. Although most of the 'ulama' support women's education to become *mujtahida*s, they disagree on whether women should become *marja'*. Some traditionalist 'ulama' reject female authority on sociological and ontological grounds, arguing that positions of authority require mental and physical strength, traits they perceive to be absent in women.[29]

Khomeini, an advocate for women's right to become *mujtahida*s, concurred with this stance. He contended that women could not be *marja'*, since a precondition for becoming a *marja'* is to be male.[30] By such reasoning, women are also barred from becoming judges, despite being encouraged to pursue the highest levels of legal studies. Morteza Motahhari, a leading advocate of women's education and confidant of Khomeini, suggested that while women's intelligence equals that of men, their heightened emotional intelligence hampers their ability to view issues objectively.[31] However, a minority of 'ulama', including Ayatollah Yusuf Sanei, contend that women can hold the same religious and political authority as men. Despite the existence of such a progressive stance, traditionalist 'ulama' continue to prevent women from attaining the title of *marja'*.[32]

Ashraf Boroujerdi, former member of IIZ and the Sociocultural Council for Women and Family Affairs, disputes the traditionalist 'ulama''s stance, arguing that women should indeed be permitted to become *mujtahida*s and judges. She criticizes the patriarchal notion that women are incapable of executing certain responsibilities, citing it as a direct violation of Islamic teachings. Referencing the Qur'an's position that for God virtue holds the highest value, she asserts that Islamic sacred texts do not condone a culture that prevents women from becoming religious and political authorities.[33] Islamic legal rulings concerning women, Boroujerdi argues, are not objective if they do not include Muslim women's perspectives. Faith-based activists like Boroujerdi argue that a comprehensive understanding of gender issues is necessary for issuing just legal rulings.

In a similar vein, Banu Nosrat Begom Amin (d. 1982) broke with tradition to become the first female *mujtahida,* holding *ijāza* (permission to issue legal rulings). Zohreh Sefati, another woman who became a *mujtahida*, has instructed several other renowned female scholars. An occasional collaborator with IIZ, she has founded several religious schools for women, including the Women's Theology School in Qum.[34] Sefati believes that female *mujtahida*s should indeed be allowed to attain the title of *marja' al-taqlid*; otherwise, the very purpose of practicing *ijtihād* is defeated. Sefati maintains that these very traditionalist ideas are discouraging women from becoming *mujtahida*. She proposes that women's issues can be best interpreted by a female religious scholar rather than a male religious authority.[35] She contends that women's unique perspectives and experiences necessitate interpretations from female religious scholars, as male authorities may not fully grasp or address the specific needs of women in their juristic rulings. Sefati states:

> When a *mujtahid* refers to the religious principles, the *mujtahid's* gender makes no difference in judgment. There is no room for personal feelings to interfere with the *mujtahid's* legal opinion. Therefore, having a man's spirit or a woman's spirit has nothing to do with the interpretation of law. However, in case an issue in question is related to women, there is a possibility that a female *mujtahid* might be able to understand, but not feel the issue more clearly than a male *mujtahid,* since she is also a woman. And there is a possibility that a female *mujtahid* might have a different opinion from a male *mujtahid.* But it should be noted that this is not a matter of gender but it depends on the extent of a *mujtahid's* understanding of the issues in question. If a *mujtahid* is well versed in economics, he is more likely to judge economic issues better than a *mujtahid* who is not well versed in economics.[36]

Female religious scholars like Sefati are paving the way for women to engage in religious education and aspire to the rank of *mujtahida,* a critical step toward better addressing women's issues. Currently, women are allowed to achieve the rank of *mujtahid,* but their influence is circumscribed, relegated to assuming the role of *marja'* solely for other women and issuing religious verdicts exclusive to the female population. But Zohreh Sefati and her contemporaries are challenging these restrictions, aiming to expand the scope permitted to female religious scholars.[37]

It was through the interpretive efforts of Zohreh Sefati and faith-based activists such as IIZ that the Guardian Council was persuaded to change the age of marriage from nine to thirteen for girls. Sefati substantiated her arguments through religious sources, differentiating between the ages of religious maturity and conjugal maturity. She proposed that religious maturity for girls should be recognized at age nine, when they become responsible for performing religious obligations such as praying and fasting. Conjugal maturity, however, should be set at thirteen, the age when they reach puberty and are ready to become sexually active. Drawing on women's jurisprudence, Sefati played a crucial role in the Guardian Council's decision to raise the age of marriage for young girls.[38]

This monumental change reflects the transformative power of women's active participation in religious and political institutions in Iran. Their involvement has redefined these traditionally male-dominated spaces. This was in part because the presence of women in such spaces has meant that women's issues can no longer be sidelined. Further, male 'ulama' have had to share religious institutions with their female counterparts, which has inevitably made these spheres more democratic.[39] Women have become integral in the governance and rationalization of Islamic education, thereby consolidating their place within the socioreligious sphere despite resistance from conservative forces.[40] This sustained female presence in traditionally male spaces has resulted in a fragmentation of male authority over religious knowledge, providing a platform for female religious scholars to communicate their teachings to students and the wider public.[41] Access and authority to interpret sacred scripture have created an alternative space where women can reclaim their authority and newly interpret women's issues.

In the past several decades, the notion of religious authority and knowledge has undergone systematic changes in Iran. Currently, there are two forms of religious authority. The first is the official structure, endorsed by religious and political institutions. The second is grassroots oriented, aiming to distance itself from religious establishments and institutionalized power structures.[42] This latter form of religious authority is where we find organizations such as IIZ, which are actively reinterpreting religious texts. These female activists combine various epistemic traditions, moving beyond classic Islamic law to create practices like women's jurisprudence for a broader interpretation of Islamic scripture. This growing participation in knowledge production signifies an emerging trend toward gender reform in religious discourse.

Regardless of their affiliation, these women collectively strive for gender justice. Their conceptualization of gender justice and rights discourse is informed by their lived experiences. Having lived under both the secular reign of the Pahlavi monarchy and the Islamic Republic, these faith-based activists understand that state measures can only partially secure women's rights. They believe that an inclusive approach to women's rights must also engage with religious traditions to fully legitimize them. For these activists, it is Islam, rather than the liberal nation-state, that bestows legitimacy upon women's rights.[43] Even though not all of these religious activists advocate for gender equality, they are all staunch proponents of gender justice through the reinterpretation of religious doctrines. Women in positions of religious leadership are rejecting justifications for gender discrimination enacted in the name of religion.

Women involved in official institutions and grassroots initiatives both aim to achieve gender justice, but with differing approaches. There are differences between women in official religious institutions who, because of the fragility of female authority, uphold conservative opinions and apply traditional jurisprudence, and grassroots religious activists, such as members of IIZ, who are advocating for women's jurisprudence and challenging the lack of female input in generating religious knowledge. But grassroots activists recognize that in order to advance gender justice they need to work within the structures of religious institutions and systems. Their mission is not to disregard traditional jurisprudence; instead, they advocate for a pluralistic approach to jurisprudence, fostering equal opportunities for female scholars to interpret sacred scriptures.

Female religious activists, such as members of IIZ, bring varied degrees of religious training to their roles. Some have been trained in traditional religious institutions like seminaries, others hold university degrees in law and Islamic studies, and many are professionals trained in unofficial religious spaces such as *jalasa* (community study groups). While some of these women define their activism as part of the reformist agenda, others identify themselves as traditionalists. Yet despite their varied educational backgrounds, activism, and political affiliations, they all question the infallibility of religion-based laws that perpetuate discrimination against women.

Grassroots religious activists urge female religious scholars to contribute actively to the creation of religious knowledge. They posit that the predominantly male-dominated production of religious knowledge has created a prevailing gender hierarchy and excluded women from positions of religious authority. IIZ argues that the Qur'an addresses both men and women impartially, not granting any special privilege or supremacy to men in interpreting religious scriptures. As Asma Barlas asserts, the Qur'an encourages all believers, regardless of gender, to deepen their understanding of the sacred texts.[44] Similarly these activists implore Muslim jurists to acknowledge women's experience and gender as epistemic modalities. By emphasizing the lived experience of Muslim women, they challenge policies conflicting with, or failing to reflect, their realities.

The contributions of faith-based activists have been particularly influential concerning the gendered discussion of shari'a. Women's training in Islamic sciences equips them to provide an alternative interpretation of Islamic law. Their religious knowledge and legal acumen have earned them influence and respect within scholarly circles and the broader society. Hence, the demand for justice made by faith-based activists comes from a position of power as they seek an equal platform in the sociopolitical and religious spheres.

Some of these women started their activism by writing for journals and magazines like *Zan-i Ruz, Payam-i-Hajar,* and *Zanan,* popular during the 1990s. These publications played a pivotal role in raising awareness about women's rights issues in Islam and the Iranian legal system, leading to women's increasingly influential intellectual contributions in religious circles.[45] Activists such as A'zam Taleghani, founder of *Payam-i-Hajar,* have written articles on viewing the Qur'an from a gender perspective. They openly challenge patriarchal interpretations of contentious verses, like those about polygyny, by placing them in historical context.[46] Other activists like Shahla Sherkat, the editor-in-chief of *Zanan,* have focused on reinterpreting the shari'a and challenging hegemonic authorities.[47] *Zanan* has also criticized the limitations Iranian women face when exercising their civil rights as religious, political, and judicial authorities.[48] Such writings by faith-based activists are aimed at both religious scholars and the public at large. Their interpretive efforts, publicly accessible to both men and women, pose a challenge to conservative and secular forces. Discussion of alternative interpretations of controversial verses has opened up a dialogue between traditionalist and reformist women as well as between them and male authorities. Pressures from faith-based activists have prompted male 'ulama' to reevaluate a number of discriminatory rulings that adversely affect women and have led to reinterpretation of various religious doctrines through contextualizing and historicizing the Qur'an and hadith.[49] This dialogue has been so influential that some 'ulama' now argue that the state should not prevent women from taking on roles such as judges, heads of the state, or *marja'*.[50]

Women's presence in positions of religious authority has proven to be a deterrent to nonegalitarian rulings. Increasingly, male 'ulama' champion gender egalitarianism and express their supportive stance. But women's involvement in the production of Islamic knowledge does not necessarily lead to egalitarian rulings. A number of female religious scholars are advocates of the more traditional view of complementary roles for men and women. These women, adhering to traditionalist jurisprudence, assert that gender differences translate to different legal rights and responsibilities. Hierarchal rulings are not solely derived from male reasoning; they can also emerge from the interpretation of religious texts and the particular methods of analysis employed. Therefore, women's participation in the production of Islamic knowledge should be assessed within the context of the jurisprudential tradition they propagate.

## PRINCIPLES OF SHI'I JURISPRUDENCE AND TRADITION

Over the years, the different jurisprudential traditions utilized by jurists have directly affected women's legal status. In the Shi'i tradition, the subject of jurisprudence has always been open to interpretation because of its inherent fluidity. This dynamic flexibility offers faith-based activists a platform to reevaluate and debate laws affecting women. *'Aql* (intellect), reinforced by *ijtihād* (legal reasoning), and *'adl* (justice)[51] are two primary principles of Shi'i theology and jurisprudence, with reason and intellect guiding individuals in distinguishing between just and unjust actions. Historically, Shi'i 'ulama' have employed rational criteria to make religious rulings and ethical judgments, understand sacred scripture, and conceptualize God. This tradition views God as just, and removed from the possibility of committing any acts of injustice, since injustice would be a sign of God's imperfection. Thus the doctrine of justness is regarded by Shi'i 'ulama' as the quintessence of all Islamic teachings and the cornerstone of legal precepts.

In the Shi'i tradition, what is perceived as essential by reason is also deemed necessary by revelation. This correlation has allowed Shi'i jurists to derive varying religious rulings on issues not explicitly addressed in sacred sources like the Qur'an, the Sunna of the Prophet, and the teachings of Shi'i imams.[52] While the 'ulama' concur on the importance of human rationality in discerning right from wrong, they have yet to reach a consensus on the degree to which rationality influences the act of interpreting religious scripture. Despite these varying opinions, the Shi'i 'ulama''s views have always been respected, fueling the vitality and dynamism of Shi'i jurisprudence.

Reformist religious leaders uphold the Shi'i ideals of justice and rationality, arguing that these principles should underpin religious edicts. Guided by the conviction that God would never wrong his creations and that any ruling against divine justice is void, these reformists work to revise legal rulings that lead to injustice. Female religious activists like IIZ follow this reformist tradition.

Indeed, the cultivation of intellect and justice in Shi'i jurisprudence has created a normative sphere where female faith-based activists debate sociolegal policies.[53] Shi'i jurisprudence and hermeneutics evolve in response to changing societal norms, such as economic realities and the education of women. These shifts prompt religious authorities and policymakers to reinterpret Islamic scripture in order to reform women's legal status.[54] Changing norms, coupled with economic obligations and inflation, have impelled women to actively participate in public life and have compelled Shi'i 'ulama' to modify their traditional jurisprudential methods to align with the contemporary realities.

Reformist 'ulama' like Mohsen Kadivar believe they have exhausted all options within traditional Islamic jurisprudence to address the rights of modern women.[55] Kadivar asserts that traditional jurisprudence falls short of effectively addressing the needs of a modern society.[56] According to him, the inconsistencies that arise out of the conflict between modern perceptions of rights and traditional Islamic jurisprudence highlight the need for new jurisprudence that can better address the complexities of the modern world.[57]

In Iran, the reformist movement was informally initiated by the founder of the Islamic Republic of Iran, Ayatollah Khomeini, and though it had humble beginnings and was initially ostracized, it gradually gained traction among religious scholars and the public. Since the 1990s, progressive reformist views have permeated the ranks of reformist 'ulama' and activists.[58] Consequently, debates between traditionalist and reformist 'ulama' and intellectuals have intensified in recent years. While traditionalists have dominated the field of Islamic knowledge and religious institutions in Iran, reformists have been progressively influencing the realm of legal tradition.[59]

The need for innovative legal frameworks to address contemporary issues in Iranian society has sparked a revival of a more dynamic approach to jurisprudence. In Iran, there are at present two predominant types of jurisprudence: traditional and reformist. Traditional jurisprudence, supported by a majority of 'ulama', prioritizes conventional precepts over human rationality and justice. Adherents of traditionalist jurisprudence limit the use of reasoning to cases that have not been addressed by previous jurists or texts. In contrast, reformist jurisprudence acknowledges the need to adapt to evolving social conditions and is inherently more dynamic. This strand, supported by reformist 'ulama' and faith-based activists, aims to revive the legal pluralism of the Islamic tradition, exemplifying the intellectual but tradition-bound movement of contemporary Iranian jurisprudential thought.

Several distinguishing factors set the reformists apart from the more traditionalist jurists. First, they advocate for jurisprudence to adopt an epistemology that incorporates science and rationalism. Second, they are driven by a desire to use dynamic jurisprudence to foster a more egalitarian and modern understanding of Islamic legal tradition. Central to their mission is the reformation of legal rulings concerning gender justice, which is at the heart of this movement.[60] Moreover, reformist 'ulama' address issues fundamental to the modernization of Muslim societies. They have pioneered a dynamic jurisprudence in Shi'i Iran, integrating traditional Islamic methodologies with human reason and justice and advocating for indigenous reformation within the Shi'i tradition.

The pluralistic nature of reformist approach is also reflected in the efforts of IIZ to advance a women's jurisprudence that seeks a refreshed interpretation of shari'a, taking into account factors such as the real-life experiences of women. In their quest, these activists merge modernity with tradition, and feminism with faith-driven activism, envisioning a gender justice that respects both contemporary values and enduring traditions. When IIZ members advocate for a revision of Islamic legal rulings, they do so in a way that signifies their religious commitment. These faith-based activists critique hierarchical rulings employed by male jurists, arguing that legal rulings related to women should be deemed invalid if they neglect the perspectives of female jurists. IIZ further emphasizes that reliance on historical legal rulings may be entirely unfounded or, even if valid, may no longer apply because of contextual and temporal changes. While shari'a is seen as indisputable because of its status as divine law, human understanding of it is fallible and open to amendment through a complex interplay of theological, legal, moral, and empirical reasoning.[61] For these activists, women's jurisprudence serves as a tool to align religious edicts more closely with the principles of gender justice.

The dynamic nature of Shi'i jurisprudence, as highlighted by faith-based activists, seeks to pave the way for the reinterpretation of Islamic rulings. These activists, represented by groups like IIZ, see women's jurisprudence as an effective tool for achieving legal reform in contemporary Iran. They argue for a departure from traditional views that deem shari'a laws immutable, instead emphasizing the use of *ijtihād* as a means to produce new legal rulings. These activists caution that if traditionalists maintain their strict adherence to conventional paradigms, refusing to adapt to changing societal realities, they risk becoming obsolete in the face of modern societal demands.[62]

For members of IIZ, the traditional interpretation of Islamic law, which has inadvertently cultivated a gender hierarchy and been integrated into modern legal systems, no longer aligns with the realities of today's society. These activists challenge the orthodox interpretations of the Qur'an by male jurists, advocating a transition from literal interpretation toward the ethical teachings of the scripture. With their efforts rooted firmly in the principles of Islam, these women aim to instigate reform within the realm of Islamic law, not just as a societal necessity but also as a religious imperative. Accordingly, Islamic law should stand as a testament to Islamic values like justice and dignity while also authentically reflecting the experiences of contemporary Iranian women. In the works of these faith-based activists, a significant shift in Shi'i legal theory is discernible. This shift is characterized by prioritization of the Qur'an, the application of the principles of justice and reason to discern principles of law, and an acknowledgment of the context-specific nature of previous laws. These principles collectively form activists' primary interpretive tools in their mission to amend discriminatory legal rulings.

In their pursuit of greater rights for women, the proponents of women's jurisprudence have met with considerable resistance from the advocates of traditional jurisprudence. This opposition, however, has not deterred them. They argue that applying traditional rulings to contemporary issues not only causes undue hardship but also is contrary to the core message of the Qur'an. These activists urge scholars to focus on the Qur'anic messages and principles in light of evolving social, economic, and political conditions. While addressing the contentious issue of women's rights in Islam, they argue that principles of humanity and justice must be prioritized in Islamic rulings. To ensure sustainable and effective change, they assert the importance of disentangling patriarchal structures from Islamic principles. The main challenge for activists like the women in IIZ is to reform the Islamic legal system in a manner that is neither patriarchal nor secular.

Faith-based activists in IIZ are seeking to shift the legal paradigm, traditionally distorted by male norms, and make it more inclusive and balanced by incorporating women's perspectives and experiences. They challenge the practicality of traditional jurisprudential methods without entirely dismissing them and offer an alternative methodology within the broader Islamic intellectual tradition. By giving primacy to human intellect, upholding the principle of justice, incorporating a female perspective, and contextualizing revelation, these faith-based activists are advancing change within the confines of the Shi'i tradition.

Faith-based activists reinterpret sacred texts to further women's rights causes. They adopt a dynamic perspective, considering the viewpoints of nonreligious experts, such as psychologists and sociologists, when addressing religious rulings. This stands in contrast to traditionalist scholars, who oppose the integration of non-Islamic knowledge and norms when issuing legal rulings.[63] Despite facing opposition from traditionalists, faith-based activists seek to harmonize Islamic legal traditions with contemporary legal needs, aiming to update women's legal standing in light of changing sociopolitical and economic circumstances.

Faith-based activists enhance their engagement in hermeneutic projects by utilizing women's jurisprudence as a means to critique gender hierarchy and articulate a more inclusive understanding of gender roles. Their interpretation of Islam substantially deviates from the inflexible understanding of gender constructs promoted by traditionalist 'ulama'. Embracing a more inclusive stance toward women's agency within existing norms, faith-based activists offer an alternative that transcends the perspectives presented by secular feminists. Their approach to achieving gender justice embodies the contemporary women's movement in Iran, which is distinctively neither secular nor feminist. Rather, its vision of gender justice is grounded in an Islamic framework, arising authentically from within the community and not perceived as secular, Western, or externally imposed.

The post-Revolution era witnessed an unprecedented shift in Iran's modern history, with traditional women gaining access to religious knowledge and thereby altering the power dynamic between the state, women, and 'ulama'. Women previously marginalized in the Pahlavi era found themselves empowered and actively involved in the country's social, political, and religious institutions. These women continue to create opportunities by engaging in domains historically dominated by men. Their participation has been transformative both for these women and for the institutions they inhabit. Realizing the transformative potential of education in enhancing living conditions—including achieving financial independence, delaying marriage, selecting marital partners, and securing reproductive autonomy—women from traditional backgrounds increasingly have begun to see education as a beacon of hope and opportunity.[64]

## FAITH-BASED ACTIVISM AND THE REVERBERATIONS OF CHANGE

Since the 1979 Revolution, women's religious activism in Iran has undergone three distinct phases in relation to the state. The initial phase, spanning from the years preceding the Revolution until the 1990s, can be categorized as "conformist." During this phase, female religious activists categorically supported the state's gender policy and often defended the political and religious establishment. Given their experience of persecution and marginalization under Pahlavi rule, these activists were hesitant to challenge the postrevolutionary state's policy toward women. The second phase emerged after the Iran-Iraq War and persisted until 2005. Characterized as "revisionist," this phase witnessed a growing disillusionment among religious women as they started to question state policies affecting women and became more actively involved in civil society organization and politics. The third phase, commencing in 2005 and extending to the early 2020s, can be characterized as "pragmatist." In this period, women from various ideological and political backgrounds have formed coalitions in their effort to advance women's causes. These women have acknowledged that uniting and equipping themselves with necessary religious knowledge to challenge discriminatory laws are key to addressing their concerns. IIZ has been a pioneering organization in this movement.

The distinct phases of women's activism in post-Revolution Iran reflect the determined efforts of faith-based activists to advance women's rights within the framework of their faith. The heightened awareness that has emerged through over four decades of activism has fostered a unique gender consciousness among religious Iranian women. As evidenced in Iran, manifestations of political Islam have created a space where modern Muslim women can embrace the cause of gender justice without feeling that they have compromised their religion or heritage.[65] Faith-based activists' approach differentiates itself from secularism while simultaneously challenging the constraints imposed by the traditionalists in positions of power.

Although Western scholarship, particularly during the 1980s, has presented a binary view of religious and secular activism in postrevolutionary Iran, the reality on the ground offers different stories. The faith-based activists involved in IIZ have succeeded in disrupting this dichotomy and blurring the line between secular and Islamist activism. While a number of prominent feminists maintain that the theocratic nature of the postrevolutionary state has sidelined women, faith-based activists argue that the dynamic nature of the Shi'i tradition has led to the emergence of a new level of awareness on gender justice in Iran. Having been actively involved in the Revolution and subsequently in women's rights movements, faith-based activists have the means to mobilize and penetrate religious and political domains. Armed with extensive legal and religious knowledge, women's rights activists disrupt nonegalitarian interpretations of sacred scriptures.[66]

Among the unique privileges held by faith-based activists is their inherent shield against accusations of being antireligious. That is an indictment often levied against secular activists, who, despite their hard work on women's rights from the start of the twentieth century, were perceived as being Westernized and un-Islamic by the masses and later by the state. Indeed, secular feminists in Iran kept the conversation on women's rights issues alive until religious activists were ready to engage with the inner workings of the system. Faith-based activists have succeeded in strategically distancing themselves from accusations of being un-Islamic, while simultaneously challenging the Orientalist narrative that labels Islam as incompatible with modernity.

For these Iranian women, with their increasing gender consciousness, the answer to whether shari'a law and gender justice can coexist in modern Iran is an emphatic yes. Legal anthropologist Ziba Mir-Hosseini frames this discourse within the context of a more prominent intellectual and ideological struggle between followers of a rigid understanding of Islam that clings to traditional jurisprudence and proponents of a more flexible Islam, not only tolerant but actively adapting to meet the needs of individuals in a modern society.[67] She posits that, in contemporary Iran, individuals willing to interpret Islamic texts differently hold the potential to effect meaningful change.

One influential method employed by faith-based activists in fostering change is a gendered reading of sacred scriptures. These activists assert that, like any other form of knowledge, religious knowledge is contingent on those who produce it, influenced by their biases, their errors, and the sociopolitical context of its production. Female faith-based activists argue that many historical and religious mandates restricting women to traditional roles stem from misinterpretations of religious scriptures derived from patriarchal structures. They assert that while some of these regulations might have been justifiable within specific cultural and contextual confines, their relevance has since diminished, necessitating considerable reform. Recent years have seen faith-based activism lead to more egalitarian interpretations of Islam, particularly regarding women's legal standing. Consequently, a number of 'ulama' and prominent political figures are reconsidering their conservative views on women's issues. Emboldened by their religious knowledge, these women publicly challenge the 'ulama' and the state, advocating for amendments in biased legal rulings affecting women.

The gendered interpretation of Islamic law is changing because of the reciprocal influence exerted by women, 'ulama', and the state on each other. Pressure from IIZ has compelled both conservative political and religious authorities to reassess existing inequalities and to appease their demands. The coexistence of moderate and conservative positions has empowered faith-based activists to employ the interpretive framework provided by the Shi'i tradition to contest conservative hegemonic structures. IIZ's use of rationality and ethical principles in their reinterpretation of religious texts has granted them greater flexibility in adopting alternative viewpoints. These activists exemplify the vibrant community of religious authorities advocating an indigenous reformation within the Shi'i tradition.

In Iran, the dynamic relationship among women, 'ulama', and the state continues to evolve as IIZ activists participate in production of religious knowledge, advocating for an inclusive interpretation of religious texts. For these faith-based activists, women's jurisprudence has opened a normative space within which the state policies and social practices affecting women can be debated and contested. IIZ activists understand that successfully advancing women's rights necessitates grounding those rights in Shi'i tradition and Islamic jurisprudence rather than secular ideals. These female activists strive to promote women's jurisprudence to foster an egalitarian culture that recognizes women's rights and prohibits gender discrimination. Incorporating women's lived experiences in their interpretive endeavors, these activists contribute toward the democratizing of the production of religious knowledge.

IIZ's participation in faith-based activism serves as a response to the discrimination faced by women and is crucial in deconstructing traditional paradigms and renegotiating gender roles in contemporary Iran. IIZ maintains that achieving gender justice in Iran is most effectively approached through a religious framework. Faith-based activists from diverse epistemic traditions are addressing prejudicial laws and regulations affecting women's legal status, and in doing so, they are striving to reassert their authority and reclaim their positions as political and religious authorities. The participation of female scholars in the Islamic tradition and Muslim societies has profound implications for societal development and gender justice. Women's faith-based activism and their contributions to religious knowledge have influenced legal and political institutions as well as the nature of lawmaking in Shiʻi Iran. Pressure from groups like IIZ has compelled the state to reconsider some policies contributing to gender hierarchy and inequality to placate these increasingly vocal challengers.

# Notes

## INTRODUCTION

1. In Islamic legal terminology, *ijtihād* refers to reasoning by an expert in Islamic law to find a solution to a legal question and produce or justify a legal judgment.

2. For more on idealizations of women's activism, see Lila Abu-Lughod, "The Romance of Resistance: Tracing Transformations of Power through Bedouin Women," *American Ethnologist* 17, no. 1 (1990): 208–26.

3. Richard Martin and Abbas Barzegar, *Islamism: Contested Perspectives on Political Islam* (Stanford, CA: Stanford University Press, 2010), 87–90.

4. Margot Badran, *Feminism in Islam: Secular and Religious Convergences* (Oxford: Oneworld Publications, 2009).

5. Valentine M. Moghadam, "Rhetorics and Rights of Identity in Islamist Movements," *Journal of World History* 4, no. 2 (1993): 243–64, www.jstor .org/stable/20078562.

6. Leila Ahmed, *Women and Gender in Islam: Historical Roots of a Modern Debate* (New Haven, CT: Yale University Press, 1992), 154.

7. Tooran Valimorad, "Majlis Tahqiq va Tafahhus az Muavinati Zanan-i Riasati Jumhuri ra Kilid Bizanad," *Shabaka-yi Iran Zanan*, July 20, 2020, http://iranzanan.com/2170/.

8. Orthodox Sunnite scholars, unlike their Shiʿite counterparts, believed that the "gate of *ijtihād*" had been closed since the fourth/tenth century. Although there are debates as to whether the "gate of *ijtihād*" has been fully closed, within the orthodox Sunni tradition scholars have not reached a consensus on this issue. Whereas the early advocates of *ijtihād* worked within an Islamic framework, today's reformists combine knowledge of Islamic learning and scripture with secular training.

9. Ziba Mir-Hosseini, "Muslim Women's Quest for Equality: Between Islamic Law and Feminism," *Critical Inquiry* 32, no. 4 (2006): 637.

10. Ziba Mir-Hosseini, "Religious Modernists and the 'Woman Question': Challenges and Complicities," in *Twenty Years of Islamic Revolution: Political and Social Transition in Iran since 1979*, ed. Eric Hooglund (Syracuse, NY: Syracuse University Press, 2002), 74–95.

11. Ziba Mir-Hosseini, *Islam and Gender: The Religious Debate in Contemporary Iran* (Princeton, NJ: Princeton University Press, 1999).

12. Saba Mahmood, *Politics of Piety: The Islamic Revival and the Feminist Subject* (Princeton, NJ: Princeton University Press, 2005); Lara Deeb, *An Enchanted Modern: Gender and Public Piety in Shi'i Lebanon* (Princeton, NJ: Princeton University Press, 2006).

13. Deeb, *Enchanted Modern*, 8.

14. Dale Eickelman and Jon W. Anderson, *New Media in the Muslim World: The Emerging Public Sphere* (Bloomington: Indiana University Press, 2003), 2.

15. Israt Turner-Rahman, "Consciousness Blossoming: Islamic Feminism and Qur'anic Exegesis in South Asian Muslim Diaspora Communities" (PhD diss, Washington State University, 2009).

16. Abu-Lughod, "Romance of Resistance," 47.

17. Abu-Lughod, "Romance of Resistance," 41–45.

18. Mahmood, *Politics of Piety*, 31.

19. Mahmood, *Politics of Piety*, 198.

20. Mahmood, *Politics of Piety*, 28.

21. Lila Abu-Lughod, ed., *Remaking Women: Feminism and Modernity in the Middle East* (Princeton, NJ: Princeton University Press, 1998).

22. Mahmood, *Politics of Piety*.

23. Sussan Siavoshi, "Islamist' Women Activists: Allies or Enemies?," in *Iran: Between Tradition and Modernity,* ed. Ramin Jahanbegloo (Lanham, MD: Lexington Books, 2004), 170.

24. Siavoshi, "'Islamist' Women Activists," 170.

25. Siavoshi, "'Islamist' Women Activists," 170.

26. The concept of female agency has been extensively discussed in Mahmood's *Politics of Piety,* 34–35.

27. See also a discussion of this issue in Abu-Lughod, "Romance of Resistance."

28. Zakia Salime, *Between Feminism and Islam: Human Rights and Sharia Law in Morocco* (Minneapolis: University of Minnesota Press, 2011).

29. Mir-Hosseini, "Religious Modernists," 77.

30. Judith E. Tucker, *Women, Family, and Gender in Islamic Law* (New York: Cambridge University Press, 2008), 7.

31. Arzoo Osanloo, *The Politics of Women's Rights in Iran* (Princeton, NJ: Princeton University Press, 2009), 1.

32. Osanloo, *Politics of Women's Rights,* xiv.

33. Sandra Harding, *Whose Science? Whose Knowledge? Thinking from Women's Lives* (Ithaca, NY: Cornell University Press, 1991); Dorothy Smith, *The Everyday World as Problematic: A Feminist Sociology* (Boston: Northeastern University Press, 1987).

34. Tucker, *Women, Family, and Gender,* 19.

35. Rudy Busto, "Pujando pero llegando: Rasquache Religious Thought and Scriptures," paper presented at the Transdisciplinary Theological Colloquium, New Knowing in Latina/o Philosophy and Theology, Drew University, Madison, NJ, 2008.

36. Sandy Jones, "God's Law or State's Law: Authority and Islamic Family Law Reform in Bahrain" (PhD diss., University of Pennsylvania, 2010), 10.

37. In Iranian politics, *Principlist* refers to conservative supporters of the Supreme Leader of Iran who advocate for protecting the "principles" of the Islamic Revolution's early days. The Iranian Principlists are a heterogeneous group, with divisions into conservatives, and pragmatists.

## CHAPTER I. WOMEN'S ACTIVISM

1. Mona Tajali's work also discusses how traditionalist women leverage their access to power to advocate for women's rights. See "Notions of Female Authority in Modern Shi'i Thought," *Religions* 2, no. 3 (2012): 449–68.

2. The term *shifting identification* was used by Kirin Narayan, "How Native Is a 'Native' Anthropologist?," *American Anthropologist* 95, no. 3 (1993): 671–86.

3. Jami'a-yi Zaynab (Zaynab Society) is a traditionalist women's organization established to pave the way for women's political activism and support their direct involvement in the political process.

4. Masserat Amir-Ebrahimi, "Transgression in Narration: The Lives of Iranian Women in Cyberspace," *Journal of Middle East Women's Studies* 4, no. 3 (October 2008): 89–115.

5. For more on women's experience in postrevolutionary Iran, see Ziba Mir-Hosseini, "Sharia and National Laws in Iran," in *Sharia Incorporated: A Comparative Overview of the Legal Systems of Twelve Muslim Countries in Past and Present,* ed. Jan Michiel Otto (Leiden: Leiden University Press, 2010), 319–71.

6. Amina Tawasil, "Towards the Ideal Revolutionary Shi'i Woman: The Howzevi (Seminarian), the Requisites of Marriage and Islamic Education in Iran," *Hawwa* 13, no. 1 (2015): 99–126.

7. Siavoshi, "'Islamist' Women Activists."

8. Seyyed Mohammad Hosseini Beheshti (1929–81) was an Iranian jurist, philosopher, cleric, and politician who was known as the second person in the political hierarchy of Iran after the Revolution. He was the main architect of the Constitution and the administrative structure of the Islamic Republic of Iran.

9. The "Imam's share" is one-fifth of the acquired wealth of Muslims. Shi'i imams would receive these funds from the public and use them to reinforce Islam, build mosques, libraries, and schools, and assist people.

10. Maryam Behroozi, personal interview, 2008.

11. "Mashru'-i Muzakirat-i Majlis-i Shuray-i Islami", June 27, 1992, cited in Siavoshi, "Islamist' Women Activists," 18–19.

12. Behroozi, personal interview, 2008.

13. Valimorad, personal interview, 2008.

14. Valimorad, personal interview, 2012.

15. Soheila Zolodarzadeh, "Girdhamayi Itilaf-i Islami-yi Zanan," Shabaka-yi Iran Zanan, accessed October 13, 2014, but since removed from website, www.iranzanan.com/first_point/004353.php.

16. Tajali, in "Notions of Female Authority," has also mentioned similar strategies employed by Iranian women to entice the state to reform discriminatory laws.

17. Fariba Adelkhah, *Being Modern in Iran,* trans. Jonathan Derrick (London: Hurst, 1999), 105–38.

18. Zahra Shojaei, personal interview, 2008.

19. Valimorad, personal interview, 2014.

20. Shadi Mokhtari, *The Search for Human Rights within an Islamic Framework in Iran* (Oxford: Blackwell, 2004), 475.

21. Tawasil, "Towards the Ideal Revolutionary Shi'i Woman," has reached a similar understanding regarding women involved in Iranian seminaries.

22. Kecia Ali, *Sexual Ethics and Islam: Feminist Reflections on Qur'an, Hadith, and Jurisprudence* (Oxford: Oneworld, 2006), 133.

23. Samaneh Oladi Ghadikolaei, "Women's Religious Authority in Shi'i Tradition: A Quest for Justice," in *Multi-religious Perspectives on a Global Ethic: In Search of a Common Morality,* ed. Myriam Renaud and William Schweiker (London: Routledge, 2020), 46–58.

24. A similar argument has been made by Amina Wadud in her book *Qur'an and Woman: Rereading the Sacred Text from a Woman's Perspective* (New York: Oxford University Press, 1999).

25. Valimorad, personal interview, 2021.

26. For a detailed analysis of women's interpretation of the Adam and Eve narrative, consult Siavoshi, "'Islamist' Women Activists." For more on Qur'an and gender hierarchy, refer to Breanna Ribeiro, "Islamic Feminism: A Discourse of Gender Justice and Equality" (PhD diss., Linfield College, 2014).

27. Valimorad, personal interview, 2021.

28. For more information on the topic of equality in the Qur'an, see Karen Bauer, "The Male Is Not Like the Female (Q 3:36): The Question of Gender Egalitarianism in the Qur'an," *Religion Compass* 3, no. 4 (2009): 637–54.

29. Fadak was a fertile piece of land from northern Arabia that came under Muslim control after the Battle of Khaybar. Shi'is believe Prophet Muhammad left the land to his daughter Fatima. But after the Prophet's death, the first caliph Abu Bakr confiscated Fadak, which led to a lifelong dispute over who was the legitimate owner of the land.

30. Valimorad, personal interview, 2012.

31. Masoomeh Ebtekar, "Tahlil-i Mafhum-i Rijal," Shabaka-yi Iran Zanan, accessed November 3, 2013, but since removed from website, www.iranzanan.com/first_point/004325.php.

32. Ali Shariati, *Fatimah Fatimah ast* (Tehran: Bunyad-i Shariati, 2001), 79. See also Bizaa Zaynab Ali, "Contemporary Karbala Narratives and the Changing Gender Dynamics in Shi'i Communities," Columbia Academic Commons, 2011, https://academiccommons.columbia.edu/doi/10.7916/D87S7WZ3.

33. Shariati, *Fatimah Fatimah ast*; Ali, "Contemporary Karbala Narratives."

34. Deeb, *Enchanted Modern*. See also Abir Hamdar, "Jihad of Words: Gender and Contemporary Karbala Narratives," *Yearbook of English Studies* 39, no. 17 (2009): 98.

35. Khaled Abou El Fadl, *Speaking in God's Name: Islamic Law, Authority, and Women* (Oxford: Oneworld, 2001).

36. *Hadith* refers to a collection of Islamic traditions containing sayings attributed to Prophet Muhammad that is revered and received as a major source of guidance.

37. The translation of verse 4:34 provided in this book is by Abdullah Yusuf Ali (d. 1953). He is the author of the most popular Qur'an translation in the English language. Abdullah Yusuf Ali, *The Holy Qur'an: Text, Translation and Commentary*, De Luxe ed. (Washington, DC: Islamic Center, 1978). Parenthetical and bracketed interpolations are both the translator's.

38. This issue has also been raised by Barbara Stowasser in her book *Women in the Qur'an, Traditions, and Interpretations* (Oxford: Oxford University Press, 1996).

39. For more on misinterpretations of the Qur'an, see Asma Barlas, *"Believing Women" in Islam: Unreading Patriarchal Interpretations of the Qur'ān* (Austin: University of Texas Press, 2002).

40. Hamid Mavani, in his article "Paradigm Shift in Twelver Shi'i Legal Theory (*uṣūl al-fiqh*): Ayatollah Yusef Saanei," *Muslim World* 99, no. 2 (2009): 335–55, mentions that reformist 'ulama' such as Ayatollah Sanei also argue for giving precedence to the Qur'an over hadith.

41. *Nahj al-Balagha,* comp. al-Sharif al-Radi, trans. Sayed Ali Reza (Rome: European Islamic Cultural Center, 1984), 204.

42. Mavani, "Paradigm Shift."

CHAPTER 2. THE INTERSECTION OF LAW,
THE STATE, AND WOMEN'S ACTIVISM IN IRAN

1. John Esposito, *Islam: The Straight Path* (New York: Oxford University Press, 1991), 75.

2. John Esposito, *Women in Muslim Family Law* (Syracuse, NY: Syracuse University Press, 1982).

3. Lynn Welchman, *Women and Muslim Family Laws in Arab States: A Comparative Overview of Textual Development and Advocacy* (Amsterdam: Amsterdam University Press, 2007), 12.

4. Tucker, *Women, Family, and Gender,* 223.

5. Jones, "God's Law," 4. Jones is drawing from Wael B. Hallaq, "Juristic Authority vs. State Power: The Legal Crises of Modern Islam," *Journal of Law and Religion* 19, no. 2 (2004): 243–58.

6. Jones, "God's Law."

7. Zohreh T. Sullivan, "Eluding the Feminist, Overthrowing the Modern? Transformations in Twentieth-Century Iran," in *Remaking Women: Feminism and Modernity in the Middle East,* ed. Lila Abu-Lughod (Princeton, NJ: Princeton University Press, 2015), 215–42.

8. Afsaneh Najmabadi, "(Un)Veiling Feminism," in *Secularisms,* ed. Janet Jakobsen and Ann Pellegrini (Durham, NC: Duke University Press, 2008), 39–57.

9. Najmabadi, "(Un)Veiling Feminism."

10. Najmabadi, "(Un)Veiling Feminism."

11. Ervand Abrahamian, *Iran between Two Revolutions* (Princeton, NJ: Princeton University Press, 1982); Abbas Amanat, "Constitutional Revolution; Intellectual Background," in *Encyclopaedia Iranica*, online ed., 1992, www.iranicaonline.org/articles/constitutional-revolution-i.

12. Mehrangiz Kar, "Iran's Constitutional Obstacles to Realizing Human Rights and Democracy," part 2, *Muftah* magazine, 2010, http://muftah.org/345/, site no longer accessible.

13. Muhammad Qasim Zaman, *The Ulama in Contemporary Islam: Custodians of Change* (Princeton, NJ: Princeton University Press, 2002).

14. Amanat, "Constitutional Revolution."

15. Ann K. S. Lambton, *Qajar Persia: Eleven Studies* (London: I. B. Tauris, 1987).

16. Amanat, "Constitutional Revolution."

17. Amir Arjomand, "The Ulama's Traditionalist Opposition to Parliamentarianism, 1907–1909," *Middle Eastern Studies* 17, no. 2 (1981): 174–90.

18. Amanat, "Constitutional Revolution."

19. Vanessa Martin, *Islam and Modernism: The Iranian Revolution of 1906* (London: I. B. Taurus, 1989).

20. Amanat, "Constitutional Revolution."

21. F. Adamiyat, *Fikr-i Azadi wa Muqaddama-yi Nahzat-i Mashrutiyyat,* Tehran, 1340/1961, cited in Vanessa Martin, "Constitutional Revolution: Events," in *Encyclopaedia Iranica*, vol. 6, fasc. 2 (London: Encyclopaedia Iranica Foundation, 1992).

22. Leila Seradj, "'Upsetting the Idea of Centuries': The Origins of the Women's Movement in Iran, 1850–1925" (MA thesis, Tufts University, 2013).

23. Janet Afary, *The Iranian Constitutional Revolution, 1906–1911: Grassroots Democracy, Social Democracy and the Origins of Feminism* (New York: Columbia University Press, 1996).

24. Kar, "Iran's Constitutional Obstacles," part 3.

25. Laurence Lockhart, "The Constitutional Laws of Persia: Outline of Their Origin and Development," *Middle East Journal* 13, no. 4 (1959): 372–89.

26. Marianne Boe, *Family Law in Contemporary Iran: Women's Rights Activism and Shari'a* (London: I. B. Tauris, 2015), 135.

27. Hamideh Sedghi, *Women and Politics in Iran: Veiling, Unveiling, and Reveiling* (New York: Cambridge University Press, 2007); Martin, "Constitutional Revolution: Events."

28. Ali Shamim, *Iran during the Qajar Monarchy: The Thirteenth Century and the First Half of the Fourteenth Century* (Tehran: Zar Yab, 2008).

29. M. Khodadad, *The Role of Women in the Constitutional Revolution* (Tehran: Farhang-i Iliya, 2008); Sedghi, *Women and Politics,* 44.

30. Parvin Paidar, *Women and the Political Process in Twentieth-Century Iran* (Cambridge: Cambridge University Press, 1995), 67–68.

31. Z. Afarai, *Iranian Women's Forum in Constitutional Revolution,* trans. J. Usefiyan (Tehran: Banoo, 1998).

32. Badr al-Muluk Bamdad, *From Darkness into Light: Women's Emancipation in Iran,* trans. F. R. C. Bagley (Hicksville, NY: Exposition Press, 1977), 47–48.

33. Nikki Keddie and Yann Richard, *Roots of Revolution: An Interpretive History of Modern Iran* (New Haven, CT: Yale University Press, 1981).

34. Louise Halper, "Law and Women's Agency in Post-revolutionary Iran," *Harvard Journal of Law and Gender* 28 (2005): 85.

35. S. Maknun, *Feminism in Iran* (Tehran: Office of Human Science Research Center, 2000).

36. Ervand Abrahamian, *A History of Modern Iran* (New York: Cambridge University Press, 2008), 92.

37. Robin Wright, *The Last Great Revolution: Turmoil and Transformation in Iran.* (New York: Random House, 2010).

38. Akhavi Shahrough and Sussan Siavoshi, "Iran," in *The Oxford Encyclopedia of the Islamic World,* January 2012, www.oxfordreference.com/display/10.1093/acref/9780197669419.001.0001/acref-9780197669419-e-199?rskey=kekfHf&result=196.

39. J. Miklos, *The Iranian Revolution and Modernization,* National Security Essay Series 83–2 (Washington, DC: National Defense University Press, 1983), 25, https://apps.dtic.mil/sti/tr/pdf/ADA131627.pdf.

40. Shahrough and Siavoshi, "Iran."

41. Azadeh Kian, "Gendered Khomeini," in *A Critical Introduction to Khomeini,* ed. Arshin Adib-Moghaddam (Cambridge: Cambridge University Press, 2014), 180.

42. Naser Yeganeh, "Civil Code," in *Encyclopaedia Iranica,* online ed., 1991, www.iranicaonline.org/articles/civil-code.

43. A. Saleh, "Quwwa-yi Muqannana wa Quwwa-yi Qazaiyyah," in Iranshahr, vol. 2, ed. Kumisiyun-i Milli-yi Yunisku (UNESCO) dar Iran. (Tehran, 1964), 956–1013, cited in Yeganeh, "Civil Code."

44. The authoritative Shi'i texts include al-Muhaqqiq al-Hilli's *Shara'i' al-Islam* and Shahid al-Thani's *Sharh al-Lum'a al-Dimashqiyya*; see Najm al-Din Ja'far b. al-Hasan al-Muhaqqiq al-Hilli, *Shara'i' al-Islam fi Masa'il al-Halal wa al-Haram,* 2nd ed., 2 vols. (Tehran: Intisharat-i Istiqlal, 1409 AH); *Al-Rawda al-Bahiyya fi Sharh al-Lum'a al-Dimashqiyya* (Qum: Daftar-i Tablighat-i Islami-yi Howza-yi 'Ilmi-yi Qum, 1412 AH).

45. Mir-Hosseini, "Sharia and National Laws," 318–71.

46. Akbar Aghajanian, "Divorce in Modern Persia," in *Encyclopaedia Iranica,* vol. 7, fasc. 4, 443–48, and vol. 7, fasc. 5, 449–51 (London: Encyclopaedia Iranica Foundation, 1995).

47. Seyedeh Nosrat Shojaei et al., "Women in Politics: A Case Study of Iran," *Journal of Politics and Law* 3, no. 2 (September 2010): 257–68.

48. Mir-Hosseini, "Sharia and National Laws," 352.

49. Sen McGlinn, "Family Law in Iran," unpublished manuscript, University of Leiden, 2001.

50. McGlinn, "Family Law in Iran"; Mir-Hosseini, "Sharia and National Laws," 352.

51. Halper, "Law and Women's Agency," 85.

52. Mir-Hosseini, "Sharia and National Laws," 339.

53. Seradj, "'Upsetting the Idea of Centuries.'"

54. Homa Hoodfar, *The Women's Movement in Iran: Women at the Cross-roads of Secularization and Islamization* (Grabels Cedex, France: Women Living Under Muslim Laws, 1999).

55. Mehrangiz Kar, *Crossing the Red Line: The Struggle for Human Rights in Iran* (Costa Mesa, CA: Blind Owl Press, 2007).

56. Paidar, *Women and the Political Process.*

57. Majid Mohammadi, *Judicial Reform and Reorganization in 20th Century Iran: State-Building, Modernization, and Islamicization* (New York: Routledge, 2008); Boe, *Family Law.*

58. Minoo Moallem, *Between Warrior Brother and Veiled Sister: Islamic Fundamentalism and the Politics of Patriarchy in Iran* (Berkeley: University of California Press, 2005).

59. Nima Naghibi, *Rethinking Global Sisterhood: Western Feminism and Iran* (Minneapolis: University of Minnesota Press, 2007).

60. *Kashf-i hijab* (unveiling) was a decree issued by Reza Shah in 1936 requiring that women be unveiled in public and that any religious symbols like the hijab be forcibly removed from women's heads.

61. Sullivan, "Eluding the Feminist," 216.

62. Halper, "Law and Women's Agency," 122.

63. Najmabadi, "Unveiling Feminism."

64. Anna-Chaido Aloumani, "Changing Role of Women in Iran" (MA thesis, University of Kansas, 2006).

65. Louis Beck and Guity Nashat, *Women in Iran: From 1800 to the Islamic Republic* (Chicago: University of Illinois Press, 2004), 65.

66. Kian, "Gendered Khomeini."

67. Shojaei et al., "Women in Politics."

68. Shojaei et al., "Women in Politics."

69. Hamid Enayat, "Political Participation of Women in Iran: A Sociological Study" (PhD diss., Panjab University, Chandigarh, 2001).

70. Maknun, *Feminism in Iran,* 189.

71. Paidar, *Women and the Political Process*; Kian, "Gendered Khomeini."

72. Halper, "Law and Women's Agency," 103.

73. Paidar, *Women and the Political Process,* 5–6; Halper, "Law and Women's Agency," 214.

74. Halper, "Law and Women's Agency," 134.

75. ʿAlī ibn Abi Talib was the cousin and son-in-law of Muhammad and is considered the first Shiʿite imam.

76. Raymond Anderson, "Ayatollah Ruhollah Khomeini, the Unwavering Iranian Spiritual Leader," *New York Times,* June 4, 1989.

77. Homa Omid, *Islam and the Post-revolutionary State of Iran* (London: Palgrave Macmillan, 1994), 62.

78. Jeffrey Usman, "The Evolution of Iranian Islamism from the Revolution through the Contemporary Reformers," *Vanderbilt Journal of Transnational Law* 35, no. 5 (2002): 1686.

79. Hamid Algar, *Constitution of the Islamic Republic of Iran* (Berkeley, CA: Mizan Press, 1980), 8.

80. Said Amir Arjomand, "Civil Society and the Rule of Law in the Constitutional Politics of Iran under Iranian President Mohammad Khatami," Iran Chamber Society, 2000, www.iranchamber.com/government/articles/civil_society_politics_iran_khatami.php.

81. Naser Katouzian, *Godar-i bar Inqilab-i Iran.* (Tehran, 1981), 168; Said Amir Arjomand, "Constitution of the Islamic Republic," in *Encyclopedia Iranica,* online ed., 1992, https://iranicaonline.org/articles/constitution-of-the-islamic-republic.

82. Arjomand, "Constitution of the Islamic Republic."

83. Arjomand "Constitution of the Islamic Republic."

84. Kar, "Iran's Constitutional Obstacles," part 4.

85. Asef Bayat, *Making Islam Democratic: Social Movements and the Post-Islamist Turn* (Stanford, CA: Stanford University Press, 2007).

86. The book was published by Ayatollah Montazeri's office in Qum and has also been made available on his website: Husayn Ali Montazeri, *Hukumat-i Dini va Huquq-i Insan* (Qum: Arghavan-i Danish, 2008). www.amontazeri.com/farsi/frame4.asp.

87. Bahman Keshavarz, "Guardian Council May Approve Citizenship Rights Charter," International Campaign for Human Rights in Iran, January 2, 2014, www.iranhumanrights.org/2014/01/bahman-keshavarz/.

88. Article 11.

89. Article 54.

90. Article 83.

91. Article 103.

92. Asghar Schirazi, *The Constitution of Iran: Politics and the State in the Islamic Republic* (London: I. B. Tauris, 1997).

93. The Islamic penal code and personal status law underwent substantial change.

94. Halper, "Law and Women's Agency," 117–20.

95. Ziba Mir-Hosseini, "Women and Politics in Post-Khomeini Iran: Divorce, Veiling and Emerging Feminist Voices," in *Women and Politics in the Third World*, ed. Haleh Afshar (London: Routledge, 1996), 142–45; Halper, "Law and Women's Agency," 101.

96. Ziba Mir-Hosseini, *Marriage on Trial: A Study of Islamic Family Law: Iran and Morocco Compared* (London: I. B. Tauris, 1993); Halper, "Law and Women's Agency," 101.

97. Nikki Keddie, "Women in Iran since 1979," *Social Research: An International Quarterly* 67, no. 2 (Summer 2000): 405–38.

98. Mohsen Sadr, *Khatarat-i Sadr-al-Ashraf* (Tehran: Vahid, 1985), 211–14.

99. In the Islamic tradition a *mahr* is a gift made by the groom to the bride at the time of the marriage contract.

100. Kian, "Gendered Khomeini."

101. Mustafa Muhaqqiq-Damad, *Barrasi-yi Fiqhi-yi Huquq-i Khanavada* (Tehran: Markaz-i Nashr-i Ulum-i Islami, 1986)

102. Ziba Mir-Hosseini, "When a Woman's Hurt Becomes an Injury: Hardship as Grounds for Divorce in Iran," *HAWWA (Journal of Women of the Middle East and the Muslim World)* 5, no. 1 (2007): 111–26.

103. Mir-Hosseini, "Sharia and National Laws," 356.

104. Mir-Hosseini, "Sharia and National Laws," 356.

105. Kian, "Gendered Khomeini," 181.

106. Ruhollah Mousavi Khomeini, sermon in Qum, April 27, 1979, *Payam-i Zan,* no. 3 (1992): 39.

107. Ruhollah Mousavi Khomeini, sermon, September 19, 1979, in *Sahifa-yi Nur* (Tehran: Sazman-i Madarik-i Farhangi-yi Inqilab-i Islami, 1989), 11:136.

108. Ruhollah Mousavi Khomeini, sermon, February 1, 1979, in *Sahifa-yi Nur,* 7:120.

109. Kian, "Gendered Khomeini," 181.

110. Moallem, *Between Warrior Brother and Veiled Sister.*

111. Kian, "Gendered Khomeini," 182.

112. Ruhollah Mousavi Khomeini, sermon in Tehran, March 16, 1981, in *Sahifa-yi Nur,* 14:130; Kian, "Gendered Khomeini," 182.

113. Ruhollah Mousavi Khomeini, declaration issued March 12, 1982, in *Sahifa-yi Nur,* 17:211.

114. Kian, "Gendered Khomeini," 182.

115. Ruhollah Mousavi Khomeini, sermon to a group of women in Qum, March 7, 1980, in *Sahifa-yi Nur,* 5:177, cited in Kian, "Gendered Khomeini," 182.

116. Ruhollah Mousavi Khomeini, sermon in Shemiran, July 12, 1980, in *Gozidah-ha-yi az Maqalat-i Payam-i Hajar,* no. 1 (Tehran: Jami'at-i Zanan-i Inqilab-i Islami, 1982). 6, 77; Kian, "Gendered Khomeini," 182.

117. Mir-Hosseini, "Muslim Women's Quest."

118. Mir-Hosseini, "Muslim Women's Quest."

119. Sullivan, "Eluding the Feminist," 232.

120. Ruhollah Mousavi Khomeini, sermon, December 7, 1978, in *Sahifa-yi Nur,* 4:34; Kian, "Gendered Khomeini."

121. Sullivan, "Eluding the Feminist," 224.

122. Kian, "Gendered Khomeini," 188.

123. Kian, "Gendered Khomeini," 188.

124. Nikki Keddie, *Modern Iran: Roots and Results of Revolution* (New Haven, CT: Yale University Press, 2006), 292–94.

125. Tara Povey and Elaheh Rostami-Povey, eds., *Women, Power and Politics in 21st Century Iran* (Farnham, Surrey: Ashgate, 2012).

126. Keddie, *Modern Iran,* 292–94.

127. Mir-Hosseini, "Muslim Women's Quest," 629–45.

128. Kian, "Gendered Khomeini," 190; Mahsa Shekarloo, "Iranian Women Take On the Constitution," *Middle East Report Online* 21 (2005), https://merip.org/2005/07/iranian-women-take-on-the-constitution/.

129. Mir-Hosseini, "Sharia and National Laws," 340.

130. Shahindokht Molaverdi, personal interview, 2014.

131. Roksana Bahramitash, "Iranian Women during the Reform Era (1994–2004): A Focus on Employment," *Journal of Middle East Women's Studies* 3, no. 2 (2007): 86–109.

132. Article 41 of the Iranian Constitution.

133. Valimorad, personal interview, 2014.

134. Elahe Koulaei, "Manshur-i Huquq-i Shahrvandi be Huquq-i Zanan Tavajjuh-i Kafi Namikunad," Shabaka-yi Iran Zanan, accessed December 30, 2016, but since removed from website, www.iranzanan.com/first_point/005093.php.

135. Koulaei, "Manshur-i Huquq-i Shahrvandi."

136. Valentine Moghadam, "Women in the Islamic Republic of Iran: Legal Status, Social Positions, and Collective Action," paper presented at the conference "Iran after 25 Years of Revolution," Woodrow Wilson International Center for Scholars, Washington, DC, 2004, 16–17, www.wilsoncenter.org/sites/default/files/media/documents/event/ValentineMoghadamFinal.pdf.

137. Mir-Hosseini, "Sharia and National Laws," 318–71.

## CHAPTER 3. ITILAF-I ISLAMI-YI ZANAN AND THE FAMILY LAW CONTROVERSY

1. In her work "God's Law," Jones similarly explores the dynamic interplay between religious scholars, female activists, and the state in shaping family law in Bahrain.

2. Boe, *Family Law*.

3. Anwar Zainah, *Wanted: Equality and Justice in the Muslim Family* (Selangor, Malaysia: Musawah, 2009), 180.

4. Zainah, *Wanted*, 181.

5. Ezzat Sadat Mir Khani, "Buhran-i Hoviyat dar Vahid-i Khanavada," Shabaka-yi Iran Zanan, accessed May 18, 2009, but since removed from website, www.iranEIZ.com/first_point/001691.php.

6. Valimorad, personal interview, 2014.

7. Tucker, *Women, Family, and Gender*, 38–82.

8. Shahla A'zazi, personal interview, 2008.

9. A'zazi, personal interview, 2008.

10. A'zazi, personal interview, 2008.

11. Valimorad, personal interview, 2014.

12. Tucker, *Women, Family, and Gender*, 7.

13. Rema Hammami, "Gender Equality and Muslim Women: Negotiating Expanded Rights in Muslim Majority and Immigrant Contexts," in *Development and Equity: An Interdisciplinary Exploration by Ten Scholars from Africa, Asia and Latin America*, ed. Dick Foeken et al. (Leiden: Brill, 2014), 123.

14. For more on the limitations of the gender equality model, see Hammami, "Gender Equality," 122.

15. Anver Emon, "The Paradox of Equality and the Politics of Difference: Gender Equality, Islamic Law and the Modern Muslim State," in *Gender and Equality in Islamic Law: Justice and Ethics in the Islamic Legal Tradition*, ed. Lena Larsen et al. (London: I. B. Tauris, 2013), 237–58.

16. On this point, see also the Oslo Coalition on Freedom of Religions or Belief, "Justice through Equality: Building Religious Knowledge for Reform of Muslim Family Laws," report on the Oslo Coalition's Muslim Family Law project, Norwegian Centre for Human Rights, University of Oslo, May 2013, www.iknowpolitics.org/en/knowledge-library/report-white-paper/justice-through-equality-building-religious-knowledge-legal.

17. "People, be mindful of your Lord, who created you from a single soul, and from it created its mate, and from the pair of them spread countless men and women far and wide; be mindful of God, in whose name you make requests of one another. Beware of severing the ties of kinship: God is always watching over you" (Qur'an 4:1).

18. Ezzat Sadat MirKhani, "Khanavada dar Buhran," Shabaka-yi Iran Zanan, accessed May 7, 2010, but since removed from website, www.iranEIZ com/first_point/001691.php.

19. Qur'an 9:70; 10:44; 29:40; and 30:9.

20. For more on patriarchal reading of the Qur'an, see Barlas, *"Believing Women in Islam."*

21. A similar argument has been made by Ribeiro, "Islamic Feminism."

22. On this point, see also Margot Badran, "Between Secular and Islamic Feminism: Reflections on the Middle East and Beyond," *Journal of Middle East Women's Studies* 1, no. 1 (2005): 6–28.

23. Arzoo Osanloo, "From Status to Rights: The Shifting Dimensions of Women's Affairs and Family Law in Iran," in *Feminist Activism, Women's Rights and Legal Reform,* ed. Mulki Al-Sharmani (London: Zed Books, 2014), 128.

24. Boe, *Family Law.*

25. Mir-Hosseini, *Marriage on Trial.*

26. Osanloo, "From Status to Rights," 134.

27. Osanloo, *Politics of Women's Rights.*

28. Osanloo, "From Status to Rights," 136.

29. Boe, *Family Law,* 63.

30. Family Protection Bill, 2007.

31. Introduction to Family Protection Bill, 2007.

32. Mir-Hosseini, "Sharia and National Laws," 357.

33. Molaverdi, personal interview, 2008.

34. Valimorad, personal interview, 2008.

35. Tooran Valimorad, "Itilaf-i Islami-yi Zanan 'alayh-i Maddah 23 Qanun-i Hamayat-i Khanavada," Shabaka-yi Iran Zanan, accessed March 4, 2009, but since removed from website, www.iranEIZ.com/first_point/001634 .php.

36. Tooran Valimorad, "Ta'yin-i Mujazat dar Layih-yi Jadid-i Hamayat az Khanavada," Shabaka-yi Iran Zanan, accessed May 12, 2010, but since removed from website, www.iranEIZ.com/first_point/002159.php.

37. Arzoo Osanloo, "From Status to Rights: The Shifting Dimensions of Women's Affairs and Family Law in Iran," in *Feminist Activism, Women's Rights and Legal Reform,* ed. Mulki Al-Sharmani (London: Zed Books, 2014), 126.

38. Valimorad, personal interview, 2009.

39. Valimorad, personal interview, 2009.

40. Tooran Valimorad, "Janjal Piramun-i Maddah-yi 23 Layih-yi Hamayat az Khanavada," Shabaka-yi Iran Zanan, accessed January 29, 2010, but since removed from website, www.iranEIZ.com/first_point/001634.php.

41. Itilaf-i Islami-yi Zanan, "Namah bi Ra'is-Jumhur az Zanan-i Jumhuri-Khah," Shabaka-yi Iran Zanan, accessed January 16, 2010, but since removed from website, www.iranEIZ.com/point_of_view/cat_7/001914.php.

42. Osanloo, "From Status to Rights," 137.

43. Tooran Valimorad, "Haq-i Talaq-i Zanan Hamchanan Hal-nashudah Baqi-mandah ast," Shabaka-yi Iran Zanan, accessed October 2, 2012, but since removed from website, www.iranEIZ.com/first_point/002124.php.

44. Valimorad, personal interview, 2012.

45. A *mujtahida* is a female religious authority who has reached the highest level of religious authority and can perform *ijtihād* and issue a legal decree (fatwa).

46. Valimorad, personal interview, 2012.

47. Itilaf-i Islami-yi Zanan, "Lavayih-i Janjali dar Qanun-i Hamayat az Khanavada Nabayad Tasvib Shavad," Shabaka-yi Iran Zanan, accessed May 1, 2010, but since removed from website, www.iranEIZ.com/first_point/001763.php.

48. Valimorad, personal interview, 2008.

49. Maryam Behroozi, "Pishnahadat barayi Eslah-i Qanun-i Hamayat az Khanavada," Shabaka-yi Iran Zanan, accessed August 3, 2010, but since removed from website, www.iranEIZ.com/point_of_view/cat_6/001759.php.

50. Boe, *Family Law,* 70.

51. Shahindokht Molaverdi, "Kastiha-yi Qanun-i Hamayat az Khanavada," Shabaka-yi Iran Zanan, accessed November 4, 2012, but since removed from website, www.iranEIZ.com/first_point/002195.php.

52. Partners who engage in temporary marriage must predetermine the terms and duration of the contract. A married man can enter a temporary marriage with multiple women, while a woman is limited to having one temporary partner at a time.

53. In Islamic law *diya* is the financial compensation paid to the victim or their heirs in cases of murder, bodily harm, or property damage.

CHAPTER 4. ISLAMIC FAMILY LAW AND GENDER POLITICS

1. Mir-Hosseini, *Marriage on Trial,* 31.

2. Schirazi, *Constitution of Iran,* 166–69.

3. McGlinn, "Family Law in Iran."

4. Qur'an 4:3.

5. Civil Code, Article 1034.

6. *Idda* is a period of waiting where a woman remains celibate after separating from her husband in order to ensure that she is not pregnant.

7. Muhammad ibn Isma'il al-Bukhari, *Sahih al-Bukhari*, vol. 7, bk. 62, *Al-Nikah* (Cairo: Al-Azhar, 1989).

8. Shahid al-Awwal [Muhammad b. Makki al-Jizzini al-'Amili], *Al-Lum'a al-Dimashqiyya fi Fiqh al-Imamiyya* (Beirut: Dar al-Turath al-Islami, 1410 AH), 2:85.

202 | Notes to Pages 110–115

9. Shahid al-Thani [Zayn al-Din al-Juba'i al-'Amili], *Masalik al-Afham fi Shara'i' al-Islam* (Qum: Mu'assasat al-Ma'arif, 1416 AH).

10. Civil Code, Article 1035.

11. Civil Code, Article 103.

12. Civil Code, Article 1040.

13. M. A. Ansari-Pur, "Iran," in *The Yearbook of Islamic and Middle Eastern Law*, vol. 4 (London: Kluwer Law International, 1997–98), 242; Family Protection Bill, Article 23.

14. Najm al-Din Ja'far b. al-Hasan al-Muhaqqiq al-Hilli, *Shara'i' al-Islam fi Masa'il al-Halal wa al-Haram*, 2nd ed., 2 vols. (Tehran: Intisharat-i Istiqlal, 1409 AH), 2:495, nos. 20–22.

15. Cited in Mir-Hosseini, *Islam and Gender,* 252.

16. Civil Code, Article 1210.

17. Civil Code, Article 1041.

18. Abu 'Ali Muhammad b. Ahmad b. al-Junayd al-Katib al-Iskafi (4th c. AH) believed that a mother and a maternal grandmother could also assume the role of wali. Cited in Shahid al-Thani, *Al-Rawda al-Bahiyya fi Sharh al-Lum'a al-Dimashqiyya* (Qum: Daftar-i Tablighat-i Islami-yi Huwza-yi 'Ilmi-yi Qum, 1412 AH), vol. 2; hereafter *Sharh al-Lum'a al-Dimashqiyya.*

19. al-Muhaqqiq al-Hilli, *Shara'i' al-Islam*, 2: 504, nos. 93-94.

20. Muhammad bin al-Hasan bin 'Ali bin al-Husayn al-Hurr al-'Amili, *Wasa'il al-Shi'a*, vol. 14, "Bab al-Nikah," hadith 9 (Tehran: Islamiyah, 1376 AH).

21. al-Hasan ibn Yusuf ibn al-Mutahhar al-Hilli, *Mukhtalaf al-Shi'a fi Ahkam al-Shari'a*, 10 vols. (Qum: Markaz-i Tahqiqat-i Ulum-i Islami, 1991), 7:141–42.

22. I. K. A. Howard, "Mut'a Marriage Reconsidered in the Context of the Formal Procedures for Islamic Marriage," *Journal of Semitic Studies* 20, no. 1 (1975): 84–85.

23. Abu Ja'far Muhammad Ibn al-Hasan al-Tusi, *al-Tibyan fi Tafsir al-Qur'an*, 10 vols. (Beirut: Dar Ihya' al-Turath al-Arabi, 1409 AH); Sayyad Muhammad Kazim Yazdi, *'Urwa al-Wuthqa*, 2 vols. (Sayda: Matba'at 'Irfan, 1348–49 AH), 2:361; al-Hasan ibn Yusuf ibn al-Mutahhar al-Hilli, *Tadhkirat al-Fuqaha'* (Tehran: al-Maktabat al-Murtadawiyya, 1388 AH), vol. 2.

24. Abu Ja'far Muhammad Ibn al-Hasan al-Tusi, *Al-Nihaya fi Mujarrad al-Fiqh wa-al-Fatawa*, trans. Mohammad-Taqi Danishpazhuh, 2 vols. (Tehran, 1964).

25. Shahid al-Thani, *Masalik al-Afham*, 1:358.

26. Ruhollah Mousavi Khomeini, *Risalah Tawdih al-Masa'il* (Tehran: Intisharat Ilmi, 1981), question 2376; Ruhollah Mousavi Khomeini, *Tahrir al-Wasilah*, 2 vols. (Najaf: Dar al-Kutub al-'Ilmiyyah, 1390 AH), 2:254.

27. Civil Code, Article 1071.

28. Civil Code, Article 1072.

29. Civil Code, Article 1074.

30. According to Article 1062, marriage takes place by proposal and acceptance in words that explicitly convey the intention of marriage.

31. Under Islamic law a guardian has the power to give his children in marriage without their consent until they reach the age of puberty. This right of coercion is known as *jabr*.

32. Khomeini, *Risalah Tawdih al-Masa'il*, question 2375.

33. McGlinn, "Family Law in Iran."

34. Civil Code, Article 1070.

35. Valimorad, personal interview, 2019.

36. Sayyidah Zahra Iftikharzadih, "Tajrubi-yi Zisti-yi Zanan dar Izdivaj-i Zudhingam," *Pazhuhisnamah-yi Madadkari-yi Ijtimai*, no. 3 (Spring 2015): 109–56.

37. Shahindokht Molaverdi, "Chalish-ha-yi Pish Ruy-i Layiha-yi Hamayat az Khanavada," Shabaka-yi Iran Zanan, accessed January 7, 2011, but since removed from website, www.iranzanan.com/first_point/002195.php.

38. Article 1041 of the Civil Code states that "marriage of girls before reaching the age of thirteen and boys before reaching the age of fifteen is subject to the permission of the guardian and on condition of taking the child's best interest into consideration and approval of the relevant court."

39. Zohreh Sefati, "Niyazmand-i Baznigari va Islah-i Ahkam-i Fiqhi-yi Banuvan Hastim," Shabaka-yi Iran Zanan, April 3, 2021, http://iranzanan.com/2996/.

40. Mir-Hosseini, *Islam and Gender*, 182.

41. al-Muhaqqiq al-Hilli, *Shara'i' al-Islam*, 2: 493, nos. 13–15.

42. Ayatollahs Sistani, Motahhari, and Khomeini have issued a verdict stating that for a divorce to be valid, it needs to be performed in the presence of two witnesses.

43. Article 1064.

44. al-Hilli, *Tadhkirat al-Fuqaha'*, 2:582; Muhammad Hasan ibn Baqir Najafi, *Jawahir al-Kalam fi Sharh Shara'i al-Islam* (Najaf: Dar al-Kutub al-Islamiya, 1377 AH), 29:141.

45. Yazdi, *'Urwa al-Wuthqa*.

46. McGlinn, "Family Law in Iran."

47. Tucker, *Women, Family, and Gender*, 50.

48. Boe, *Family Law*.

49. al-Hilli, *Mukhtalaf*, 7:163–66.

50. Khomeini, *Tahrir al-Wasilah*, 2:302.

51. Sayyid Muhammad-Sa'id al-Tabataba'i al-Hakim, *Minhaj al-Salihin*, (Najaf, 1365 AH), 2:305.

52. Civil Code, Article 1128.

53. Article 1068.

54. Article 1069.

55. Qur'an 4:4; 2:237; 4:24.

56. This hadith is cited in Seyed Mostafa Malihi et al., "The Ability and Financial Commitment of the Husband in Payment of Dowry," *Journal of Social Issues and Humanities* 2, no. 3 (March 2014): 172.

57. Ziba Mir-Hosseini, "Tamkin: Stories from a Family Court in Iran," in *Everyday Life in the Muslim Middle East*, 2nd ed., ed. Donna Lee Bowen and Evelyn A. (Bloomington: Indiana University Press, 2002), 136, 138.

58. Najafi, Jawahir al-Kalam, 31:107–8; Shahid al-Thani, *Sharh al-Lum'a al-Dimashqiyya*, 2:100.

59. Shahid al-Thani, *Sharh al-Lum'a al-Dimashqiyya*, 2:100.

60. Khomeini, *Tahrir al-Wasilah*, 2:300, question 14.

61. Burhan al-Din 'Ali ibn Abi-Bakr al-Marghinani, *al-Hidaya: Sharh Bidayat al-Mubtadi,* 4 vols. (Cairo: Dar al-Salam, 2000), 2:489–90.

62. al-Hilli, *Mukhtalaf,* 7:178–79.

63. Civil Code, Article 1091.

64. Civil Code, Article 1093.

65. Civil Code, Article 1094.

66. al-Hurr al-'Amili, *Wasa'il al-Shi'a,* vol. 14, "Bab al-Mahr," secs. 48, 49, and 50.

67. Civil Code, Article 1095.

68. al-Hurr al-'Amili, *Wasa'il al-Shi'a,* vol. 14, "Bab al-Mut'a," sec. 4; Najafi, *Jawahir al-Kalam,* 30:162.

69. Najafi, *Jawahir al-Kalam,* 30:166.

70. al-Hilli, *Mukhtalaf,* 7:149.

71. Khomeini, *Risalah Tawdih al-Masa'il,* question 2420.

72. Shahid al-Thani, *Masalik al-Afham,* 1:421.

73. Shahid al-Thani, *Masalik al-Afham,*1:421.

74. al-Hilli, *Mukhtalaf,* 7:153–54.

75. Muhammad Baqir Majlisi, *Bahar al-Anwar* (Tehran: Islamiyah, 1376 SH), 103:349.

76. Malihi, "Ability and Financial Commitment," 172.

77. Boe, *Family Law.*

78. Mir-Hosseini, *Marriage on Trial,* 73.

79. Mir-Hosseini, *Marriage on Trial,* 81.

80. Jamila Hussain, *Islam: Its Law and Society*, 2nd ed. (Sydney: Federation Press, 2004), 94–96.

81. Mir-Hosseini, *Marriage on Trial,* 81.

82. Asad Allah Jolaei, "Azadi-yi 67 Hezar Zindani-yi Ghayr-i Amd," *Alef* magazine, February 2013, http://old.alef.ir/vdccsoqsm2bqmx8.ala2.html?17txt.

83. al-Tusi, *al-Nihaya,* 497–502.

84. Tucker, *Women, Family, and Gender,* 57.

85. Howard, "Mut'a Marriage Reconsidered," 82–92.

86. al-Tusi, *al-Nihaya,* 498.

87. Mir-Hosseini, *Marriage on Trial,* 162–91.

88. Civil Code, Articles 1075 to 1080.

89. Shahla Haeri, "Temporary Marriage: An Islamic Discourse on Female Sexuality in Iran," *Social Research* 59, no. 1 (1992): 75–102.

90. Shahla Haeri, "Mota," in *Encyclopaedia Iranica,* online ed., 2005, https://iranicaonline.org/articles/mota.

91. Khomeini, *Risalah Tawdih al-Masa'il,* questions 2421 and 2423.

92. Tucker, *Women, Family, and Gender,* 58.

93. al-Hurr al-'Amili, *Wasa'il al-Shi'a,* 14:458.

94. al-Hurr al-'Amili, *Wasa'il al-Shi'a,* vol. 14.

95. Khomeini, *Tahrir al-Wasilah,* 2:290; al-Hasan ibn Yusuf ibn al-Mutahhar al-Hilli, *Tahrir al-Ahkam* (Mashhad: Mu'assasat Al al-Bayt, 1985), 2:26.

96. Shahid al-Thani, *Sharh al-Lum'a al-Dimashqiyya,* 2:88.

97. Civil Code Article, 1076.

98. Civil Code Article, 1077.

99. Tucker, *Women, Family, and Gender,* 58.

100. Article 1095.

101. Civil Code, Article 1097; Khomeini, *Risalah Tawdih al-Masa'il,* question 2431.

102. Khomeini, *Risalah Tawdih al-Masa'il,* question 2422.

103. Article 1096.

104. Haeri, "Mota."

105. Khomeini, *Risalah Tawdih al-Masa'il,* question 2427.

106. The *'idda* period in a temporary marriage is two menstrual cycles (Civil Code, Article 1120).

107. Khomeini, *Risalah Tawdih al-Masa'il,* question 2425.

108. al-Tusi, *al-Nihaya,* 497–502.

109. Haeri, "Mota."

110. Haeri, "Mota."

111. Mir-Hosseini, "Sharia and National Law in Iran."

112. Amin Banani, *The Modernization of Iran* (Stanford, CA: Stanford University Press, 1961).

113. McGlinn, "Family Law in Iran."

114. Juliet Williams, "Unholy Matrimony? Feminism, Orientalism, and the Possibility of Double Critique," *Signs* 34, no. 3 (2009): 619.

115. Shahla Haeri, "Temporary Marriage and the State in Iran: An Islamic Discourse on Female Sexuality," *Social Research: An International Quarterly* 59 (1992): 201–23.

116. Magdalena Rodziewicz, "The Legal Debate on the Phenomenon of 'White Marriages' in Contemporary Iran," *Anthropology of the Middle East* 15, no. 1 (2020): 50–63.

117. Constitution, Article 10.

118. Mohammad Nayyeri, "Gender Inequality and Discrimination: The Case of Iranian Women," Iran Human Rights Documentation Center, March 5, 2013, https://iranhrdc.org/gender-inequality-and-discrimination-the-case-of-iranian-women/.

119. Valimorad, personal interview, 2014.

120. The word *remarriage* as used here refers to polygynous marriage.

121. Valimorad, personal interview, 2014.

122. Tooran Valimorad, "Taadud-i Zawjat va Bayadha va Nabayadha," Shabaka-yi Iran Zanan, November 23, 2019, http://iranzanan.com/135/; Zibai-Nijad, "Namah-yi Rais-i Markaz-i Tahqiqat va Mutalaat-i Zanan va Khanavada bi Rais-i Majlis dar Irtibat ba Layah-yi Hamayat az Khanavada," Shabaka-yi Iran Zanan, September 20, 2022, http://iranzanan.com/2353/.

## CHAPTER 5. NAVIGATING ISLAMIC FAMILY LAW

1. Qur'an 30:21.

2. Abu l-Qasim Payanda, Nahj al-Fasaha (Tehran: Intisharat-i 'Ilmi, 1945).

3. al-Hurr al-'Amili, *Wasa'il al-Shi'a,* vol. 11, "Bab al-Jihad."

4. Civil Code, Article 1104.

5. Civil Code, Article 940.

6. Civil Code, Article 1107.

7. Qur'an 65:7; al-Hurr al-'Amili, *Wasa'il al-Shi'a*, vol. 14, "Bab al-Nafaqa," sec. 1.

8. al-Hilli, *Mukhtalaf*, 7:304.

9. Halper, "Law and Women's Agency."

10. Najafi, *Jawahir al-Kalam*, 31:304; Al-Hasan ibn Yusuf ibn al-Mutahhar al-Hilli, *Qawa'id al-Ahkam fi Masa'il al-Halal wa al-Haram* (Tehran, 1315 AH), 3:267.

11. Najafi, *Jawahir al-Kalam*, 31:312; Shahid al-Thani, *Masalik al-Afham*, "Bab al-Nafaqa."

12. Najafi, *Jawahir al-Kalam*, 31:311.

13. Civil Code, Article 1111.

14. al-Hilli, *Mukhtalaf*, 7:300; Civil Code, Articles 1129 and 1130.

15. Civil Code, Article 1085.

16. Muhammad ibn Hassan ibn Yusuf al-Hilli, *Izzah al-Fawaid fi Sharh Mushkilat al-Qawa'id*, (Qum: Ismaili, 1387), 3:267; Shahid al-Thani, *Masalik al-Afham*, "Bab al-Nafaqa"; Najafi, *Jawahir al-Kalam*, 31:304.

17. al-Hilli, *Mukhtalaf*, 7:320; Tucker, *Women, Family, and Gender*, 51.

18. Civil Code, Article 1108.

19. Tucker, *Women, Family, and Gender*, 55.

20. Basim Musallam, *Sex and Society in Islam: Birth Control before the Nineteenth Century* (Cambridge: Cambridge University Press, 1983), 33.

21. Khomeini, *Risalah Tawdih al-Masa'il*, question 2418.

22. Civil Code, Articles 1106–8.

23. Khomeini, *Risalah Tawdih al-Masa'il*, question 2412.

24. Civil Code, Article 1108.

25. Civil Code, Article 1127.

26. Civil Code, Article 1114.

27. Najafi, *Jawahir al-Kalam*, 31:339.

28. Civil Code, Article 1115.

29. Qur'an 4:19 and 65:6.

30. Civil Code, Article 1117.

31. Constitution, Principle 28.

32. "Qanun-i Guzarnama," Markaz-i Pazhuhishha-yi Majlis Shuray-i Islami, accessed 2014, http://rc.majlis.ir/fa/law/show/96904.

33. al-Hakim, *Minhaj al-Salihin*, 2:316.

34. al-Hilli, *Mukhtalaf*, 7:322; Khomeini, *Tahrir al-Wasilah*, 2:302; Shahid al-Thani, *Sharh al-Lum'a al-Dimashqiyya*, 2:112.

35. Khomeini, *Risalah Tawdih al-Masa'il*, question 2416.

36. Itilaf-i Islami-yi Zanan, "Karha-yi bar Zamin Mandah dar Huzih-yi Zanan," Shabaka-yi Iran Zanan, March 2, 2022, http://iranzanan.com/3410/.

37. Itilaf-i Islami-yi Zanan, "Baznagari dar Qanun-i Madani," Shabaka-yi Iran Zanan, accessed May 8, 2013, but since removed from website, www.iranzanan.com/first_point/005901.php.

38. Valimorad, personal interview, 2014.

39. Civil Code, Articles 1103 and 940.

40. Valimorad, personal interview, 2014.

41. A similar argument has been put forth by Margot Badran, *Feminists, Islam, and Nation: Gender and the Making of Modern Egypt* (Princeton, NJ: Princeton University Press, 1995).

42. McGlinn, "Family Law in Iran," 56.

43. Civil Code, Articles 946–48.

44. Tucker, *Women, Family, and Gender*, 161.

45. "Layih-yi Himayat az Khanavada," Markaz-i Pazhuhishha-yi Majlis Shuray-i Islami, accessed 2014, http://rc.majlis.ir/fa/law/show/97187.

46. Qur'an 4:34 and 2:228.

47. Tucker, *Women, Family, and Gender*, 84.

48. Qur'an 2:231 and 4:19.

49. Civil Code, Article 1120; Najafi, *Jawahir al-Kalam*, 32:10; al-Hilli, *Tadhkirat al-Fuqaha'*, "Bab al-Talaq."

50. Civil Code, Articles 1150, 1143–4; Khomeini, *Risalah Tawdih al-Masa'il*, questions 2524 and 2525.

51. Mir-Hosseini, *Marriage on Trial*, 38; Civil Code, Article 1145; Khomeini, *Risalah Tawdih al-Masa'il*, question 2522.

52. Situations where the wife is granted divorce by compensating her husband (*khul'*) are also considered irrevocable.

53. Civil Code, Article 1148.

54. al-Hurr al-'Amili, *Wasa'il al-Shi'a*, 18:400.

55. McGlinn, "Family Law in Iran," 61.

56. Muhaqqiq-Damad, *Barrasi-yi Fiqhi-yi Huquq-i Khanavada*, 205.

57. Civil Code, Article 1140; Khomeini, *Risalah Tawdih al-Masa'il*, question 2499.

58. al-Hurr al-'Amili, *Wasa'il al-Shi'a*, vol. 15, "Bab al-Talaq."

59. Civil Code Article 1134; Khomeini, *Risalah Tawdih al-Masa'il*, question 2543.

60. Khomeini, *Tahrir al-Wasilah*, 1:274.

61. Muhaqqiq-Damad, *Barrasi-yi Fiqhi-yi Huquq-i Khanavada*, 207.

62. Civil Code, Article 1136.

63. Najafi, *Jawahir al-Kalam*, 32:4.

64. al-Hurr al-'Amili, *Wasa'il al-Shi'a*, vol. 15, "Bab al-Talaq," secs. 18 and 37.

65. al-Hilli, *Izzah al-Fawaid*, 3;310; Shahid al-Thani, *Sharh al-Lum'a al-Dimashqiyya*, 2:127.

66. Civil Code, Article 1138.

67. al-Hurr al-'Amili, *Wasa'il al-Shi'a*, vol. 15, "Bab al-Talaq," sec. 35.

68. Civil Code, Article 1119.

69. Civil Code, Article 1133.

70. Mir-Hosseini, *Marriage on Trial*, 57, 209–210.

71. Azadeh Kian-Thiebaut, *Les femmes iraniennes entre Islam, état et famille* (Paris: Maisonneuve et Larose, 2002), 126.

72. Halper, "Law and Women's Agency," 100.

73. Ziba Mir-Hosseini, "Family Law. ii. In Islam," In *Encyclopaedia Iranica*, vol. 9, fasc. 2 (London: Encyclopaedia Iranica Foundation, 1999), 184–96.

74. Halper, "Law and Women's Agency," 100.
75. Mir-Hosseini, "Women and Politics," 142–45.
76. Mir-Hosseini, *Marriage on Trial*, 61.
77. McGlinn, "Family Law in Iran," 70.
78. al-Hurr al-ʿAmili, *Wasaʾil al-Shiʿa*, 15:487.
79. Civil Code, Article 1146.
80. Khomeini, *Risalah Tawdih al-Masaʾil*, question 2530.
81. al-Hurr al-ʿAmili, *Wasaʾil al-Shiʿa*, vol. 15, "Bab al-Khulʿ wa al-Mubaraʾah," sec. 4.
82. al-Hurr al-ʿAmili, *Wasaʾil al-Shiʿa*, 15:497.
83. Najafi, *Jawahir al-Kalam*, 33:41; al-Hurr al-ʿAmili, *Wasaʾil al-Shiʿa*, vol. 15, "Bab al-Khulʿ wa al-Mubaraʾah," sec. 1.
84. Najafi, *Jawahir al-Kalam*, 33:41; Khomeini, *Tahrir al-Wasilah*, 2:352.
85. Najafi, *Jawahir al-Kalam*, 33:90.
86. al-Hilli, *Mukhtalaf*, 7:391.
87. Civil Code, Article 1147; Khomeini, *Risalah Tawdih al-Masaʾil*, question 2535.
88. McGlinn, "Family Law in Iran," 65.
89. Civil Code, Article 1130.
90. Civil Code, Article 1156.
91. McGlinn, "Family Law in Iran," 67.
92. Civil Code, Article 1122.
93. Civil Code, Article 1121.
94. Civil Code, Article 1122.
95. Civil Code, Article 1126.
96. Civil Code Article 1121.
97. Civil Code, Article 1123.
98. Civil Code, Article 1126.
99. Mir-Hosseini, *Islam and Gender*, 62, 162, 164–65; Civil Code, Article 1129.
100. Civil Code, Article 1150 and 1151; Khomeini, *Risalah Tawdih al-Masaʾil*, questions 2512 and 2513.
101. Khomeini, *Risalah Tawdih al-Masaʾil*, question 2516.
102. Civil Code, Article 1152; Khomeini, *Risalah Tawdih al-Masaʾil*, question 2515.
103. Khomeini, *Risalah Tawdih al-Masaʾil*, question 2520; al-Hurr al-ʿAmili, *Wasaʾil al-Shiʿa*, 15:451; Qurʾan 2:234.
104. Civil Code, Article 1153; Khomeini, *Risalah Tawdih al-Masaʾil*, question 2514, 2518; Qurʾan 65:4.
105. Civil Code, Article 1148 and 1149.
106. Civil Code, Article 1149.
107. Article 1156.
108. Article 1109; Al-Hurr al-ʿAmili, *Wasaʾil al-Shiʿa*, vol. 14, "Bab al-Nafaqa," sec. 8.
109. Khomeini, *Tahrir al-Wasilah*, 2:315; Civil Code, 1113.
110. Civil Code, Article 1116.
111. Civil Code, Article 1179.

112. Civil Code, Article 1178.

113. Civil Code, Article 1176.

114. Khomeini, *Risalah Tawdih al-Masa'il*, question 2491.

115. Khomeini, *Risalah Tawdih al-Masa'il*, question 2487.

116. Except for cases where an individual aged fifteen years or older can display their maturity to a judge (Civil Code Article 1210).

117. M. Shafai, Mut'a va Athar-i Huquqi va Ijtimai-yi an (Tehran: Markaz-i Nashr-i Kitab, 1962), 164–68, cited in Ziba Mir-Hosseini, "Family Law. iii. In Modern Persia," in *Encyclopaedia Iranica*, online ed., 1999, www.iranicaonline.org/articles/family-law#iii.

118. Civil Code, Article 1169.

119. Previously, mothers retained custody of their daughters until the age of seven, but fathers were awarded custody of sons once the boy reached the age of two.

120. Shirin Ebrahimi, "Child Custody '(*Hizanat*)' under Iranian Law: An Analytical Discussion," *Family Law Quarterly* 39, no. 2 (2005): 459–76.

121. Civil Code, Article 1174.

122. Civil Code, Article 1175.

123. Civil Code, Article 1170.

124. Civil Code, Article 1171.

125. Fatemeh Hashemi, "Mutalabat-i Zanan az Ra'is-jumhur Rouhani," Shabaka-yi Iran Zanan, accessed June 18, 2010, but since removed from website, www.iranzanan.com/first_point/004465.php.

126. "Qanun-i Madani," Markaz-i Pazhuhishha-yi Majlis Shuray-i Islami, accessed March 13, 2008, http://rc.majlis.ir/fa/law/show/92778.

127. Mir-Hosseini, "Sharia and National Laws," 354.

128. Paidar, *Women and the Political Process*.

129. Ebrahimi, "Child Custody '(*Hizanat*)'."

130. Civil Code, Article 1199.

131. Civil Code, Article 1173. Article 1184 was amended in 2000 to give the court the power to place restrictions on the authority of the guardian.

132. Civil Code, Article 1183.

133. Itilaf-i Islami-yi Zanan, "Zanan va Qanun-i Madani," Shabaka-yi Iran Zanan, accessed August 8, 2014, but since removed from website, www.iranzanan.com/first_point/005901.php.

134. Civil Code, Articles 1182 and 1184–87.

135. Mir-Hosseini, "Sharia and National Laws," 355; Mir-Hosseini, *Marriage on Trial*, 17.

136. Valimorad, personal interview, 2014.

137. Civil Code, Articles 1130–33.

138. Masoomeh Abad, "Dastrisi-yi Zanan bi Talaq," Shabaka-yi Iran Zanan, accessed July 12, 2012, but since removed from website, www.iranzanan.com/first_point/003322.php?q=print.

139. Muhammad Janfishan, "Afzayish-i Talaq-i 'Atifi," Shabaka-yi Iran Zanan, accessed February 1, 2014, but since removed from website, www.iranzanan.com/cultural/cat-116/005724.php.

140. Valimorad, personal interview, 2014.

141. Mir-Hosseini, *Islam and Gender*, 275.
142. Mir-Hosseini, *Marriage on Trial*, 57.


CONCLUSION

1. Hilary Kalmbach, "Social and Religious Change in Damascus: One Case of Female Islamic Religious Authority," *British Journal of Middle Eastern Studies* 35, no. 1 (2008): 37–57.
2. Kalmbach, "Social and Religious Change."
3. Abdulaziz Sachedina, "Woman, Half-the-Man? Crisis of Male Epistemology in Islamic Jurisprudence," in *Perspectives on Islamic Law, Justice, and Society*, ed. R.S. Khare (Lanham, MD: Rowman and Littlefield, 1999), 149.
4. Keiko Sakurai, "Women's Empowerment and Iranian-Style Seminaries in Iran and Pakistan," in *The Moral Economy of the Madrasa: Islam and Education Today*, ed. Keiko Sakurai and Fariba Adelkhah (New York: Routledge, 2011), 32.
5. Kalmbach, "Social and Religious Change," 37–57.
6. These *maktab*s included Maktab-i Narjis in Mashhad; the Maktab-i Tawhid, and the women's section of the Dar al-Tabligh in Qum; the Maktab-i Fatimah, established in Isfahan; and the Maktab-i Zahra in Shiraz. Cited in Sakurai, "Women's Empowerment," 34.
7. Sakurai, "Women's Empowerment," 34.
8. "Gardahami-yi Mudiran va Mas'ulan-i Hawza-ha-yi 'Ilmiyya-yi Khaharan-i Sarasar-i Kishvar," *Payam-i Hawza*, no. 14, 1997, www.hawzah.net/Per/Magazine/PH/014/pho1404.asp.
9. Sakurai, "Women's Empowerment."
10. Tawasil, "Towards the Ideal Revolutionary Shi'i Woman," 105.
11. Adelkhah, *Being Modern in Iran;* Afsaneh Najmabadi, "Crafting an Educated Housewife in Iran," in Abu-Lughod, *Remaking Women*, 91–125; Sullivan, "Eluding the Feminist," 215–42.
12. Golnar Mehran, "The Paradox of Tradition and Modernity in Female Education in the Islamic Republic of Iran," *Comparative Education Review* 47, no. 3 (2003): 269–86; Golnar Mehran, "Shi'a Education in Iran," in *Teaching Islam: Textbooks and Religion in the Middle East*, ed. G. Starrett and E.A. Doumato (Boulder, CO: Lynne Rienner, 2007), 53–70; David Menashri, *Education and the Making of Modern Iran* (Ithaca, NY: Cornell University Press, 1992).
13. Roksana Bahramitash, "Saving Iranian Women: Orientalist Feminism and the Axis of Evil," in *Security Disarmed: Critical Perspectives on Gender, Race, and Militarization,* ed. Sandra Morgen, Barbara Sutton, and Julie Novkov (New Brunswick, NJ: Rutgers University Press, 2008), 101–10; Maryam Poya, *Women, Work and Islamism: Ideology and Resistance in Iran* (New York: Zed Books, 1999); Sullivan, "Eluding the Feminist."
14. Tawasil, "Reading as Practice: The Howzevi (Seminarian) Women in Iran and Clair de Lune," *Anthropology and Education Quarterly* 50, no. 1 (2019): 69.

15. Mohammad Khatami, "Zanan va Mardan Mutafavit Hastand, amma Zan Jins-i Duvvum Nist va Mard Bartar Nist," Zan-i Ruz, no. 1629 (1997), 8–10; Mehran, "Paradox of Tradition."

16. Mehran, "Paradox of Tradition," 271.

17. Roksana Bahramitash, "Islamic Fundamentalism and Women's Economic Role: The Case of Iran," International Journal of Politics, Culture and Society, 16, no. 4 (2003): 551–68.

18. Monique Girgis, "Women in Pre-revolutionary, Revolutionary and Post-revolutionary Iran," Iran Chamber Society, 1996, www.iranchamber.com/society/articles/women_prepost_revolutionary_iran1.php.

19. Girgis, "Women."

20. Halper, "Law and Women's Agency," 85.

21. Sullivan, "Eluding the Feminist."

22. Tajali, "Notions of Female Authority."

23. Tawasil, "Towards the Ideal Revolutionary Shi'i Woman," 107.

24. Tawasil, "Reading as Practice," 78.

25. Tawasil, "Towards the Ideal Revolutionary Shi'i Woman," 106.

26. Sakurai, "Women's Empowerment," 39.

27. Sakurai, "Women's Empowerment," 40.

28. Keiko Sakurai, "Shi'ite Women's Seminaries (Howzeh-Ye 'Elmiyyeh-Ye Khahran) in Iran: Possibilities and Limitations," Iranian Studies 45, no. 6 (2012): 738.

29. Sakurai, "Shi'ite Women's Seminaries," 744.

30. Ruhollah Mousavi Khomeini, Maqam-i Zan az Didgah-i Imam Khomeini (Tehran: Muassasah-yi Tanzim va Nashr-i Asar-i Imam Khomeini, 2001).

31. Morteza Motahhari, Nizam-i Huquq-i Zan dar Islam (Tehran: Daftar-i Intisharat-i Islami, 1980), 111–12.

32. Mirjam Kunkler, "What Iran Wants from Female Religious Authority: Piety—Yes, Expertise in Fiqh—No," openDemocracy, February 13, 2012, www.opendemocracy.net/5050/mirjam-k%C3%BCnkler/what-iran-wants-from-female-religious-authority-piety-yes-expertise-in-fiqh-no.

33. Ashraf Boroojerdi, interview, Shabaka-yi Iran Zanan, 2013, post no longer available on site, www.iranzanan.com/first_point/004689.php.

34. Mirjam Kunkler and Roja Fazaeli, "The Life of Two Mujtahidahs: Female Religious Authority in 20th Century Iran," in Women, Leadership and Mosques: Contemporary Islamic Authority, ed. Masooda Bano and Hilary Kalmbach (Leiden: Brill, 2011), 127–60.

35. Sakurai, "Shi'ite Women's Seminaries," 743.

36. Zohreh Sefati, interview by Keiko Sakurai, June 6, 2011, cited in Sakurai, "Shi'ite Women's Seminaries," 743.

37. For more information on women as religious authorities, see Moojan Momen, "Women. iii: In Shi'ism," in Encyclopaedia Iranica, online ed., 2011, https://iranicaonline.org/articles/women-shiism.

38. Kunkler and Fazaeli, "Life of Two Mujtahidahs."

39. Sakurai, "Women's Empowerment," 53.

40. Adelkhah, *Being Modern in Iran,* chap. 5; Sakurai, "Women's Empowerment."

41. Dale F. Eickelman and James Piscatori, *Muslim Politics* (Princeton, NJ: Princeton University Press, 1996), 131; Sakurai, "Women's Empowerment."

42. David Kloos and Mirjam Kunkler, "Studying Female Islamic Authority: From Top-Down to Bottom-Up Modes of Certification," *Asian Studies Review* 40, no. 4 (2016): 479–90.

43. Osanloo, *Politics of Women's Rights.*

44. Barlas, *Believing Women.*

45. Azadeh Kian, "Women and the Making of Civil Society in Post-Islamist Iran," in *Twenty Years of Islamic Revolution: Political and Social Transition in Iran since 1979,* ed. Eric Hooglund (Syracuse, NY: Syracuse University Press, 2002), 56–73; Najmabadi, "Feminism," 62; Boe, *Family Law.*

46. Foruq ibn al-Din, "Luzum-i Islah-i Qavanin-i Talaq, Ta'addud-i Zujat va Hizanat," *Payam-i Hajar,* September 10, 1992, 28–29.

47. Sullivan, "Eluding the Feminist," 236; Afsaneh Najmabadi, "Feminism in an Islamic Republic: 'Years of Hardship, Years of Growth,'" in *Islam, Gender, and Social Change,* ed. Yvonne Y. Haddad and John Esposito (New York: Oxford University Press, 1998), 59–84.

48. Kian, *Gendered Khomeini,* 189.

49. Azadeh Kian, "Gendering Shi'ism in Post-revolutionary Iran," in *Gender in Contemporary Iran: Pushing the Boundaries,* ed. Roksana Bahramitash and Eric Hooglund (London: Routledge, 2011), 24–35.

50. Yusuf Sanei, interview, Farzana, no. 10 (Winter 2000): 19–20; Mohammad Mujtahid Shabestari, *Naqdi bar Qara'at-i Rasmi az Din: Buhranha, Chalashha, Rah-i Halha* (Tehran: Tarh-i Naw, 2000), 503–4.

51. The word 'adl, which means to act equitably and justly, is also used to convey the idea of making two things equal.

52. Muhammad-Baqir Behbahani, Risalat al-Ijtihad wa al-Akhbar (Tehran, n.d.), cited in Devin Stewart, "Ejma'," in *Encyclopedia Iranica,* vol. 8, fasc. 3 (London: Encyclopaedia Iranica Foundation, 1998), updated for online ed., 2011, https://iranicaonline.org/articles/ejma.

53. For further discussion of Muslim women's advocacy for legal reform see Adila Abusharaf, "Women in Islamic Communities: The Quest for Gender Justice Research," *Human Rights Quarterly* 28, no. 3 (August 2006).

54. Poya, *Women, Work and Islamism.*

55. Yasuyuki Matsunaga, "Human Rights and New Jurisprudence in Mohsen Kadivar's Advocacy of 'New-Thinker' Islam," *Die Welt des Islams* 51, nos. 3–4 (2011): 358–81.

56. Mohsen Kadivar, *Hukumat-i Wilayi* (Tehran: Intisharat-i Niy, 1999) and *Nazariyah-ha-yi Dawlat dar Fiqh-i Shi'a* (Tehran: Intisharat-i Niy, 2001).

57. Mohsen Kadivar, *Haqq al-Nas: Islam va Huquq-i Bashar* (Tehran: Kavir, 2008), 137.

58. Mir-Hosseni, "Sharia and National Laws," 341.

59. Matsunaga, "Human Rights."

60. Matsunaga, "Human Rights."

61. For a detailed exploration of the reformist approach to dynamic juris-prudence, see Matsunaga, "Human Rights."

62. For more on the reformist perspective on Islamic jurisprudence, see Mat-sunaga, "Human Rights."

63. Mokhtari, *Search for Human Rights*, 469–79.

64. Azadeh Kian-Thiebaut, "From Islamization to the Individualization of Women in Post-revolutionary Iran," in *Women, Religion and Culture in Iran,* ed. Sarah Ansari and Vanessa Martin (Richmond, Surrey, UK: Curzon, 2002), chap. 8; Jaleh Shaditalab, "Iranian Women: Rising Expectations," *Critique: Critical Middle Eastern Studies* 14, no. 1 (Spring 2005): 35–55; Keddie, *Modern Iran;* Amir-Ebrahimi, "Transgression in Narration," 89–118.

65. Ziba Mir-Hosseini, "New Feminist Voices in Islam," *BARAZA!*, no. 4 (2010): 3–4.

66. Boe, *Family Law.*

67. Mir-Hosseini, "Muslim Women's Quest," 629–45.

# Bibliography

PRIMARY SOURCES IN PERSIAN AND ARABIC

Ali, Abdullah Yusuf. *The Holy Qur'an: Text, Translation and Commentary*. De Luxe ed. Washington, DC: Islamic Center, 1978.

Astarabadi, Muhammad 'Ali. *Risala dar Siyagh-i Aqd-i Nikah*. MS no. 3514. Kitabkhanah-i Majlis-i Shura-yi Islami, Tehran.

Behbahani, Muhammad Baqir. *Risalat al-Ijtihad wa al-Akhbar*. Tehran, n.d.

Birjandi, Muhammad Baqir. *Risala fi al-Talaq*. MS no. 3410. Mar'ashi Library, Qum.

Bojnourdi, Mousavi Muhammad. *Huquq-i Zan dar Islam*. Pazuhishgah-i Ulum-i Insani, 2004.

al-Bukhari, Muhammad ibn Isma'il. *Sahih al-Bukhari*. Cairo: Al-Azhar, 1989.

Qanun-i Madani. Markaz-i Pazhuhishha-yi Majlis Shuray-i Islami. Accessed March 13, 2008. http://rc.majlis.ir/fa/law/show/92778.

Ibn al-Din Foruq. "Luzum-i Islah-i Qavanin-i Talaq, Ta'addud-i Zujat va Hizanat." *Payam-i Hajar*, September 10, 1992, 28–29.

Iftikharzadih, Sayyidah Zahra. "Tajrubi-yi Zisti-yi Zanan dar Izdivaj-i Zudhingam" *Pazhuhishnamah-yi Madadkari-yi Ijtimai*, no. 3 (Spring 2015): 109–56.

Itilaf-i Islami-yi Zanan. Shabaka-yi Iran Zanan [website]. www.iranzanan.com.

Layih-yi Himayat az Khanavada. Markaz-i Pazhuhishha-yi Majlis Shuray-i Islami. Accessed 2014. http://rc.majlis.ir/fa/law/show/97187.

Gavahi, Zahra. *Sima-yi Zan dar Ainah-i Fiqh-i Shi'a: Pazhuhishi Piramun-i Ahkam-i Khas-i Zanan*. Tehran: Markaz-i Chap va Nashr-i Sazman-i Tablighat-i Islami, 1990.

al-Ha'iri, Sayyid Ali b. Muhammad Ali Tabataba'i. *Riyad al-Masa'il fi Bayan al-Ahkam bi-l-Dala'il*. Qum, 1292 AH.

al-Hakim, Sayyid Muhammad-Sa'id al-Tabataba'i. *Minhaj al-Salihin*. Najaf, 1365 AH.

al-Hilli, Al-Hasan ibn Yusuf ibn al-Mutahhar. *Izzah al-Fawaid fi Sharh Mush-kilat al-Qawa'id.* Qum: Isma'ili, 1387 AH.

———. *Mukhtalaf al-Shi'a fi Ahkam al-Shari'a.* 10 vols. Qum: Markaz-i Tah-qiqat-i Ulum-i Islami, 1991.

———. *Qawa'id al-Ahkam fi Masa'il al-Halal wa al-Haram.* Tehran, 1315 AH.

———. *Tadhkirat al-Fuqaha'.* Tehran: al-Maktabat al-Murtadawiyya, 1388 AH.

———. *Tahrir al-Ahkam.* Mashhad: Mu'assasat Al al-Bayt, 1985.

al-Hurr al-'Amili, Muhammad bin al-Hasan bin 'Ali bin al-Husayn. *Wasa'il al-Shi'a.* 20 vols. Tehran: Islamiyah, 1376 AH.

Isfar, Ahmad. *Zanan-i Namdar-i Shi'a.* Tehran: Rayiha-i Itrat, 2002.

Ja'fari, Muhammad Taqi, and Muhammad ibn al-Husayn Sharif al-Radi. *Tarjoma va Tafsir-i Nahj al-Balagha.* Tehran: Farhang-i Islami, 1978.

Jannati, Muhammad Ebrahim. *Adwar-i Ijtihad az Didgah-i Madhahib-i Islami.* Tehran: Kiyhan, 1993.

Javadi Amoli, Abd Allah. *Zan dar Ayinah-i Jalal va Jamal.* Qum: Markaz-i Nashr-i Isra, 1999.

Kadivar, Mohsen. *Haqq al-Nas: Islam va Huquq-i Bashar.* Tehran: Kavir, 2008.

———. *Hukumat-i Wilayi.* Tehran: Intisharat-i Niy, 1999.

———. *Nazariyah-ha-yi Dawlat dar Fiqh-i Shi'a.* Tehran: Intisharat-i Niy, 2001.

Katouzian, Naser. *Godar-i bar Inqilab-i Iran.* Tehran, 1981.

———. *Huquq-i Madani-yi Khanavada.* Tehran: Tehran University Press, 1989.

Khatami, Mohammad. "Zanan va Mardan Mutafavit Hastand, amma Zan Jins-i Duvvum Nist va Mard Bartar Nist." *Zan-i Ruz,* no. 1629 (1997).

Khayr al-Din, Adil. *Al-Alam al-Fikri lil-Imam Jafar al-Sadiq.* Beirut: Dar wa-Maktabat al-Hilal, 1993.

Khomeini, Ruhollah Mousavi. Declaration issued March 12, 1982. In *Sahifa-yi Nur,* vol.17. Tehran: Sazman-i Madarik-i Farhangi-yi Inqilab-i Islami, 1989.

———. *Maqam-i Zan az Didgah-i Imam Khomeini.* Tehran: Muassasah-yi Tanzim va Nashr-i Asar-i Imam Khomeini, 2001.

———. *Risalah Tawdih al-Masa'il.* Tehran: Intisharat Ilmi, 1981.

———. Sermon, December 7, 1978. In *Sahifa-yi Nur,* 4:34. Tehran: Sazman-i Madarik-i Farhangi-yi Inqilab-i Islami, 1989.

———. Sermon, February 1, 1979. In *Sahifa-yi Nur,* vol. 11. Tehran: Sazman-i Madarik-i Farhangi-yi Inqilab-i Islami, 1989.

———. Sermon in Qum, April 27, 1979. *Payam-i Zan,* no. 3 (1992): 39.

———. Sermon, September 19, 1979. In *Sahifa-yi Nur,* vol. 11. Tehran: Sazman-i Madarik-i Farhangi-yi Inqilab-i Islami, 1989.

———. Sermon in Shemiran, July 12, 1980. In *Gozidah-ha-yi az Maqalat-i Payam-i Hajar,* no. 1. Tehran: Jami'at-i Zanan-i Inqilab-i Islami, 1982.

———. Sermon in Tehran, March 16, 1981. In *Sahifa-yi Nur,* 14:130. Tehran: Sazman-i Madarik-i Farhangi-yi Inqilab-i Islami, 1989.

———. *Tahrir al-Wasilah,* 2 vols. Najaf: Dar al-Kutub al-'Ilmiyyah, 1390 AH.

Majlisi, Muhammad Baqir, *Bahar al-Anwar.* Vol. 103. Tehran: Islamiyah, 1376 SH.

al-Marghinani, Burhan al-Din 'Ali ibn Abi-Bakr. *Al-Hidaya: Sharh Bidayat al-Mubtadi.* 4 vols. Cairo: Dar al-Salam, 2000.

Muhaqqiq-Damad, Mustafa. *Barrasi-yi Fiqhi-yi Huquq-i Khanavada.* Tehran: Markaz-i Nashr-i Ulum-i Islami, 1986.

al-Muhaqqiq al-Hilli, Najm-al-Din Ja'far b. Hasan. *Shara'i' al-Islam fi Masa'il al-Halal wa al-Haram.* Tehran: Intisharat-i Istiqlal, 1409 AH.

Montazeri, Husayn Ali. *Hukumat-i Dini va Huquq-i Insan.* Qum: Arghavan-i Danish, 2008.

———. *Masalah-i Hijab.* Tehran: Anjuman-i Islami-yi Pizishkan, 1969.

Motahhari, Morteza. *Nizam-i Huquq-i Zan dar Islam.* Tehran: Daftar-i Intisharat-i Islami, 1980.

*Nahj al-Balagha.* Compiled by al-Sharif al-Radi. Translated by Sayed Ali Reza. Rome: European Islamic Cultural Center, 1984.

Najafi, Muhammad Hasan ibn Baqir. *Jawahir al-Kalam fi Sharh Shara'i al-Islam.* Najaf: Dar al-Kutub al-Islamiya, 1377 AH.

Qanun-i Guzarnama. Markaz-i Pazhuhishha-yi Majlis Shuray-i Islami. Accessed 2014. http://rc.majlis.ir/fa/law/show/96904.

Payanda, Abu l-Qasim. *Nahj al-Fasaha.* Tehran: 'Ilmi Publications, 1945.

Sadr, Mohsan. *Khatarat-i Sadr-al-Ashraf.* Tehran: Vahid, 1985.

Sanei, Yusuf. *Ahkam-i Banuvan: Mutabiq ba Fatava-yi Marja'-i 'Aliqadr-i Hazrat-i Ayatollah al-'Uzma Hajj Shaykh Yusuf Sanei.* Qum: Maysam Tammar, 2001.

———. Interview. *Farzana.* no. 10 (Winter 2000): 19–20.

———. *Qaymumat-i Mader.* Qum: Mu'assasah-yi Farhangi-yi Fiqh-i Thaqalayn, 2005.

Shabestari, Mohammad Mujtahid. *Naqdi bar Qara'at-i Rasmi az Din: Buhranha, Chalishha, Rah-i Halha.* Tehran: Tarh-i Naw, 2000.

Shafai, M. *Mut'a va Athar-i Huquqi va Ijtimai-yi an.* Tehran: Markaz-i Nashr-i Kitab, 1962.

Shafi'i, Muhammad ibn Idris. *Al-Risala.* Edited by A. M. Shakir. Cairo: Mustafa al-Babi al-Halabi, 1940.

Shahid al-Awwal [Muhammad b. Makki al-Jizzini al-'Amili]. *Al-Lum'a al-Dimashqiyya fi Fiqh al-Imamiyya.* Beirut: Dar al-Turath al-Islami, 1410 AH.

Shahid al-Thani [Zayn al-Din al-Juba'i al-'Amili]. *Masalik al-Afham fi Shara'i' al-Islam.* Qum: Mu'assasat al-Ma'arif, 1416 AH.

———. *Al-Rawda al-Bahiyya fi Sharh al-Lum'a al-Dimashqiyya.* Vol.2. Qum: Daftar-i Tablighat-i Islami-yi Huwza-yi 'Ilmi-yi Qum, 1412 AH.

Shariati, Ali. *Fatimah Fatimah ast.* Tehran: Bunyad-i Shariati, 2001.

Turkaman, Muhammad. *Rasa'il, I'lamiyah-ha, Maqalat va Ruznamah-yi Shaykh Shahid Fazlullah Nuri.* Tehran: Rasa, 1983.

al-Tusi, Abu Ja'far Muhammad Ibn al-Hasan. *Al-Nihaya fi Mujarrad al-Fiqh wa-al-Fatawa.* Translated by Mohammad-Taqi Danishpazhuh, 2 vols. Tehran, 1964.

———. *Al-Tibyan fi Tafsir al-Qur'an,* 10 vols. Beirut: Dar Ihya' al-Turath al-Arabi, 1409 AH.

Yazdi, Sayyad Muhammad Kazim. 'Urwa al-Wuthqa, 2 vols. Sayda: Matba'at 'Irfan, 1348–49 AH.


SECONDARY SOURCES

Abou El Fadl, Khaled. *Speaking in God's Name: Islamic Law, Authority and Women.* Oxford: Oneworld, 2001.

Abrahamian, Ervand. *A History of Modern Iran.* New York: Cambridge University Press, 2008.

Abu-Lughod, Lila, ed. *Remaking Women: Feminism and Modernity in the Middle East.* Princeton, NJ: Princeton University Press, 1998.

———. "The Romance of Resistance: Tracing Transformations of Power through Bedouin Women." *American Ethnologist* 17, no. 1 (1990): 208–26.

Abusharaf, Adila. "Women in Islamic Communities: The Quest for Gender Justice Research." *Human Rights Quarterly* 28, no. 3 (2006): 714–28.

Abu Zayd, Nasr. *Reformation of Islamic Thought: A Critical Analysis.* Amsterdam: Amsterdam University Press, 2006.

Adelkhah, Fariba. *Being Modern in Iran.* Translated by Jonathan Derrick. London: Hurst, 1999.

Afarai, Z. *Iranian Women's Forum in Constitutional Revolution.* Translated by J. Usefiyan. Tehran: Banoo, 1998.

Afary, Janet. *The Iranian Constitutional Revolution, 1906–1911: Grassroots Democracy, Social Democracy and the Origins of Feminism.* New York: Columbia University Press, 1996.

———. *Sexual Politics in Modern Iran.* Cambridge: Cambridge University Press, 2009.

Aghajanian, Akbar. "Divorce in Modern Persia." In *Encyclopaedia Iranica*, vol. 7, fasc. 4, 443–48, and vol. 7, fasc. 5, 449–51. London: Encyclopaedia Iranica Foundation, 1995.

Ahmad, A. Ahmad. *The Fatigue of the Shari'a.* New York: Palgrave Macmillan, 2012.

Ahmed, Leila. *Women and Gender in Islam: Historical Roots of a Modern Debate.* New Haven, CT: Yale University Press, 1992.

Algar, Hamid. *Constitution of the Islamic Republic of Iran.* Berkeley, CA: Mizan Press, 1980.

———. *Islam and Revolution: Writings and Declarations of Imam Khomeini.* Berkeley, CA: Mizan Press, 1981.

Ali, Bizaa Zaynab. "Contemporary Karbala Narratives and the Changing Gender Dynamics in Shi'i Communities." Columbia Academic Commons, 2011. https://academiccommons.columbia.edu/doi/10.7916/D87S7WZ3.

Ali, Kecia. *Marriage and Slavery in Early Islam.* Cambridge, MA: Harvard University Press, 2010.

———. *Sexual Ethics and Islam: Feminist Reflections on Qur'an, Hadith, and Jurisprudence.* Oxford: Oneworld Publication, 2006.

Aloumani, Anna-Chaido. "Changing Role of Women in Iran." MA thesis, University of Kansas, 2006.

Amanat, Abbas. "Constitutional Revolution; Intellectual Background." In *Encyclopaedia Iranica*, online ed., 1992. www.iranicaonline.org/articles/constitutional-revolution-i.

Amir-Ebrahimi, Masserat. "Transgression in Narration: The Lives of Iranian Women in Cyberspace." *Journal of Middle East Women's Studies* 4, no. 3 (October 2008): 89–115.

Amir-Moezzi, Mohammad Ali. *The Divine Guide in Early Shi'ism: The Sources of Esotericism in Islam.* Albany: State University of New York Press, 1994.

An-Na'im, Abdullahi. *Islamic Family Law in a Changing World: A Global Resource Book.* London: Zed, 2002.

Ansari-Pur, M. A. "Iran." In *The Yearbook of Islamic and Middle Eastern Law,* vol. 4. London: Kluwer Law International, 1997–98.

Anwar, Zainah. *Wanted: Equality and Justice in the Muslim Family.* Selangor, Malaysia: Musawah, 2009.

Arjomand, Amir. *After Khomeini: Iran under His Successors.* Oxford: Oxford University Press, 2009.

———. "Civil Society and the Rule of Law in the Constitutional Politics of Iran under Khatami—Iranian President Mohammad Khatami." Iran Chamber Society, 2000. www.iranchamber.com/government/articles/civil_society_politics_iran_khatami.php.

———. "Constitution of the Islamic Republic." In *Encyclopaedia Iranica,* online ed., 1992. https://iranicaonline.org/articles/constitution-of-the-islamic-republic.

———. "The Ulama's Traditionalist Opposition to Parliamentarianism, 1907–1909." *Middle Eastern Studies* 17, no. 2 (1981): 174–90.

Asad, Talal. *Formations of the Secular: Christianity, Islam, and Modernity.* Stanford, CA: Stanford University Press, 2003.

Badran, Margot. "Between Secular and Islamic Feminism/s: Reflections on the Middle East and Beyond." *Journal of Middle East Women's Studies* 1, no. 1 (2005): 6–28.

———. *Feminism in Islam: Secular and Religious Convergences.* Oxford: Oneworld Publications, 2009.

———. *Feminists, Islam, and Nation: Gender and the Making of Modern Egypt.* Princeton, NJ: Princeton University Press, 2005.

Bahramitash, Roksana. "Iranian Women during the Reform Era (1994–2004): A Focus on Employment." *Journal of Middle East Women's Studies* 3, no. 2 (2007): 86–109.

———. "Islamic Fundamentalism and Women's Economic Role: The Case of Iran." *International Journal of Politics, Culture and Society* 16, no. 4: (2003): 551–68.

———. "Saving Iranian Women: Orientalist Feminism and the Axis of Evil." In *Security Disarmed: Critical Perspectives on Gender, Race, and Militarization,* edited by Sandra Morgen, Barbara Sutton, and Julie Novkov, 101–10. New Brunswick, NJ: Rutgers University Press, 2008.

Bamdad, Badr al-Moluk. *From Darkness into Light: Women's Emancipation in Iran.* Translated by F. R. C. Bagley Hicksville. New York: Exposition Press, 1977.

Banani, Amin. *The Modernization of Iran.* Stanford, CA: Stanford University Press, 1961.

Bano, Masooda, and Hilary Kalmbach. *Women, Leadership and Mosques: Changes in Contemporary Islamic Authority.* Leiden: Brill, 2012.

Barlas, Asma. *"Believing Women" in Islam: Unreading Patriarchal Interpretations of the Qur'ān.* Austin: University of Texas Press, 2002.

———. "Reading the Qur'an: Challenges and Possibilities for Muslim Women." Paper presented at the Symposium on Gender, Race, Islam, and the "War on Terror," Simon Fraser University, 2006.

Bauer, Karen. *Gender Hierarchy in the Qur'ān: Medieval Interpretations, Modern Responses.* New York: Cambridge University Press, 2015.

———. "The Male Is Not Like the Female (Q 3:36): The Question of Gender Egalitarianism in the Qur'an." *Religion Compass* 3, no. 4 (2009): 637–54.

Bayat, Asef. *Making Islam Democratic: Social Movements and the Post-Islamist Turn.* Stanford, CA: Stanford University Press, 2007.

Beck, Louis, and Guity Nashat. *Women in Iran: From 1800 to the Islamic Republic.* Chicago: University of Illinois Press, 2004.

Boe, Marianne. *Family Law in Contemporary Iran: Women's Rights Activism and Shari'a.* London: I. B. Tauris, 2015.

Busto, Rudy. "Pujando pero llegando: Rasquache Religious Thought and Scriptures." Paper presented at the Transdisciplinary Theological Colloquium, New Knowing in Latina/o Philosophy and Theology, Drew University, Madison, NJ, 2008.

Butler, Judith. *Gender Trouble: Feminism and the Subversion of Identity.* New York: Routledge, 2010.

Calder, Norman. "Judicial Authority in Imami Shi'i Jurisprudence." *Bulletin British Society for Middle Eastern Studies* 6, no. 2 (1979): 104–8.

Chaido, Anna. *Changing Role of Women in Iran.* Lawrence: University of Kansas Press, 2006.

Coulson, Noel. *Conflicts and Tensions in Islamic Jurisprudence.* Chicago: University of Chicago Press, 1969.

Deeb, Lara. *An Enchanted Modern: Gender and Public Piety in Shi'i Lebanon.* Princeton, NJ: Princeton University Press, 2006.

Ebadi, Shirin. *Iran Awakening: A Memoir of Revolution and Hope.* New York: Random House, 2006.

Ebrahimi, Shirin. "Child Custody '(*Hizanat*)' under Iranian Law: An Analytical Discussion." *Family Law Quarterly* 39, no. 2 (2005): 459–76.

Eickelman, Dale, and James Piscatori. *Muslim Politics.* Princeton, NJ: Princeton University Press, 1996.

———. *New Media in the Muslim World: The Emerging Public Sphere.* Bloomington: Indiana University Press, 2003.

Emon, Anver. "The Paradox of Equality and the Politics of Difference: Gender Equality, Islamic Law and the Modern Muslim State." In *Gender and Equality in Islamic Law: Justice and Ethics in the Islamic Legal Tradition,* edited by Ziba Mir-Hosseini, Kari Vogt, Lena Larsen, and Christian Moe, 237–58. London: I. B. Tauris, 2013.

Enayat, Hamid. "Political Participation of Women in Iran: A Sociological Study." PhD diss., Panjab University, Chandigarh, 2001.

Esposito, John. *Islam: The Straight Path*. New York: Oxford University Press, 1991.

———. "Muslim Family Law Reform: Towards an Islamic Methodology." *Islamic Studies* 15, no. 1 (1976): 19–51.

———. *Women in Muslim Family Law*. Syracuse, NY: Syracuse University Press, 1982.

Fadel, Mohammad. "Muslim Reformists, Female Citizenship, and the Public Accommodation of Islam in Liberal Democracy." *Politics and Religion* 5, no. 1 (2012). https://doi.org/10.1017/S1755048311000617.

Fatemi, Mohammad Ghari S. "Autonomy and Equal Right to Divorce with Specific Reference to Shī'ī Fiqh and the Iranian Legal System." *Islam and Christian–Muslim Relations*, 17, no. 3 (2005): 280–95.

Fischer, Michael. *Iran: From Religious Dispute to Revolution*. Cambridge, MA: Harvard University Press, 1980.

Girgis, Monique. "Women in Pre-revolutionary, Revolutionary and Post-revolutionary Iran." Iran Chamber Society, 1996. www.iranchamber.com/society/articles/women_prepost_revolutionary_iran1.php.

Gribetz, Arthur. *Strange Bedfellows: Mut'at al-Nisā and Mut'at al-Hajj: A Study Based on Sunnī and Shī'ī Sources of Tafsīr, Hadīth and Fiqh*. Berlin: K. Schwarz, 1994.

Haddad, Yvonne Yazbeck, and John L. Esposito. *Islam, Gender, and Social Change*. New York: Oxford University Press, 1998.

Haeri, Shahla. *Law of Desire: Temporary Marriage in Shi'i Iran*. Syracuse, NY: Syracuse University Press, 1989.

———. "Mota." In *Encyclopaedia Iranica*, online ed., 2005. https://iranicaonline.org/articles/mota.

———. "Temporary Marriage: An Islamic Discourse on Female Sexuality in Iran." *Social Research* 59, no. 1 (1992): 75–102.

———. "Temporary Marriage and the State in Iran: An Islamic Discourse on Female Sexuality." *Social Research: An International Quarterly* 59 (1992): 201–23.

———. "Women, Law and Social Change in Iran." In *Women in Contemporary Muslim Societies*, edited by J.I. Smith, 209–34. Lewisburg, PA: Bucknell University Press, 1980.

Hairi, Abdul Hadi. *Shi'ism and Constitutionalism in Iran*. Leiden: Brill, 1977.

Hallaq, Wael. *Authority, Continuity, and Change in Islamic Law*. Cambridge: Cambridge University Press, 2001.

———. "Juristic Authority vs. State Power: The Legal Crises of Modern Islam." *Journal of Law and Religion* 19, no. 2 (2004): 243–58.

Halper, Louise. "Law and Women's Agency in Post-revolutionary Iran." *Harvard Journal Law and Gender* 28 (2005): 1137–90.

Hamdar, Abir. "Jihad of Words: Gender and Contemporary Karbala Narratives." *Yearbook of English Studies* 39, no. 17 (2009): 84–100.

Hammami, Rema. "Gender Equality and Muslim Women: Negotiating Expanded Rights in Muslim Majority and Immigrant Contexts." In *Development and Equity: An Interdisciplinary Exploration by Ten Scholars from Africa, Asia and Latin America, edited by Dick Foeken, Ton Dietz, Leo Haan, and Linda Johnson, 118–31. Leiden: Brill, 2014.

Hammer, Juliane. "Identity, Authority, and Activism: American Muslim Women Approach the Qur'ān." Muslim World 98, no. 4 (2008): 443–64.

Harding, Sandra. Whose Science? Whose Knowledge? Thinking from Women's Lives. Ithaca, NY: Cornell University Press, 1991.

Hinchcliffe, Doreen. "Legal Reforms in the Shi'i World: Recent Legislation in Iran and Iraq." Malaya Law Review 10:2 (1968): 292–305.

Hirschkind, Charles. The Ethical Soundscape: Cassette Sermons and Islamic Counterpublics. New York: Columbia University Press, 2006.

Hoodfar, Homa. The Women's Movement in Iran: Women at the Crossroads of Secularization and Islamization. Grabels Cedex, France: Women Living Under Muslim Laws, 1999.

Howard, I. K. A. "Mut'a Marriage Reconsidered in the Context of the Formal Procedures for Islamic Marriage." Journal of Semitic Studies 20, no. 1 (1975): 82–92.

Hussain, Jamila. Islam: Its Law and Society. 2nd ed. Sydney: Federation Press, 2004.

Ibrahim, Celene. Women and Gender in the Qur'an. New York: Oxford University Press, 2020.

Jackson, Sherman. "Legal Pluralism between Islam and the Nation-State: Romantic Medievalism or Pragmatic Modernity?" Fordham Law Journal 30, no. 1 (2006): 158–76.

Jones, Sandy. "God's Law or State's Law: Authority and Islamic Family Law Reform in Bahrain." PhD diss., University of Pennsylvania, 2010.

Kahf, Mohja. Western Representations of the Muslim Woman: From Termagant to Odalisque. Austin: University of Texas Press, 1999.

Kalmbach, Hilary. "Social and Religious Change in Damascus: One Case of Female Islamic Religious Authority." British Journal of Middle Eastern Studies 35, no. 1 (2008): 37–57.

Kamali, Mohammad Hashim. Principles of Islamic Jurisprudence. Cambridge: Islamic Texts Society, 2003.

Kandiyoti, Deniz. Women, Islam, and the State. Philadelphia: Temple University Press, 1991.

Kar, Mehrangiz. Crossing the Red Line: The Struggle for Human Rights in Iran. Costa Mesa, CA: Blind Owl Press, 2007.

———. "Iran's Constitutional Obstacles to Realizing Human Rights and Democracy." Parts 1–4. Muftah magazine, 2010, site no longer accessible. http://muftah.org/345/.

Keddie, Nikki. Modern Iran: Roots and Results of Revolution. New Haven, CT: Yale University Press, 2003.

———. "Women in Iran since 1979." Social Research: An International Quarterly 67, no. 2 (Summer 2000): 405–38.

Keddie, Nikki, and Yann Richard. Roots of Revolution: An Interpretive History of Modern Iran. New Haven, CT: Yale University Press, 1981.

Keshavarz, Bahman. "Guardian Council May Approve Citizenship Rights Charter." International Campaign for Human Rights in Iran, January 2, 2014. www.iranhumanrights.org/2014/01/bahman-keshavarz/.

Khodadad, M. *The Role of Women in the Constitutional Revolution*. Tehran: Farhang-i Iliya, 2008.

Kian, Azadeh. *Les femmes iraniennes entre Islam, état et famille*. Paris: Maisonneuve et Larose, 2002.

———. "Gendered Khomeini." In *A Critical Introduction to Khomeini*, edited by Arshin Adib-Moghaddam, 170–92. Cambridge: Cambridge University Press, 2014.

———. "Gendering Shiʿism in Post-revolutionary Iran." In *Gender in Contemporary Iran: Pushing the Boundaries*, edited by Roksana Bahramitash and Eric Hooglund, Iranian Studies Series, 24–35. London: Routledge, 2011.

———. "Women and the Making of Civil Society in Post-Islamist Iran." In *Twenty Years of Islamic Revolution: Political and Social Transition in Iran since 1979*, edited by Eric Hooglund, 56–73. Syracuse, NY: Syracuse University Press, 2002.

Kian-Thiebaut, Azadeh. "From Islamization to the Individualization of Women in Post-revolutionary Iran." In *Women, Religion and Culture in Iran*, edited by Sarah Ansari and Vanessa Martin, chap. 8. Richmond, Surrey, UK: Curzon, 2002.

Kloos, David, and Mirjam Kunkler. "Studying Female Islamic Authority: From Top-Down to Bottom-Up Modes of Certification." *Asian Studies Review* 40, no. 4 (2016): 479–90.

Kunkler, Mirjam. "What Iran Wants from Female Religious Authority: Piety— Yes, Expertise in Fiqh—No." openDemocracy, February 13, 2012.

Kunkler, Mirjam, and Roja Fazaeli. "The Life of Two *Mujtahidahs*: Female Religious Authority in 20th Century Iran." In *Women, Leadership and Mosques: Contemporary Islamic Authority*, edited by Masooda Bano and Hilary Kalmbach, 127–60. Leiden: Brill, 2011.

Kunkler, Mirjam, and Devin J. Stewart, eds. *Female Religious Authority in Shiʿi Islam: Past and Present*. Edinburgh: Edinburgh University Press, 2021.

Kurzman, Charles. *Liberal Islam: A Sourcebook*. Oxford: Oxford University Press, 1998.

Lambton, Ann. *Qajar Persia: Eleven Studies*. London: I. B. Tauris, 1987.

Lockhart, Laurence. "The Constitutional Laws of Persia: An Outline of Their Origin and Development." *Middle East Journal* 13, no. 4 (1959): 372–89.

Mahmood, Saba. *Politics of Piety: The Islamic Revival and the Feminist Subject*. Princeton, NJ: Princeton University Press, 2005.

Maknun, S. *Feminism in Iran*. Tehran: Office of Human Science Research Center, 2000.

Malihi, Seyed Mostafa, et al. "The Ability and Financial Commitment of the Husband in Payment of Dowry." *Journal of Social Issues and Humanities* 2, no. 3 (2014).

Martin, Richard, and Abbas Barzegar. *Islamism: Contested Perspectives on Political Islam*. Stanford, CA: Stanford University Press, 2010.

Martin, Vanessa. "Constitutional Revolution: Events." In *Encyclopaedia Iranica*, vol. 6, fasc. 2. London: Encyclopaedia Iranica Foundation, 1992.

———. *Islam and Modernism: The Iranian Revolution of 1906*. London: I. B. Tauris, 1989.

Matsunaga, Yasuyuki. "Human Rights and New Jurisprudence in Mohsen Kadivar's Advocacy of 'New-Thinker' Islam." *Die Welt des Islams* 51, nos. 3–4 (2011): 358–81.

Mavani, Hamid. "Paradigm Shift in Twelver Shiʿi Legal Theory (uṣūl al-fiqh): Ayatullah Yusef Saanei." *Muslim World* 99, no. 2 (2009): 335–55.

McAuliffe, Jane. "Chosen of All Women: Mary and Fatima in Qurʾanic Exegesis." *Islamochristiana Roma* 7 (1981): 19–28.

McGlinn, Sen. "Family Law in Iran." Unpublished manuscript, University of Leiden, 2001.

Mehran, Golnar. "The Paradox of Tradition and Modernity in Female Education in the Islamic Republic of Iran." *Comparative Education Review* 47, no. 3 (2003): 269–86.

———. "Shiʿa Education in Iran." In *Teaching Islam: Textbooks and Religion in the Middle East*, edited by G. Starrett and E. A. Doumato, 53–70. Boulder, CO: Lynne Rienner, 2007.

Menashri, David. *Education and the Making of Modern Iran*. Ithaca, NY: Cornell University Press, 1992.

Miklos, J. *The Iranian Revolution and Modernization*. National Security Essay Series 83-2. Washington, DC: National Defense University Press, 1983. https://apps.dtic.mil/sti/tr/pdf/ADA131627.pdf.

Mir-Hosseini, Ziba. "Family Law. ii. In Islam." In *Encyclopaedia Iranica*, vol. 9, fasc. 2. London: Encyclopaedia Iranica Foundation, 1999.

———. "Family Law. iii. In Modern Persia." In *Encyclopaedia Iranica*, online ed., 1999. www.iranicaonline.org/articles/family-law#iii.

———. *Islam and Gender: The Religious Debate in Contemporary Iran*. Princeton, NJ: Princeton University Press, 1999.

———. *Marriage on Trial: A Study of Islamic Family Law: Iran and Morocco Compared*. London: I. B. Tauris, 1993.

———. "Muslim Women's Quest for Equality: Between Islamic Law and Feminism." *Critical Inquiry* 32, no. 4 (2006): 629–45.

———. "New Feminist Voices in Islam." *BARAZA!*, no. 4 (2010): 3–4.

———. "Religious Modernists and the 'Woman Question': Challenges and Complicities." In *Twenty Years of Islamic Revolution: Political and Social Transition in Iran since 1979*, edited by Eric Hooglund, 74–95. Syracuse, NY: Syracuse University Press, 2002.

———. "Sharia and National Laws in Iran." In *Sharia Incorporated: A Comparative Overview of Legal Systems in Twelve Muslim Countries in Past and Present*, edited by Jan Michiel Otto, 319–71. Leiden: Leiden University Press, 2010.

———. "Tamkin: Stories from a Family Court in Iran." In *Everyday Life in the Muslim Middle East*, 2nd ed., edited by Donna Lee Bowen and Evelyn A. Early, 136–51. Bloomington: Indiana University Press, 2002.

———. "When a Woman's Hurt Becomes an Injury: Hardship as Grounds for Divorce in Iran." *HAWWA (Journal of Women of the Middle East and the Muslim World)* 5, no. 1 (2007): 111–26.

———. "Women and Politics in Post-Khomeini Iran: Divorce, Veiling and Emerging Feminist Voices." In *Women and Politics in the Third World*, edited by Haleh Afshar, 142–70. London: Routledge, 1996.

Moallem, Minoo. *Between Warrior Brother and Veiled Sister: Islamic Fundamentalism and the Politics of Patriarchy in Iran.* Berkeley: University of California Press, 2005.

Modarressi, Hossein. "Rationalism and Traditionalism in Shi'i Jurisprudence: A Preliminary Survey." *Studia Islamica* 59 (1984): 141–58.

Moghadam, Valentine. "Rhetorics and Rights of Identity in Islamist Movements." *Journal of World History* 4, no. 2 (1993): 243–64.

———. "Women in the Islamic Republic of Iran: Legal Status, Social Positions, and Collective Action." Paper presented at the conference "Iran after 25 Year of Revolution: A Retrospective and a Look Ahead," Woodrow Wilson International Center for Scholars, Washington, DC, 2004. www.wilsoncenter.org/sites/default/files/media/documents/event/ValentineMoghadamFinal.pdf.

Mohammadi, Majid. *Judicial Reform and Reorganization in 20th Century Iran: State-Building, Modernization and Islamicization.* London: Routledge, 2008.

Mokhtari, Shadi. *The Search for Human Rights within an Islamic Framework in Iran.* Oxford: Blackwell, 2004.

Momen, Moojan. "Women. iii: In Shi'ism." In *Encyclopaedia Iranica,* online ed., 2011. https://iranicaonline.org/articles/women-shiism.

Murata, Sachiko. *Temporary Marriage (Mut'a) in Islamic Law.* Qum: Ansariyan Publications, 1991.

Musallam, Basim. *Sex and Society in Islam: Birth Control before the Nineteenth Century.* Cambridge: Cambridge University Press, 1983.

Naghibi, Nima. *Rethinking Global Sisterhood: Western Feminism and Iran.* Minneapolis: University of Minnesota Press, 2007.

Najmabadi, Afsaneh. "Crafting an Educated Housewife in Iran." In *Remaking Women: Feminism and Modernity in the Middle East,* edited by Lila Abu-Lughod, 91–125. Princeton, NJ: Princeton University Press, 1998.

———. "Feminism in an Islamic Republic: 'Years of Hardship, Years of Growth.'" In *Islam, Gender, and Social Change,* edited by Yvonne Y. Haddad and John Esposito, 59–84. New York: Oxford University Press, 1998.

———. "(Un)Veiling Feminism." In *Secularisms,* edited by Janet Jakobsen and Ann Pellegrini, 39–57. Durham, NC: Duke University Press, 2008.

———. "Veiled Discourse—Unveiled Bodies." *Feminist Studies* 19, no. 3 (Autumn 1993): 487–518.

———. "*Zanhā-yi Millat*: Women or Wives of the Nation?" *Iranian Studies* 26, nos. 1–2 (Winter-Spring 1993): 51–71.

Narayan, Kirin. "How Native Is a 'Native' Anthropologist?" *American Anthropologist* 95, no. 3 (1993): 671–86.

Nayyeri, Mohammad. "Gender Inequality and Discrimination: The Case of Iranian Women." Iran Human Rights Documentation Center, March 5, 2013. https://iranhrdc.org/gender-inequality-and-discrimination-the-case-of-iranian-women/.

Oladi Ghadikolaei, Samaneh. "Women's Religious Authority in Shi'i Tradition: A Quest for Justice." In *Multi-religious Perspectives on a Global Ethic: In Search of a Common Morality*, edited by Myriam Renaud and William Schweiker, 46–58. London: Routledge, 2020.

Omid, Homa. *Islam and the Post-revolutionary State in Iran*. London: Palgrave Macmillan, 1994.

Osanloo, Arzoo. "From Status to Rights: The Shifting Dimensions of Women's Affairs and Family Law in Iran." In *Feminist Activism, Women's Rights and Legal Reform*, edited by Mulki Al-Sharmani, 125–50. London: Zed Books, 2014.

———. *The Politics of Women's Rights in Iran*. Princeton, NJ: Princeton University Press, 2009.

Oslo Coalition on Freedom of Religions or Belief. "Justice through Equality: Building Religious Knowledge for Reform of Muslim Family Laws." Report on the Oslo Coalition's Muslim Family Law project, Norwegian Centre for Human Rights, University of Oslo, May 2013. www.iknowpolitics.org/en/knowledge-library/report-white-paper/justice-through-equality-building-religious-knowledge-legal.

Paidar, Parvin. *Women and the Political Process in Twentieth-Century Iran*. Cambridge: Cambridge University Press, 1995.

Povey, Tara, and Elaheh Rostami-Povey. *Women, Power and Politics in 21st Century Iran*. Farnham, Surrey: Ashgate, 2012.

Poya, Maryam. *Women, Work and Islamism: Ideology and Resistance in Iran*. New York: Zed Books, 1999.

Quraishi, Asifa, and Frank Vogel. *The Islamic Marriage Contract: Case Studies in Islamic Family Law*. Cambridge, MA: Harvard University Press, 2008.

Rahman, Fazlur, and Ebrahim Moosa. *Revival and Reform in Islam*. Oxford: Oneworld, 1999.

Ribeiro, Breanna. "Islamic Feminism: A Discourse of Gender Justice and Equality." PhD diss., Linfield College, 2014.

Rodziewicz, Magdalena. "The Legal Debate on the Phenomenon of 'White Marriages' in Contemporary Iran." *Anthropology of the Middle East* 15, no. 1 (2020): 50–63.

Sachedina, Abdulaziz. "Woman, Half-the-Man? Crisis of Male Epistemology in Islamic Jurisprudence." In *Perspectives on Islamic Law, Justice, and Society*, edited by R. S. Khare, 145–60. Lanham, MD: Rowman and Littlefield, 1999.

Sakurai, Keiko. "Shi'ite Women's Seminaries (Howzeh-Ye 'Elmiyyeh-Ye Khahran) in Iran: Possibilities and Limitations." *Iranian Studies* 45, no. 6 (2012): 727–44.

———. "Women's Empowerment and Iranian-Style Seminaries in Iran and Pakistan." in *The Moral Economy of the Madrasa: Islam and Education Today*, edited by Keiko Sakurai and Fariba Adelkhah, 32–58. New York: Routledge, 2011.

Salime, Zakia. *Between Feminism and Islam: Human Rights and Sharia Law in Morocco*. Minneapolis: University of Minnesota Press, 2011.

Schirazi, Asghar. *The Constitution of Iran: Politics and the State in the Islamic Republic*. London: I. B. Tauris, 1997.

Scott, Joan. "Deconstructing Equality-versus-Difference: Or, the Uses of Poststructuralist Theory for Feminism." *Feminist Studies* 14, no. 1 (1988): 33–50.

Sedghi, Hamideh. *Women and Politics in Iran: Veiling, Unveiling, and Reveiling*. New York: Cambridge University Press, 2007.

Seradj, Leila. "'Upsetting the Idea of Centuries': The Origins of the Women's Movement in Iran, 1850–1925." MA thesis, Tufts University, 2013.

Shaditalab, Jaleh. "Iranian Women: Rising Expectations." *Critique: Critical Middle Eastern Studies* 14, no. 1 (Spring 2005): 35–55.

Shahrough, Akhavi, and Sussan Siavoshi. "Iran." In *The Oxford Encyclopedia of the Islamic World*, January 2012. www.oxfordreference.com/display/10.1093/acref/9780197669419.001.0001/acref-9780197669419-e-199?rskey=kekfHf&result=196.

Shamim, Ali. *Iran during the Qajar Monarchy: The Thirteenth Century and the First Half of the Fourteenth Century*. Tehran: Zar Yab, 2008.

Shekarloo, Mahsa. "Iranian Women Take On the Constitution." *Middle East Report Online* 21 (2005). https://merip.org/2005/07/iranian-women-take-on-the-constitution/.

Shojaei, Seyedeh Nosrat, Ku Hasnita, Ku Samsu, and Hossein Asayesh. "Women in Politics: A Case Study of Iran." *Journal of Politics and Law* 3, no. 2 (2010): 257–68.

Siavoshi, Sussan. "Islamist' Women Activists: Allies or Enemies?" In *Iran: Between Tradition and Modernity*, edited by Ramin Jahanbegloo, 168–84. Lanham, MD: Lexington Books, 2004.

Smith, Dorothy. *The Everyday World as Problematic: A Feminist Sociology*. Boston: Northeastern University Press, 1987.

Soroush, Abdolkarim. "The Evolution and Devolution of Religious Knowledge." In *Liberal Islam: A Sourcebook*, edited by Charles Kurzman, 244–54. Oxford: Oxford University Press, 1998.

Spectorsky, Susan. *Women in Classical Islamic Law: A Survey of the Sources*. Leiden: Brill, 2010.

Stewart, Devin. "Ejmā'." In *Encyclopaedia Iranica*, vol. 8, fasc. 3. London: Encyclopaedia Iranica Foundation, 1998. Updated for online ed., 2011. https://iranicaonline.org/articles/ejma.

———. *Islamic Legal Orthodoxy: Twelver Shiite Responses to the Sunnī Legal System*. Salt Lake City: University of Utah Press, 1998.

Stowasser, Barbara Freyer. *Women in the Qurʾan, Traditions, and Interpretation*. Oxford: Oxford University Press, 1994.

Sullivan, Zohreh T. "Eluding the Feminist, Overthrowing the Modern? Transformations in Twentieth-Century Iran." In *Remaking Women: Feminism and Modernity in the Middle East*, edited by Lila Abu-Lughod, 215–42. Princeton, NJ: Princeton University Press, 2015.

Tajali, Mona. "Notions of Female Authority in Modern Shiʿi Thought." *Religions* 2, no. 3 (2012): 449–68.

———. *Women's Political Representation in Iran and Turkey: Demanding a Seat at the Table.* Edinburgh: Edinburgh University Press, 2022.

Tawasil, Amina. "Reading as Practice: The Howzevi (Seminarian) Women in Iran and Clair de Lune." *Anthropology and Education Quarterly* 50, no. 1 (2019): 66–83.

———. "Towards the Ideal Revolutionary Shi'i Woman: The Howzevi (Seminarian), the Requisites of Marriage and Islamic Education in Iran." *Hawwa* 13, no. 1 (2015): 99–126.

Thurlkill, Mary. *Chosen among Women: Mary and Fatima in Medieval Christianity and Shíite Islam.* Notre Dame, IN: University of Notre Dame Press, 2007.

Tucker, Judith. *Women, Family, and Gender in Islamic Law.* Cambridge: Cambridge University Press, 2008.

Turner-Rahman, Israt. "Consciousness Blossoming: Islamic Feminism and Qur'anic Exegesis in South Asian Muslim Diaspora Communities." PhD diss., Washington State University, 2009.

Usman, Jeffrey. "The Evolution of Iranian Islamism from the Revolution through the Contemporary Reformers." *Vanderbilt Journal of Transnational Law* 35, no. 5 (2002): 1678–1730.

Wadud, Amina. *Inside the Gender Jihad: Women's Reform in Islam.* Oxford: Oneworld, 2006.

———. *Qur'an and Women: Rereading the Sacred Text from a Woman's Perspective.* New York: Oxford University Press, 1999.

Webb, Gisela. *Windows of Faith: Muslim Women Scholar-Activists in North America.* Syracuse, NY: Syracuse University Press, 2000.

Welchman, Lynn. *Women and Muslim Family Laws in Arab States: A Comparative Overview of Textual Development and Advocacy.* Amsterdam: Amsterdam University Press, 2007.

Williams, Juliet. "Unholy Matrimony? Feminism, Orientalism, and the Possibility of Double Critique." *Signs* 34, no. 3 (2009): 611–32.

Wright, Robin. *The Last Great Revolution: Turmoil and Transformation in Iran.* New York: Random House, 2001.

Yeganeh, Naser. "Civil Code." In *Encyclopaedia Iranica,* online ed., 1991. www.iranicaonline.org/articles/civil-code.

Zainah, Anwar. *Wanted: Equality and Justice in the Muslim Family.* Selangor, Malaysia: Musawah, 2009.

Zaman, Muhammad Qasim. *The Ulama in Contemporary Islam: Custodians of Change.* Princeton, NJ: Princeton University Press, 2002.

# Index

Founded in 1893,
UNIVERSITY OF CALIFORNIA PRESS
publishes bold, progressive books and journals
on topics in the arts, humanities, social sciences,
and natural sciences—with a focus on social
justice issues—that inspire thought and action
among readers worldwide.

The UC PRESS FOUNDATION
raises funds to uphold the press's vital role
as an independent, nonprofit publisher, and
receives philanthropic support from a wide
range of individuals and institutions—and from
committed readers like you. To learn more, visit
ucpress.edu/supportus.